THE OCCULT
ELV

"This is the kind of book that sh[...]
to see that things are not what they seem to be, especially with the
King of rock 'n' roll. Everything we thought we knew, we didn't.
The truth is way, *way* stranger."

JEFFREY J. KRIPAL, AUTHOR OF *HOW TO THINK IMPOSSIBLY*

"Miguel takes the ever-impressive depth of esoteric knowledge and
insight he's known for and applies it to a pop culture cornucopia
of unexpected threads spiraling out from the King himself. It's
easy to forget that the magical fabric of reality can be found in
unexpected places, and what we have here is a grand, bedazzled,
suit-shaped reminder. Hallelujah!"

GREG CARLWOOD, HOST OF *THE HIGHERSIDE CHATS*

"Miguel writes with sincerity balanced by a sense of humor and
pop sensibilities balanced by knowledge of esoteric traditions.
Even well-read Elvis fans will find surprises in this romp of an
informative read about a man many Americans still call the King."

RONNIE PONTIAC, ASTROLOGER AND AUTHOR OF
AMERICAN METAPHYSICAL RELIGION AND
COAUTHOR OF *THE MAGIC OF THE ORPHIC HYMNS*

"Memphis, Egypt, was a center of the mystery cults of Osiris,
which were the ancient world's favorite venue for sex, drugs, and
rock 'n' roll. Given that Osiris was the King of the Gods and the
God of Kings, it's no accident that Memphis, Tennessee, would
give rise to the King of Rock 'n' Roll. Who better than the knowledgeable Miguel Conner to rip the lid off the esoteric roots of

these modern mysteries of Rock and its King? There have been tens of thousands of books written about Elvis and his lasting magic, but none that truly cut to the core of the King's enduring appeal like this one!"

CHRISTOPHER KNOWLES, AUTHOR OF
THE SECRET HISTORY OF ROCK 'N' ROLL

"*The Occult Elvis* takes us on a thrilling and surprising journey of the wide range of occult, religious, and mystical subjects that greatly interested Elvis Presley throughout the different phases of his life. This is an important book to read, not only for fans wanting to learn more about his unstoppable drive to become somebody great and his remarkable triumph over the hardscrabble life that he was born into, but also for those who are spiritually awakening and want to know more about how Elvis discovered and integrated that other reality into his life and music. Through his passionate and concise exploration of the inner world of rock music's most iconic and influential artist, Connor tells a fascinating story—of how Elvis cultivated his deep desire to know and experience the mysterious in the name of serving his beloved family, the many people he cared about, and his fans across the world—and in doing so, successfully reminds us of how deeply connected the occult and the divine are to rock and roll."

PAUL WYLD, SINGER, SONGWRITER, AND AUTHOR OF
JIM MORRISON, SECRET TEACHER OF THE OCCULT

"The public never knew the complexity of Elvis, who spent seven years with members of the Memphis Mafia. If you want a sneak peek behind the cape, you must step inside this book. Once again, Elvis doesn't disappoint his audience."

GAIL LYNN, EXECUTIVE PRODUCER OF
THE FILM *PROTECTING THE KING*

THE OCCULT
ELVIS

THE MYSTICAL AND MAGICAL
LIFE OF THE KING

MIGUEL CONNER

DESTINY
BOOKS

Destiny Books
Rochester, Vermont

Destiny Books
One Park Street
Rochester, Vermont 05767
www.DestinyBooks.com

Destiny Books is a division of Inner Traditions International

Cataloging-in-Publication Data for this title is available from the Library of Congress

ISBN 979-8-88850-135-1 (print)
ISBN 979-8-88850-136-8 (ebook)

Printed and bound in the United States by Lake Book Manufacturing, LLC

10 9 8 7 6 5 4 3 2 1

Text design by Virginia Scott Bowman and layout by Debbie Glogover
This book was typeset in Garamond Premier Pro with Alverata, Aviano Serif and Gill Sans MT Pro used as display typefaces

All images are the author's own, in the public domain, or credited in the caption.

To send correspondence to the author of this book, mail a first-class letter to the author c/o Inner Traditions • Bear & Company, One Park Street, Rochester, VT 05767, and we will forward the communication, or contact the author directly at **miguelconner.com**.

Scan the QR code and save 25% at InnerTraditions.com.
Browse over 2,000 titles on spirituality, the occult, ancient mysteries, new science, holistic health, and natural medicine.

For Elvis.
You needed a favor from a friend,
and I was honored to help.
The world finally knows your truth,
and now you are free.
And so is the world.

My whole life is a dream. I hope I never wake up.

ELVIS PRESLEY

They know about Elvis, the image, but not the inner me.

ELVIS PRESLEY

Truth is like the sun. You can shut it out for a time, but it ain't going away.

ELVIS PRESLEY

CONTENTS

ACKNOWLEDGMENTS

THANK YOU, thank you very much.

I had to write this, thinking in a heavy Tennessee accent. Elvis truly meant it from the bottom of his heart every time he said it. He was a kind man who was raised to appreciate kindness, and his Mama taught him we are all equal under the eyes of the Divine.

My gratitude comes from the bottom of my heart, too, and I humbly appreciate all those who helped me on this journey to finding the authentic Elvis Presley. Most of you knew him better, as I knew very little of him when I started this book on a cold February day in 2023.

So thank you, thank you very much to Gail Lynn, who planted the seeds of understanding Elvis's occult side during our interview and watered them in many discussions afterward; to Dr. HermanSJr., who believed me from the start, and pushed and coached me hard while handing out sage advice; to Tamra Lucid and Ronnie Pontiac, whose incredible, invaluable editing and suggestions turned so much lead to gold in the book; to Mitch Horowitz, who guided me to give the King justice and find proper places for his musical idol; to Gary Tillery, whose initial research on the esoteric side of Elvis and further instruction was an essential springboard; and to Maja D'Aoust: your witchery and keen scholarship helped extract the complete picture of Elvis's magical life.

And thank you, thank you very much to my Gen-X squad of high weirdness mavens and synchromystic mages: Christopher Knowles, Sean Rardin, Joanna Kujawa, Laura London, Matthew Frederick, and Matthew Schmitz. Your talent and eye for the reality behind our reality was the hot sauce the work needed. Of course, my gratitude is equal for my Millennial squad of chaos magicians with your smuggled Gnosis: Gordon White, Steven Snider, Cat Rose Neligan, and Nathan Lee Miller Foster. As for boomers? Without a doubt, Gary Lachman's knowledge and help with Rudolf Steiner was invaluable.

And thank you, thank you very much, *Aeon Byte* listeners. You heard me ramble on during live shows about Elvis, and your highly positive reactions and suggestions ensured I never looked back until I was out of the writing underworld. Whether staying up late at one in the morning or researching on Sundays, your song made me not find Eurydice until I had left the Hades building.

My last thank you—and thank you very much!—goes to the stellar staff at Inner Traditions. The entire process was a delight and rewarding learning experience. It's rare to find a company that is professional and ambitious and makes the world a better place.

PROLOGUE
IF I COULD DREAM
HOW IT STARTED

VERNON PRESLEY STEPPED OUT onto the front porch for a cigarette. He lit up and walked into the small yard, pulling his coat tighter around his body. *Sweet Jesus, it's cold*, he thought, *and that wind is like a whip*. He could see his breath as it swirled with the wild air. But the break was nice—and so were the sounds of nature, like the rustling leaves and the distant complaint of eternally invisible coyotes. The January winter night was clear, though, granting a view of the neighborhood of wooden houses interrupted by daisy pastures and stripped gum trees. What waited beyond were the cotton and corn fields of East Tupelo and a lot of poverty as the Great Depression continued to eat the dreams and futures of the common folk.

He glanced back at his home, the little two-room shack in meager Mississippi. He could hear Gladys moaning in what had been a long labor. Twins, she said! They couldn't even afford a hospital delivery. Twins! At least his mother and the midwife Edna were here to help, and then Vernon would rush to get Doctor William as soon as the babies were ready to come out.

Everything would work out, he told himself, again looking at the scenery, even though nothing had really worked out in Vernon's life, from jobs to friends to his ideas. The Good Lord would be as good as the cigarette he was having, as fast as the winter wind that was . . .

The wind? Where had it gone? Silent. Completely silent. Not even the howl of coyotes.

Instinctively, he turned toward the house and froze as if the temperature had gone so low hell had frozen over down below.

A blue glow surrounded the house. It was soft but pulsing with confidence. Almost liquid. The light was not from this world, he knew immediately. What was going on?

"Sweet Jesus," he mouthed. Vernon Presley barely realized he had dropped his cigarette. He barely knew how terrified he was and didn't notice his legs moving desperately.

Vernon entered the shack with warnings ready in his mouth, but his mind was abruptly washed with more shock as he was greeted with heat, blood stench, and Gladys's screams. He forgot everything except being in the static present. Every time he tried to talk, he could only grunt. Sounds punished his temples. *Get the doctor! Things are breaking! We must pray, Vernon! We must pray!*

Forget, a voice told him, and Vernon felt it was coming from the blue light. Was that a coyote laughing at him outside, too? The wind was back.

We must pray!

Soon, Vernon witnessed the birth of a king and a jester, delivered by a blue coronation, as was foretold. No one knew if it was the king or the jester who died shortly afterward.

INTRODUCTION
The King and I

QUENTIN TARANTINO'S 1994 CLASSIC FILM, *Pulp Fiction*, is pregnant with memorable lines that define Americana. In the original theatrical release, one example happens in the scene where Mia Wallace (Uma Thurman) videotapes a sulking Vincent Vega (John Travolta). She remarks:

> There are only two kinds of people in the world, Beatles people and Elvis people. Now Beatles people can like Elvis and Elvis people can like the Beatles, but nobody likes them both equally. Somewhere you have to make a choice. And that choice tells you who you are.

For most of my life, I considered myself a Beatles person. Revelation had different plans for me since you are reading this, and it changed who I thought I was and my views on reality itself.

I regularly viewed Elvis Presley as representing the more shallow, bombastic, and kitsch aspects of Yankee culture. He was the gimcrack Orpheus of campy consumerism, a symbol of overindulgence and empty-calories thinking, no better than anthropomorphized McDonald's or Mountain Dew. My parents were neither Beatles nor Elvis fans, focused more on big band and jazz music. When I encountered rock 'n' roll as a young teen, the Beatles and the rest of the British Invasion were my gateway drug into the storm of adolescent hope and despair. Sometimes

I even agreed with Public Enemy in "Fight the Power": "Elvis was a hero to most but he didn't mean shit to me."

My views on the King softened slightly in my twenties and thirties. I became more open-minded and could honestly appreciate his music legacy, even admitting that I liked "Suspicious Minds" (the female backup is sublime). I fully recognized that Elvis inspired musicians I admired, like David Bowie, Led Zeppelin, The Clash, Tom Petty, and the Beatles (I was still their kind of person, though). At some point, I accepted his role as a benign symbol of the USA. I loved his muse aspect in yet another Tarantino film, *True Romance* (Val Kilmer murkily played Elvis). Elvis's brief (and also murky) appearance in *Forrest Gump* was also memorable. In this film he was voiced by Kurt Russell in an uncredited role (and Russell both played the King in a 1979 John Carpenter biopic and starred with him as a child in the film *It Happened at the World's Fair*). I laughed hard and never forgot the Flying Elvis's (Utah chapter!) scenes in *Honeymoon in Vegas*. What would my life be without Nicholas Cage minus his obsession and continual copying of Elvis, especially his corny sexiness and madcap intensity? And what would my life be like without laughing with my kids watching Elvis-cipher *Johnny Bravo* on Cartoon Network? We all have six degrees of Elvis, whether we want to admit it or not.

The new century came. In my forties my attitude toward Elvis remained relatively the same—at least until 2013, when I interviewed author and artist Gary Tillery on my podcast. We chatted about his newly released "spiritual biography" of Elvis, *The Seeker King*. The book surveyed many of the unorthodox views and experiences of Elvis, none of which I had ever heard of before. I walked away with a new admiration for the King. Discovering that he was a man of spiritual depth and mystic encounters was a pleasure. However, as I focused on children and careers, he became just another rock star from a bygone era who tapped into higher energies and was caught in the headwinds of kismet and human carnality. I could learn little from Elvis at my age, and I might as well shelve him with John Lennon, Jimi Hendrix, and Jim Morrison, all cautionary tales and unusual religious case studies. I tucked away my appreciation and understanding somewhere down in my unconscious.

At least I accepted that I saw Elvis as so many others saw him: as an image of something larger than I could ever understand, a projection of my own prejudices and hopes. As Elvis biographer Peter Guralnick wrote:

> Elvis Presley may well be the most written-about figure of our time. He is also in many ways the most misunderstood, both because of our ever-increasing rush to judgment and, perhaps more to the point, simply because he appears to be so well known. It has become as impossible to imagine *Elvis* amid all our assumptions, amid all the false intimacy that attaches to a tabloid personality, as it is to separate the President from the myth of the presidency, John Wayne from the myth of the American West. "It's very hard," Elvis declared without facetiousness at a 1972 press conference, "to live up to an image." And yet he, as much as his public, appeared increasingly trapped by it.[1]

And then, in 2022, I found myself in the latter part of the Ernest Hemingway "gradually and then suddenly" trope when it came to Elvis. My adventure had truly begun.

Enter another podcast in August of that year. (For the record, I hadn't noticed that Baz Luhrmann's *Elvis* had been released.) My guest was entrepreneur and inventor Gail Lynn, who shared her new book and technology on alternative healing modalities. During my research for this interview, I found that she had dated someone in Elvis's family, and the two had produced a docudrama based on the King's final years. I mentioned this part of her life, and for some reason, we jumped right into the occult and paranormal aspects of Elvis's life. Something stirred in me, and I kept thinking of him. Less than a month later, I was deep in Ayahuasca ceremonies during a trip to visit my family in Portugal. I experienced powerful, trippy visions and out-of-body odysseys, but I must admit that I had no encounters with Elvis (or Paul) in the third heaven.

Between the shamanistic ceremonies, I walked into my aunt's living room one morning, and she suddenly asked, "What about Elvis?" I froze instantly but realized her attention was on the "telly." She was asking about the Luhrmann movie.

What about Elvis?

He began haunting me.

When I returned to the USA, Elvis kept preoccupying me. I watched the Luhrmann movie several times, reread Tillery's book (and listened to the audiobook), and couldn't play any music except Elvis for two months. I dressed up like Elvis during Halloween and even did a live podcast as him. I started talking with his accent and talking about him to friends and colleagues. Guests on my podcast would ask curiously, "When will you write a book about Elvis?"

What about Elvis?

And then one stark winter day, I knew I had two choices: listen to the voiceless message fully or . . .

I realized I had only one choice! I had to tell the untold story of a king birthed in blue light who was more than a king, with the thesis I had already told thousands of people in the podcast or personally.

What is the thesis?

AMERICA'S MAGICIAN

In my alternative circles we often debate who is history's great magic user. The list can include Solomon, Medea, Simon Magus, John Dee, Aleister Crowley, Eliphas Levi, or Dion Fortune, to name a few. Or it might be the American Jack Parsons, Marjorie Cameron, or Edgar Cayce, or one of countless Native American shamans and ill-treated witches. Entire libraries and internet space have been written about the various magical mystics who have shaped human history.

The world overlooked one magic user, the greatest one.

Per the Guralnick quote, humanity got the image of Elvis farthest from his true self, that of a country-boy, fundie Christian, fried-banana-and-peanut-butter-sandwich-eating folk hero—Johnny Appleseed with a guitar and a high sex drive.

It is time for the world to see America's Magician, for, as will be discussed, we are in a dangerous time of transition, and Elvis was essential to a previous shift. As we travel into the inner sanctum of Elvis, the eye of a sorcerer-god's storm, you will likely find a part of yourself missing all along. In a way, Elvis made America, and you are standing in his dream, and he awaits each one of us. I am confident that this work will open new vistas to your existence, dear reader, from the gifts left behind by the King to discover your authentic self and purpose.

A constellation of Elvis biographies has been written. They either skip Elvis's occult pedigree, focus solely on his (marginally) Protestant Christian faith, or include his magical side briefly and in a forgettable manner. I also should mention the "dark/occult" side of rock music works, which are also legion; many of these compendiums are excellent in research and insight, but as they focus on numerous figures at once, the bandwidth of each tends to be limited. I will not do that. This book is not a linear, conventional biography but will instead:

- Supply the supernatural, prophetic, and cosmic circumstances that gave rise to Elvis
- Catalog his extensive interest and research in alternative spiritualities
- Reveal his profound, otherworldly experiences, visionary encounters, mystic abilities, and reality-bending powers
- Showcase his arcane rituals and how they paved the way for modern spirituality and praxis
- Make the case that Elvis was part of the machinations of higher forces that transformed Western culture forever
- Provide Jungian, Steiner-oriented, alchemical, and other esoteric ideas on the rise and fall of the King, examining his self-destructive, addictive persona, and solving the perennially confounding relationship with manager Colonel Tom Parker

- Present the eerie parallels between Elvis and Philip K. Dick that underscore Elvis's remarkable abilities

The evidence comes from many sources and is corroborated by many witnesses. Even if one questions one of my arguments, it is still obvious, as Buffalo Springfield sang in "What It's Worth": "There's something happening here. . . ." But instead of not being "exactly clear," it will be so obvious.

I understand much of what Elvis was into is no longer "occult" or "magic" per se—much of it is readily available today at your average suburban strip mall. But in the context of the times and the nation's psyche, Elvis laid the ground for a new age with all its perils and opportunities.

During this apocalypse of truth, terms like *shaman*, *occultist*, *Gnostic*, *mystic*, and others will be employed when referring to Elvis. They may or may not be comparable in your view, but all refer to those who tear the veil of mundane reality and discover or experience the supernatural, the shores of the divine. Regardless, I will expand the context of these terms as Elvis tore down the veils of mundane reality in his heterodox explorations and paranormal encounters. Sometimes, I will use the term *high weirdness*, as it involves traditional occultism paired with modern technology, conspiracy theory, psychedelics, and pop culture—an apt term when dealing with magic users of the late twentieth century like Robert Anton Wilson, Terence McKenna, Kenneth Grant, and others; and indeed Elvis, but he will tower above them all again.

But first, magic should be addressed before our magical mystery tour (am I still a Beatles person? You'll find out at the end).

IT'S A KINDA MAGIC

Magic is a polysemous word, meaning it can have multiple meanings or senses depending on the context in which it is used, making it challenging to define or interpret. Other polysemous words, especially in alternative circles, include *love*, *pagan*, and even *occult* (is anything really hidden in the internet age?). Magic and the terms mentioned are also abused, weaponized, and tossed around carelessly for spiritual sophistry or social media cred. Gandalf performs magic, but going to Disneyland can be considered magic. In Late Antiquity, magic was whatever the Roman Empire, either pagan or Christian, deemed unsanctioned ritual practice. These days, magic is considered parlor or sleight-of-hand tricks. Between Roman times and David Blaine, magic has taken many protean definitions.

John Michael Greer, one of today's most respected magicians and occultists, highlights the confusing situation of understanding magic:

> It's very difficult to talk about magic in modern industrial society and be understood clearly. That's not because magic is innately difficult to understand. It's because our culture has spent the last two thousand years or so doing its level best not to understand it.[2]

Greer does grant a workable definition for modernity, directly quoting famed occultist Dion Fortune, who herself is riffing off Aleister Crowley: "Magic is the art and science of causing changes in consciousness in accordance with will."

You could say magic is the esoteric way of thriving for or explaining salvation, enlightenment, or the Hellenistic idea of "metanoia," the turning about toward what is good and purposeful. That definition provides some elasticity if used outwardly, able to include, for example, Soviet propaganda, corporate advertising, or even mass hallucinations. It provides the strict materialist wriggle room to pierce normative reality and push the bounds of human imagination, so long as humans somewhat agree with empirical reality.

In *How to Become a Modern Magus*, Don Webb distinguishes between sorcery (*goeteia*) and magic (*theurgia*).[3] The former is the manipulation of matter by some arcane ritual or invocation to higher forces. He writes on those who practice *goeteia*:

They have thrown their pennies into wells, kissed the Blarney stone, or in a petty fit stepped on a crack expressing rage at their mother. However, sorcery does work from some—so sorcerous cookbooks exist in numerous traditions from Hoodoo to Anton LaVey's *Satanic Bible*. The sorcerer is not interested in self-change, only in play. The sorcerer knows the basic formula: extreme emotion plus symbolic manipulation produces events.[4]

This sensibility conforms with Dion Fortune's definition, making magic a telekinetic art, a tweaking of quantum probability fields by cosplaying ancient sages. In the end, magic is about transformation—taking a person to their ultimate potential as both a mortal and immortal.

There is a saying that goes, "We practice religion; they practice magic." In other words, it's only transgressive when theological foes attain supernatural powers. Put another way, as ancient magic researcher Robert Conner writes: "Religion is magic for the masses while magic is religion for the individual."[5]

Magic can then be divided into these levels:

- Parlor or sleight-of-hand tricks (modern-day)
- Psychic self-actualization or individuation that might or might not be supernatural, a power that can possibly be utilized outwardly toward a person or group (Fortune)
- The manipulation of matter and reality through uncanny means (Webb)
- A transformation into what we are at full potential, even beyond being human (Webb)

As with the terms *love* or *pagan*, a whole book could be written on magic (and excellent ones have been written). Yet this rubric removes most of the smell in the polysemous word. If all else fails, one can lean on the ancient Egyptian definition of magic, which can be defined as "an action which seeks to obtain its goods by methods outside the simple laws of cause and effect."[6]

What does all this Golden Dawn-ish talk have to do with Elvis?

Elvis encompassed all the bullet points mentioned, as I will argue, and in ways not matched by any practitioner in Western culture. Like all notable magic users, he was a seer and theologian whose life was hectic with eerie encounters. He was a genuine seeker, as Tillery rightly describes in his book.

No matter how you cut the Tarot deck, Elvis was a magician. Magic and Elvis are almost inseparable, as you will find out in the following chapters.

But first, a little earthly history.

1
A Quick History of Elvis Presley

Black velvet and that little boy's smile
Black velvet with that slow southern style
A new religion that'll bring ya to your knees
Black velvet if you please

ALANNAH MYLES, "BLACK VELVET"

THIS CHAPTER MUST BE DONE. I know that for many readers who are fans, having to go through the history of Elvis is like the obligatory viewing of the alley death of Thomas and Martha Wayne in a Batman flick, or yet another childhood bio of Clark Kent in a Superman narration. We get it—do we have to do it again?

This biography is micro, breaking down the life stages of the ever-reinventing King of Rock 'n' Roll. It will work as a reference once we go down the rabbit hole that is the magical side of his life.

CHILD ELVIS

Elvis Aron Presley was born in Tupelo, Mississippi, on January 8, 1935. He was the only living child of Vernon and Gladys Presley. His twin brother, Jesse Garon Presley, was born thirty-five minutes earlier but was stillborn. The Presley family was poor, and Vernon worked odd jobs to support his family, from sharecropping to running moonshine. Gladys took small jobs when she was able.

Elvis was extremely close to his parents, especially his mother. The family attended the Assembly of God Church, where he found his initial musical inspiration. Elvis was shy and introverted as a young boy. His passion was music, reflected in often singing at school or church.

The Presleys continued to live in poverty during that time, with Vernon even spending time away in jail for altering a check from an employer. In 1948, when Elvis was thirteen, the family moved to Memphis, Tennessee. Elvis was exposed to the sounds of blues, country, and gospel music there. As a teenager, he frequented Beale Street, an African-American music and culture hub. The music in that area had a profound impact on his musical style.

ROCKABILLY ELVIS

In 1953, with no formal music training and no ability to read music, working as a truck driver, Elvis paid four dollars to record two songs at the Memphis Recording Service, owned by Sun Records founder Sam Phillips. His first session was unremarkable. Nevertheless, Phillips saw potential in Elvis's unique blend of country and blues. He invited the youth back to record a second time. During his second recording session, in July 1954, Elvis recorded his breakthrough hit, "That's All Right (Mama)." The song became a local hit, leading to appearances on regional radio and television programs. Shortly after, Elvis signed a recording contract with RCA Records and released his first single, "Heartbreak Hotel," for the label in 1956. The song became an instant hit, reaching number one on the pop charts. Other chart-topping classics soon followed, like "Hound Dog," "All Shook Up," and "Don't Be Cruel."

Elvis's career skyrocketed in the following years, helping make rock music mainstream and ubiquitous. He became a cultural icon known for his suggestive dance moves and unique sound. His music mated several styles, including blues, country, and gospel. His charisma and sex appeal made him a favorite among teenagers and adults alike. Elvis's popularity was further fueled by appearances on television programs like *The Ed Sullivan Show*, which introduced him to a national audience and made him a household name.

ARMY ELVIS

Elvis served in the army after being drafted in 1958. His two-year service stint was a significant interruption in his career, tragically marked by the sudden death of his mother Gladys. He also became interested in more unconventional spirituality, healing modalities, and martial arts. He returned to the music scene in 1960 with a renewed focus and passion.

MOVIE STAR ELVIS

Elvis's first stint as an actor was in *Love Me Tender*, released in 1956. After leaving the army and as his music career cooled down in the 1960s, he went on to star in more than thirty films. Though his film career was not as impactful as his music career, his movies were extremely popular with his fans and cemented his status as a pop icon.

Despite releasing mostly campy musicals, Elvis was one of the highest-paid movie stars of his era. At one point, he earned a million dollars per picture plus a guarantee of 50 percent of the profit. His movies were mainly moneymakers.

During this time, Elvis expanded his spirituality, embracing an eclectic array of rituals and viewpoints.

VEGAS ELVIS

Elvis reinvented himself one last time after his 1968 Christmas television special (or *'68 Comeback Special*, as it's chiefly known). Once again, he became the most famous solo artist in the country. He focused on Las Vegas shows outside of touring, all monstrous successes, still releasing hit songs like "Suspicious Minds," "In the Ghetto," and "Burning Love."

FAT ELVIS

By 1975, Elvis's growing drug consumption, unhealthy lifestyle, and mental disorders began to take their toll. He could not lose weight as in the past, and his behavior became erratic. From the greatest performer on Earth, he became a show curiosity and the epitome of the aged, decaying rock star, a parody of what once made him edgy and groundbreaking.

PERSONAL LIFE

As the greatest male star in the world, Elvis's personal life was the continual subject of tabloid rumors and speculation. He dated several women, including actress Ann-Margret in the early 1960s. His most significant relationship was with Priscilla Beaulieu, whom he met when Priscilla was just fourteen years old while Elvis was serving in the army in Germany. The two continued corresponding, and she began dating Elvis after returning to the USA. They married in 1967, conceiving Lisa Marie Presley the following year. As with most celebrities, their marriage was challenging, ultimately ending in 1973.

The effects of divorce and the demands of his renewed fame were the main drivers of Elvis's self-destruction in the following years.

DEATH AND LEGACY

On August 16, 1977, at forty-two, Elvis Presley died of an apparent heart attack at his home in Memphis. His death rocked the world. Fans around the globe mourned his passing. In the years since his death, Elvis's popularity has only grown, and he is still considered one of the most impactful cultural figures in the history of popular music. He remains one of the highest-selling solo artists of all time with over a billion records sold worldwide.

That was simple. Thomas and Martha Wayne are forever being killed in some future screenplay, while Superman grows corn as a teen—and maybe we can include the spider biting Peter Parker for good measure—but Elvis lives forever in so many retellings. You drove here to see the freakshow, I assume. Now it's time to witness the magician and his life.

Let's start by finding the fonts from which the magic came, which would later crown the King, who was not really a king.

2
THE APOCALYPTICAL WORLD THAT CREATED ELVIS

At the Crossroads of Heaven and Hell

> *Tears obliterate upon a throne*
> *Hills obliterate upon a throne*
> *Wipe that seat, fan it down*
> *Ripped and married and killed away*
> *The King will walk on Tupelo*
> *The King will walk on Tupelo*
> *And carry the burden of Tupelo*
>
> NICK CAVE AND THE BAD SEEDS, "TUPELO"

NOTHING HAPPENS IN A VACUUM—not even vacuums. To understand the magician, whether it's Merlin or Circe, we must understand the forces of their time—their innate power and desires. A boy cannot retrieve a sword from a stone unless destiny writes some of his script.

LOST TWIN AND FOUND DAEMON

Straight out of the gate, Samsara welcomed Elvis with death and tragedy. When his identical twin, Jesse, died at birth at 4:35 a.m. on January 8, 1935, it took Elvis half an hour to come out into this world of temporality. The arduous labor occurred after a long and complicated pregnancy that forced Gladys to quit her job. Gladys let out a long, piercing wail while the midwife carried the dead infant to the back room. As for the once and future King, he was snugly wrapped in a shoebox. So worried were Glady and Vernon about the surviving newborn Elvis that they placed him in the warmest place in the house: the oven. After little Elvis was taken to the hospital, Gladys discovered that she would be unable to have another child. She later said, "When one twin died, the one that lived got all the strength of both."[1]

Jesse, named after Vernon's father, was placed in a small coffin to be later buried in an unmarked grave at Priceville Cemetery. The surviving twin was named Elvis after Vernon's middle name. The Presleys had planned to make the middle names of their twins, Garon and Aaron, rhyme with a long *a*. When their physician completed the birth certificate two days later, he followed their pronunciation, resulting in the name Elvis Aron Presley. Despite this unique spelling on his birth certificate, Elvis later stated that he preferred the conventional spelling of his middle name. Although the unusual spelling was recorded on his Social Security card and US Army records, his tombstone reads Elvis Aaron Presley.[2]

A shy and lonely child who often stuttered, one of Elvis's forms of solace was visiting the grave of his older twin with his father. Gladys never visited Jesse, only grieving through church visits. As a child, Elvis never spoke to anyone about Jesse except to one friend, James Ausborn. At age four or five, he started hearing a voice in his mind, which he recognized as Jesse. As an adult, he frequently referred to this voice as his "psychic twin" or "original bodyguard." He contended that this voice instructed him to love, care for, and understand other humans and their perspectives. Jesse became his conscience or alter ego.[3] Moreover, he became a "mystical figure, neither fully alive nor completely dead, possessed of supernatural powers of healing and human goodness, a spirit more than an entity, to be used for inspiration and guidance."[4]

From an esoteric standpoint, Jesse became the mask of Elvis's daemon (or daimon), an ancient Greco-Roman concept of a higher, timeless self or spirit guide that helps a mortal navigate life and eventually reintegrate with the divine realms. This symbiotic entity also possesses the spectral LinkedIn profiles of the guardian angel: genius, animal guide, and higher self, among others, depending on cultures across the globe. The daemon can be akin to the muse, which to the ancients was an ontological reality and conscious force. As Anthony Peake discusses in *The Daemon*, this semi-independent existence communicates through dreams, synchronicity, déjà vu, visions, and other unconventional means. It often takes familiar forms or voices to those it seeks to shepherd in the material world. The daemon spoke to Socrates about the weather and showed Niels Bohr a vision of the path of electrons orbiting around the nucleus. Sometimes, the daemon helps its lower self avoid death, and sometimes it foretells death itself, as happened with the poet Percy Shelly, who was warned by his daemon (taking the form of his doppelgänger) about his demise during a shipwreck.[5]

Describing the daemon as accurately as possible, we can turn to another mercurial bard like Elvis, W. B. Yeats, from his *Words Upon the Window Pane*:

> Daimon is timeless, it has present before it [a man's] past and future, or it has no present and is that past and future, and as the dramatisations recede from his waking mind and from the dreams that reproduce his waking desires they begin to express that knowledge.[6]

In a more streamlined manner, astrologist Cat Rose Neligan describes the daemon not as an entity but as an "altered state of consciousness that a human (or even a god) could be in. It was something that took hold of us and worked through us."[7] As the mind expands into nonlocal places, a new language guides the journey in reality, and it's not often a linear native vocabulary.

But can a dead brother become the manifestation of this helpful and inspirational supernal force? Ancestors guiding the living is a tale as old as civilization, but the answer is yes when it comes to siblings, as happened to another historic artist: William Blake. His dead brother Robert appeared in visions and assisted him in crafting both his poetry and legendary print art.[8]

Elvis's daemon (or two, as revealed in the next chapter) wasn't as vocally ubiquitous as with past mystics. It must also be considered that due to his culture and fame, he was always wary whom he spoke to about the supernatural; he only opened up about spirituality in his late twenties. Plus, as Neligan explains, the daemon is the force that stirs the call of a person's destiny in the rigid machinery of fate, a pull from the mundane to the impactful. The daemon is the part of us that reminds us why we are here, and that plea is often voiceless.[9]

James Hollis, one of today's leading Jungian authorities, explains well the fate-call of the daemon in relation to Elvis:

> We may not wish to be called, but we are all to something, and like listening to the Daimon, it is better to respond than to flee. Artists who follow their path do not "choose" to be an artist in face of suffering, uncertainty, failure, impoverishment, and cultural marginalization, but real artists do serve the calling.[10]

For Elvis, the pull of providence was immensely strong. Straight out of that cosmic portal, Elvis was thrust into a haunted world of spirit guides, voices in his head, and the eternal reminder of death. He constantly wondered about Jesse and what might have been. In a way, Elvis's entire life was an extended requiem for his twin.

The psychological impact would be oceanic on the mind of Elvis, who said about losing Jesse, "I've always felt part of me was missing."[11] As clinical psychologist Peter O. Whitmer (himself a twinless twin and the first drummer for the band The Turtles) writes in *Inner Elvis*:

Elvis's twin's death at birth was a tragedy that triggered a process that made his dead sibling the bedrock, the singular driving force in his life.[12]

Jesse's early departure also had permanent spiritual ramifications, a primary driver in the occult side of Elvis. In the mystical arenas, he could find the means to reunite and commune with his sibling. In this interaction, Elvis felt Jesse would provide the secrets to the meaning of life.[13]

A popular trope details that twins are united more than other siblings, sometimes in paranormal ways. The loss of a twin can be highly damaging to the survivor. But what makes twins so bonded, especially those who only know each other in the dark comfort of a womb? Whitmer answers this:

Sonograms have clearly shown what is called "interfetal stimulation," or the touching by twins of each other's feet, hands, and lips. Given the anatomy of the "sensory strip," such contact is quite significant. Twins can excite each other in the most basic ways in the intimate world they share before birth. The sensations they offer each other are quantitatively and qualitatively different from those experienced by the single fetus. It has been hypothesized that actual "interfetal communication" takes place. Researchers suggest there is a dominant twin, one who is first to react to external sounds. The dominant fetus passes along information to its twin. . . . The precise mechanism for such communication is not yet fully understood.[14]

We may never know who the alpha between Elvis and Jesse was, but they were intimately bonded from conception, and a premature separation leads to permanent trauma. Whitmer goes on to break down the deterministic path of a twinless twin, which indeed parallels the life of Elvis, and reveals what destined him to be history's greatest rock star and a seeker of expanded consciousness:

- An over-attached mother, yet a powerful son-mother bond
- A driven, high-intensity personality
- A need for attention and success, always balanced by imposter syndrome, gives them the tendency to give their wealth away
- The inability to have intimate relationships because they are subconsciously committed to their lost sibling for life
- The experience of always suffering an inner torment of unresolved grief and internal blame and trying to understand on a larger, even cosmic scale

When Liberace met Elvis in 1956, as the King's career was exploding, he explained that he had also lost his twin at birth. This tragedy fueled Liberace's desire for flamboyance, overworking, and overachievement. Instead of telling Elvis how to curb this wild spirit, Liberace told him to lean into it and just be unique in his success.[15]

Jesse never left the Elvis building.

THE QUEEN'S GAMBIT

As biographer and journalist Alanna Nash wrote about Gladys Love Smith, Elvis's mother:

> In rock-and-roll mythology, she is the proud, all-suffering Madonna, the commoner who birthed a king and died too soon, knocking his world off its axis. Like her famous son, her first name is all that's needed. Elvis called her "my best gal," but in the deepest psychological sense, she was not only his best gal, but also his only one.[16]

That's a problem many Elvis biographers skip over, and we shall unpack why.

Born in 1912, Gladys was on the surface a typical Southern farmland gal, doing her best in Tupelo, Mississippi, in the highs and lows of the first half of the twentieth century. One could characterize Gladys

as playful but lazy within family circles, timid and deferent in the public arena, and impulsive when it came to men's attention (to the point
where she eloped in her teens with a married man and came to her
senses two days later, becoming the talk of the town).[17]

Extremes ruled her personality, an affliction her famous son would
inherit. She was a "lively, passionate young woman who hoped to make
a good impression and be accepted by others." At the same time, her
mood could immediately shift into a storm most would rather avoid.
As Memphis Mafia member Lamar Fike said, "Everybody in that family was scared of Gladys and her temper." Beyond bipolar tugs, Glady
was often filled with overwhelming anxiety, another trait Elvis would
inherit (in fact, it was gargantuan nerves that gave Elvis his famous
leg and hip moves, not something he orchestrated on purpose as part
of his act). Her anxiety could intensify to the point that her worries
became intense paranoias and illusory threats, and these were sometimes coupled with "prophetic dreams and mystical intuitions." She
once spoke of "dark things" in the bushes of her property and had
them cut down."[18]

Gladys found dancing therapeutic, as did many in her small town.
On Saturday nights, neighbors would clear the rooms of furniture and
play the hand-cranked Victrola, booming Jimmie Rodgers recordings.
Glady would brandish her "buck dance," moving in a trancelike frenzy
as if possessed by some animal spirit. Her style was sensual and certainly improper, yet very cathartic during the hardships of the Great
Depression, described as an "Irish jig with the strut of a rooster designed
to draw the hen's attention."[19]

Her father's death in 1931 darkened Gladys, then nineteen, even
more. With more farming responsibilities and four younger siblings, her
anxiety skyrocketed. The disorder manifested in her body as collapsing health and paralysis. Part of her simply couldn't deal with reality.
The one thing that saved her and would save her many other times
from a complete mental breakdown would be immersing herself in
her faith. She began attending the Assembly of God Church after her

father's passing. The worship place started in a tent on an empty lot in her neighborhood. By 1937, it was a wooden building on Adams Street, built by the preacher—a man who happened to be Elvis's great-uncle, the husband of Gladys's aunt. From the start, its Pentecostal intensity grounded her soul.[20] As Whitmer summarizes:

> The vortex of anxiety that would, over the years, rise slowly to engulf Gladys was her primary defining psychological characteristic. It first showed in a nervous, startled hypervigilance that seemed inconsistent with her laziness, and in socially impulsive behavior that later, through involvement with the Assembly of God Church, evolved into a lifestyle of rule-bound traditionalism.

Whitmer further writes that this was "regular for the Assembly of God Church, the beating heart of the Holiness Movement, the same faith that would mold the characters of Jimmy Swaggart and Jerry Lee Lewis. It is a style of worship whereby catharsis, not chant, and movement, not meditation, is the practice of the day. After days of labor in the fields and in the mills, this is an elixir for the soul."[21]

Glady's total embracing of the Christian theurgy of intense prayer, healing hands, constant guitar music, outdoor woodland services, speaking in tongues as the Holy Spirit possessed, and epic sermons would be shared with Jesse and Elvis—especially as attendance became daily a few months before giving birth.[22]

Thus, Gladys subjected her unborn children to prolonged exposure to music, rhythms, and movement. Elvis and Jesse were linked to Gladys physically through the placenta and spiritually, soaking in the soulful sounds and stirring emotions for months before they were born. A celestial beat must have been embedded within them from the womb. This was a kingdom unto itself—human and guitar noises in an endless gospel celebration—exhilarating, vigorous, spirited, and ceaseless except for brief periods when Gladys allowed herself some sleep.[23]

Elvis and Jesse constantly bonding and communicating with each other, even perhaps dancing together in the womb, became a form of initiation into Christian magic (which I will explain further in this chapter). The initiation, especially spiritual music, also doubled as a form of primordial comfort. As Nash writes:

> Elvis, then, instinctively began moving to music before he was born. He learned to communicate, to feel good, through instruments and voices. While he was still in the womb, music became a dynamic and primary way of expressing himself in his relationship with his twin, his mother, and all that defined his world.[24]

When Jesse died and Elvis became the only child, Gladys kept Elvis in another kind of womb, a psychic one. Elvis and Gladys became so close that, as Nash states, it was "almost as if Gladys had been Elvis's twin and not Jessie." Gladys enveloped Elvis with attention and smothered him with her presence, refusing to allow any relative, including Vernon, to give her a break from parenting. "Gladys had a one-track mind," offered a female cousin. "She would hold that baby so tight I thought he might suffocate. She wouldn't let nobody carry him around but her, not even Vernon."

Nash also writes: "Gladys had always been so entwined with her son that it was hard to know where she left off and he began, even for the two of them. It came both from circumstances beyond their control, and from a need that was so great and pervasive as to be encoded in their DNA."[25]

So protective was Gladys of her surviving child that Vernon was sidelined for much of their relationship. That's not hard to see, as Vernon was a somewhat withdrawn, ambitionless, and poorly regarded man by his peers. With his father being a classic beta male and wallflower in character, Elvis became the King out of the gate, crowned by his very own mother.[26] Nothing changed once Elvis reached the Everest of fame, except Vernon was "basically jealous of Elvis."[27] But there was nothing to be jealous of as Elvis inherited a powerful and sometimes visionary anxiety that saw figures beyond reality, along with a tendency toward manic behavior.

Many have dismissed Gladys's behavior as proper for a woman who lost a child and then learned she would never conceive again. Others might say Elvis was just a mama's boy with his Southern honor. Yet even Elvis admitted the attention was over the top and constraining: "My mama never let me out of her sight. I couldn't go down to the creek with the other kids. Sometimes when I was little, I used to run off. Mama would whip me, and I thought she didn't love me."[28]

Abuse must be considered, especially when a relationship becomes so mutually codependent that the two become one identity without defined personality borders, the child feeling guilty that he is the surviving twin and the mother creating a Borg-like world that engulfs him in total, ubiquitous safety.[29]

In everyday parlance, one might call Gladys's approach helicopter parenting: the overprotective, ever-present manner of raising kids that hinders their ability to learn by going beyond boundaries. From a serious, psychological perspective, it is dramatically dubbed "lethal enmeshment." What is lethal enmeshment exactly? It refers to a situation in which, due to issues in marriage or life, a mother will utilize a child to fulfill her emotional needs. This shift is where the smothering happens, beyond overprotection. The child is not allowed to gradually break away, explore the world, and develop their sense of self. The child becomes the surrogate partner of the mother. Simultaneously, and because they neglect their own child's inner world until later in life, these children tend to be trapped in a duality of child and caretaker adult, constantly feeling "both eight and eighty." It is almost like they permanently create two personalities that are always at odds: one to satisfy the mother, the other to satisfy the child. Whitmer writes: "The adult survivor of lethal enmeshment is a divided personality. One side remains in hazy yet profound contact with the world of his infancy. The most visible part, however, plays out the role of pseudo-mature parent."[30]

A child such as Elvis would undergo emotional tensions, mood swings, and vast confusion later during the sexual stages of life. Not surprisingly, lethal enmeshment survivors tend to be self-destructive, incredibly impulsive, workaholic, addiction-prone, and unable to nurture lasting relationships.[31] As seen and will further be seen, everything was more significant in force and effect with Elvis—double the trouble.

Here would be easy to stop wondering how Elvis became Elvis, about his eagerness for spiritual experiences and his visionary anxiety that saw "dark things." Still, it's just the start of an incredible continuity of polarities that continued to crown and crucify his psyche, almost like he had no choice but to become the character of Elvis Presley. It will be more apparent as we deal with Gladys's true power in the following chapters, including her archetypal power.

Would Elvis have cared, given this information? As mentioned earlier, a king was born and so was a jester, delivered by a blue coronation, and regardless of who survived, their roles were lonely and set in stone before any sword was yanked from a stone. In a less wordy way, Elvis once said stoically, "People will come from miles around to see a freak."[32]

You drove to this particular freakshow, remember?

THE ARCHON OF POVERTY

I don't regard money or position as important. But I can never forget the longing to be someone. I guess if you are poor, you always think bigger and want more than those who have everything when they are born.

ELVIS PRESLEY

Until the money poured in and he could buy Gladys a Cadillac, Elvis Presley lived an economic life we today would associate with a developing country. Such poverty existed in America and still does.

The Great Depression blanketed the country with pain and

uncertainty. Its dark sorcery was magnified in Tupelo—a dirt-poor land where the main work was picking cotton or stitching clothes at the local textile mill for two dollars a day. The Presleys were classic poor whites, a state that had cursed the family for generations, on the "wrong side of the tracks in a wrong-side-of-the-tracks town."[33] Long vanquished were the Chickasaw tribe and buffalo; long finished were the British and French battles; almost forgotten were the Civil War and snail-pace industrialization. What always remained was the punishing poverty of the first half of the twentieth century.

As Gabor and Daniel Maté argue in *The Myth of Normal*, poverty is traumatic *and* epigenetic; in other words, it alters our genes negatively and is passed down to our offspring. Mental disorders, health issues, and stress continue from generation to generation, all caused by scarcity, urban blight, and discrimination.[34] Gladys and Vernon were merely punching bags for what I call the Archon of Poverty (based on the ancient Gnostic ideas of the archons, celestial beings who trap humans in crushing fate to feed off their souls and negative feelings). Gladys, unable to afford a hospital visit, had no choice but to give birth to Elvis and Jesse at home in East Tupelo, rudely separated from Tupelo proper by the city dump. Vernon's mother and two other women, including one midwife, helped with the delivery until a doctor arrived.

Vernon had built the tiny house himself in a neighborhood with unpaved streets across the tracks from Tupelo proper. The home consisted of two small rooms enclosed by whitewashed wood walls. The structure, having no foundation, was propped up on cinder blocks, and the surrounding yard was barren dirt. Coal oil lamps provided all the light, and there was no heating. Water came from a hand-cranked pump outside. The only toilet was an outhouse. That was yet another harshness Elvis met as soon as he entered the world.

Finances were challenging, but with Gladys taking care of Elvis, matters worsened, with the nineteen-year-old Vernon being the single breadwinner. He took odd jobs: milkman, carpenter, sharecropper,

Fig. 2.1. The home where Elvis was born.
Photo by Carol M. Highsmith.

moonshine runner, and so on. It wasn't uncommon for cornbread and water to be the family's *only* meal. At one point, Gladys fended for herself when, in 1938, Vernon spent nine months in prison in an eventually commuted sentence for altering a business check. The family lost the house, and the young mother was forced to work at a laundromat.[35] The harrowing event fused Gladys and Elvis even more, leaving yet another scar on Elvis's psyche.

After years of acute poverty, transient living, and Vernon juggling migratory jobs, sometimes in different cities (like helping build a prisoner-of-war camp in Como, Mississippi, during the height of World War II), the Presleys made their way to Memphis, Tennessee, in 1948. "We were broke, man, broke," Elvis said, "and we left Tupelo overnight. Dad packed all our belongings in boxes and put them in the trunk and on top of a 1939 Plymouth. We just headed for Memphis. Things had to be better."[36]

Finances improved slightly in the new city, with Gladys taking work as Elvis got older. However, the family still lived in New Deal–era public assistance housing and struggled at times until Elvis could start working as an older teen.[37]

The Archon of Poverty lorded over Elvis's childhood and teenage years, and the monster never completely left his mind. As Whitmer writes:

> Elvis Aaron Presley came from a family of sharecroppers. His most profound inheritance was destitution. Both sides of his family tree were rich in poverty. With this came a whole spectrum of associated deficits in terms of values, ethics, expectations, and morals. Life was bleak because it always had been. The future seemed a hostile place with a pinched horizon, where it was always someone else who was destined for better things.[38]

Between crushing penury and a desire for a long-shot breaking of karma, Elvis carried a chip on his shoulder and believed he was special regardless of the outward circumstances. The Archon of Poverty was instrumental in making him seek out music and African-American culture (as both white and Black poor shared neighborhoods in the South during the Great Depression). The Archon of Poverty made Elvis reject the "po people" dress code, the short hair and blue jean-wearing fashion of the 1950s. Instead, he sought his own look to manifest being "destined for better things": black slacks with a stripe down the pants legs, black sport coats with the collar turned up, scarves, and the piled-high hair ruled over by Vaseline.[39]

Even on a specific level, the Archon of Poverty was a guiding hand. On his eleventh birthday, in January 1946, Elvis received a guitar instead of the bicycle he wanted. "Son, wouldn't you rather have a guitar?" Gladys had asked. "It would help you with your singing, and everyone does enjoy hearing you sing." In his mother's mind, beyond worrying her son might get run over by a car, the guitar was considerably less expensive than a bicycle.[40] The Archon of Poverty and lethal enmeshment worked together this time, for this decision led Elvis to learn to become a musician. And it should be mentioned that the Archon of Poverty never gave Elvis a formal musical education—he learned from family and church—and it allowed him to be creative and syncretic with his budding talent.

The Archon of Poverty also taught Elvis constant humility, an understanding that those at the bottom deserved equality and dignity, and a rock-solid desire to improve his life continually. "Poor we were," Vernon once said. "I'll never deny that. But trash we weren't. . . . We never had any prejudice. We never put anybody down. Neither did Elvis."[41] At the same time, Gladys made sure that the big picture of Creation was what mattered to Elvis, once saying, "Son . . . always remember . . . no matter what happens when you grow up, never look down on others or think that you are better than they are, because in the eyes of God we are all equal."[41]

The Presleys, under the hoof of the Archon of Poverty, reacted by becoming insular and appearing to live in their own world. This granted Elvis a strong sense of loyalty that made him take care of family and friends after he broke incredible odds to become wealthy. His propensity for giving and being charitable is legendary, and that will be addressed later in the book, although it must be said that he displayed kindness throughout his childhood. Once, Vernon wanted to take him hunting, and Elvis cried, "Daddy, I don't want to kill birds." Elvis was also always a generous child with his possessions, even giving away his meager Christmas or birthday presents to other children in the neighborhood.[42]

With Elvis, it was not so much that he enjoyed being wealthy but that he was so grateful not to be poor. The Archon of Poverty was both a harsh and wise teacher in the King's eventual enthronement. "Shit, man, my little brother died and my mama almost died because we couldn't afford to go to no damn hospital,"[43] Elvis once said. And as Joe Moscheo wrote in *The Gospel Side of Elvis*: "Elvis never forgot the pain of poverty. He was so thankful for what came his way, and he felt compelled to share it with others."[44]

One of the ways Elvis stayed humble while being famous was by continually connecting with his past. Of the many vehicles he owned, one was a beat-up old black panel truck. He would don a black yacht cap and some sunglasses, fill up a jug of tea, and take the truck around Memphis, revisiting old haunts like his old high school or parks where he had played football.[45] For a small spell, he was no longer Elvis but just another Southerner from a hard but honest time.

CAPTAIN MARVEL

Elvis grew up during what is known as the Golden Age of Comic Books, a halcyon time between 1938 and 1956, when some of the best-known superheroes came to life: Superman, Batman, Captain America, and Wonder Woman. Jeff Kripal summarizes this era aptly in *Mutants and Mystics*:

> Nurtured by almost two decades of pulp magazines, newspaper strips, and early heroic figures like Tarzan, Prince Valiant, the Phantom, and the Shadow, the Golden Age is definitively initiated by the appearance of Superman in Action Comics #1, erupts in the summer of 1938, rolls through World War II with characters like Batman, Captain America, Captain Marvel, and Wonder Woman, and then peters out after the war, when America no longer needs its heroes.[46]

During this time, comic books were considered as fringe as extra-terrestrials and the alternative spirituality Elvis would later come to embrace. When rock 'n' roll came to the scene, comic books had become popular and were considered just as transgressive. By the 1940s, the genre was arguably the most popular form of entertainment, even if still considered somewhat fringe and adopted by outsiders. Moreover, comic books were an economic boon for the marginal classes who created them, mainly on the East Coast: Jews, Italians, and other urban minorities.

As with rock 'n' roll, religious groups pushed back against this form of entertainment, blaming it for teen delinquency and other societal afflictions. In some cities like New Orleans, Los Angeles, and Cleveland, comic books were banned or restricted during World War II, a reaction far removed from the superhero obsession and admiration that blossomed in the twenty-first century.[47]

Elvis loved reading comic books. The genre was a panacea during his, let's be honest, shitty life in Tupelo. His favorite superheroes were DC's Captain Marvel and Captain Marvel Jr., not to be confused with the female Captain Marvel of Marvel Comics. The character of the original Captain Marvel these days is closer to the successful *Shazam!* film (2019) and its (let's be honest, too) shitty sequel, *Shazam! Fury of the Gods* (2023).

The story goes as follows: Billy Batson is an unimposing young boy from humble origins chosen by an ancient wizard named Shazam to become his successor. He is bestowed the power of the gods. When Billy speaks the wizard's name, "Shazam," he is transformed into (or more accurately, possessed by some entity to become) a superhero with prodigious strength, speed, and other abilities.

The name "Shazam" is an acronym for the six legendary figures whose powers Billy inherits:

- Solomon's wisdom
- Hercules's strength
- Atlas's stamina
- Zeus's power
- Achilles's courage
- Mercury's speed

Billy must learn to balance his newfound powers with his ordinary life as a youth while facing off against dangerous villains seeking to exploit his abilities or do the typical bad-guy stuff.

It would be hard to imagine a more magical inspiration than

Captain Marvel. Jack Kirby, one of the most influential comic book superhero creators of history, based his most pagan creation, the Mighty Thor, on Captain Marvel.[48]

Captain Marvel became a very popular superhero in the Golden Age, but so was Superman. Elvis went for the high weirdness. Even Solomon, the famed monarch of Israel, is prominent in the same occult arenas that Elvis would later visit, which we shall visit in the next chapter. Many occultists and Freemasons regard Solomon as a master magician. In some ancient Gnostic texts like "The Apocalypse of Adam" and "The Testimony of Truth," Solomon controls legions of demons with powerful sorcery.

Captain Marvel Jr. would come later, originating as Freddy Freeman (subtle name). He was a disabled teen saved by Captain Marvel from the villainous Captain Nazi (another subtle name!). However, Freeman was seriously injured during the confrontation. Captain Marvel granted him part of his powers, converting him into Captain Marvel Jr. Unlike Captain Marvel, Freeman remained a teenager when transforming into his superhero alter ego.

For much of his life, Elvis remained infatuated with Captain Marvel and Captain Marvel Jr. He related to Billy Batson and later understood his transformation into a bigger-than-life figure. As Superman wore blue and red, Captain Marvel wore red and yellow with a prominent yellow thunderbolt on his chest. Captain Marvel Jr.'s suit was blue and yellow with a red cape and the famed yellow lightning bolt.

For more magic, we must consider writer Otto Binder, who didn't create Captain Marvel but crafted some of the comics' most memorable adventures. After leaving the comic book industry, Binder became an individual steeped in high weirdness, writing intensely about space exploration for NASA and Disney and becoming an adroit researcher of extraterrestrial accounts, all around the time Elvis began experiencing UFO encounters. Binder's research led him to extreme conclusions, like extraterrestrial confederacies and stereotypic alien sex involving human abduction to breed hybrid races. Binder said, "The flying saucers are here. The UFOs are real. The only thing unreal is Earth's attitude toward these significant objects and their mysterious masters, who may well be here to tell us of a brotherhood of worlds in the universe."[49] In the 1970s, Binder would interact with Ted Owens, the legendary PK Man: an individual with telekinetic, lightning-manipulation, and other powers who used a lightning insignia. In other words, Binder met his real-life Captain Marvel.[50]

In 1970, Elvis and Priscilla designed a pendant for his fourteen-carat gold necklace with a significant meaning. The pendant's prominent feature was a jagged golden bolt of lightning, with the letters TCB, standing for "taking care of business," incorporated into the design. Elvis was so pleased with the creation that he and Priscilla ordered a dozen more to distribute to his entourage and close colleagues. The logo became so meaningful to Elvis that he used it on rings, a Graceland wall, the tail of his private plane, and even his tombstone. Throughout his life, Captain Marvel's lightning logo symbolized the potential transformation of the common person.[51]

Another eldritch symbol on his necklace next to the lighting logo was a gold ankh, the ancient symbol of eternal life.[52]

Captain Marvel was magical, but was his appeal to Elvis only as an individual who transcended his meager life? It might be both the timeless story and the magic itself. As the book *Elvis Presley, Reluctant Rebel* states:

> Superhero stories tapped into adolescent fantasies of rule breaking and destruction in the name of good. They were a projection of thwarted ambition, a daydream of supremacy in a world where mountains are hard to climb and obstacles may appear insurmountable, as well as an archetypal resurgence of ancient demigods.[53]

In his book *Our Gods Wear Spandex*, Chris Knowles agrees with this assessment. Knowles further details how our beloved superheroes are nothing more than old gods and heroes modified for the modern age. The pagan gods were just the superheroes of their time:

> Few people realize, however, that explicitly magical characters are actually the earliest examples of modern superheroes. In fact, it can be

argued that all superheroes are essentially magical, since most of their powers have no basis in real science. Early superheroes like Captain Marvel, Phantasmo, and Green Lantern were unambiguously magical in origin, drawing on themes taken directly from the pulps.

Knowles sees Captain Marvel as a "pagan Sun god" involved in "Masonic, or secret-society, initiation" before meeting the wizard Shazam in an underground temple. The magician dies at the end of the Temple of Doom-ish ceremony, and Billy Batson officially becomes Captain Marvel. Knowles claims this is "the birth of Horus, the new Sun King."[54]

Perhaps Elvis did not merely love the story of Billy Batson / Freddy Freeman but *became them.* As Knowles states, Elvis adopted Captain Marvel Jr.'s hairstyle (even if other lore states he copied Tony Curtis, which makes less sense).[55] What's more, Elvis dyed his hair black, likely to appear like his secret deity (yes, ladies, he was a natural blond). And let's face it: those Las Vegas outfits parallel the two Captain Marvel costumes. Even Peter Guralnick called his show clothing Elvis's "Captain Marvel getup."[56] Although Elvis and his designer never divulged the inspiration for the Vegas Elvis look, the parallels to Captain Marvel have been speculated upon, from the mini-cape with the tall collar to the dynamic designs.[57]

I invite you to compare the images below and let your Solomonic wisdom decide.

On an interesting and ironic note, in the 1990s Freddy Freeman was recreated as Captain Marvel Jr. as an homage to Elvis, looking like none other than the King of Rock 'n' Roll. In a later story, Freeman admits to being an Elvis fan.

In my view, most biographers gloss over how important Captain Marvel was to Elvis. *Elvis for Dummies* doesn't even mention Captain Marvel or Captain Marvel Jr. Perhaps it is a generational issue. Today, the idea of superheroes being akin to gods and prime role models is mainstream. The cosplay generation at conferences and movie openings would probably have made Elvis grin. As Elvis himself once

Fig. 2.2. Captain Marvel Jr. /
Freddy Freeman, Fawcett Comics,
circa 1942. Art by Mac Raboy.

Fig. 2.3. Elvis Presley,
RCA publicity photo,
1972.

told an audience: "When I was a child, ladies and gentlemen, I was a
dreamer. I read comic books, and I was the hero of the comic book. I
saw movies, and I was the hero in the movie. So every dream that I ever
dreamed has come true a hundred times."[58]

In the King's mind, he had, in some way or another, transformed
into this most magical of beings, one who apparently materialized in
real life and is widely known in UFO and paranormal circles (don't let

go of the connection between Elvis and extraterrestrials in the next section and following chapters).

WEIRD SCIENCE, ALIEN TECH?

The Archon of Poverty drove and shaped Elvis, but ironically, wealth and progress allowed the King to ascend to his throne.

After World War II, the USA metamorphosed from a republic to an imperialistic nation gorged on capitalism. To wit, the country became very rich. The gross national product rose from $353.3 billion in 1950 to an astounding $487.7 billion in 1960. The main drivers were the automobile industry, housing, and expanding consumer goods.[59] And let's not forget military spending, too. This was the idyllic "Eisenhower America," where a family could own a house and have two cars in their garage. Millions of Americans lived the middle-class dream while immersed in rampant consumer culture. Poverty still lingered among many ethnic groups, including white and Black Americans, but even a robust African-American middle class emerged.

The postwar economic boom created a trickle-down effect from mom and dad to the kids. In other words, teenagers had more money than ever and could shape popular culture. The result was a growing rift between parents and their children. The younger generation, predictably, didn't share the values of their parents and rapidly pivoted to embracing more progressive or transgressive social issues or music. Youths could make themselves heard and have an impact.[60] As Glenn C. Altschuler writes in *All Shook Up*, before the twentieth century "teenagers did not exist." Adolescence was not much better than childhood when it came to adults having complete control of young people's lives. In the first half of the century, adolescents gained some freedom and identity because of factors like legal marriage age rising, but by "the end of World War II, the term 'teen-ager' was firmly established in the language." A new caste was created, a new social class that could move the social and political needle.[61]

On the one hand, you had parents who had survived the Great

Depression and World War II and "did not want to deny their children cars, clothes, or commercial entertainment in a more affluent age."[62] On the other hand, as Gary Tillery writes, you had a youth that was "maturing in the age of television and 3D films, of long-range missiles and flying saucers, and, most crucially, in the atomic age, with the grim specter of nuclear war threatening to obliterate humankind."[63]

Propelled into a new age that rained money and potentially might rain nuclear ash, aided by doting parents, this young, pre-boomer generation wanted to play hard and have new experiences, exploring an odd combination of existentialism and ecstasy. They were known as the Silent Generation, Traditionalists, or "Radio Babies," recognized as being born under the shadow of harsh American eras. This age group was considered purpose-driven, loyal to ideals, yet fretful about the country's prospects. Many were not quiet or willing to accept the new capitalist Eden; beyond Elvis, this list can include Martin Luther King, Jr., Noam Chomsky, Bob Dylan, Maya Angelou, and Muhammad Ali. Their heroes, from Marlon Brando to James Dean, would express their restlessness and worry. As far as music went, the old standards made no sense; all that mattered was questing the fringes for excitement. As rock historian Piero Scaruffi wrote, "White people had the money, but black people were making the most exciting music."[64] In the following section, I will show it was because diaspora African culture is where the ancient sorcery and timeless, engaging myths resided.

But beyond a younger generation possessing the resources and drive to embrace non-church music in the Bible Belt, push back against segregation, and influence fashion (eventually leading to someone as dualistic and extreme as themselves: Elvis), science was a key factor in opening the door to alternative artforms, cultures, and metaphysics.

Mass media, in the form of radio and television, allowed the fringe to become more mainstream. In 1951, the first jukebox machines that played 45 RPM records began to spread in every corner of the country. Radio stations switched from 78 to 45 RPM in 1954, facilitating music sales, production, and distribution. In the same year, Japanese electronics company TTK (which later became Sony) introduced the great destroyer of barriers and castes in entertainment: the transistor radio.[65] At the same time, African-American music became more accepted and broadcast on radio stations and jukeboxes. Hundreds of Black disc jockeys worked in radio stations. By 1959, 156 million radios were buzzing across the United States, three times the number of TV sets.[66]

As David R. Shumway writes, one can't stress enough what television did for society and the rising caste that was teens:

> Television was essential to the rise of rock & roll and its trans-formation of American popular music. Because TV could convey the visual excitement of rock & roll performances, popular music shifted from a primarily aural mass experience to one in which the visual field held equal primacy. Television had a profound impact on everyday life in America; its rapid penetration of American homes was unprecedented, the number of households with TV increasing from 0.66 percent in 1948, to 64 percent in 1955, and to 90 percent by the end of the decade.[67]

Moreover, television connected growing suburbia while allowing the middle class to experience different forms of entertainment and art at a safe distance. American culture was forever transformed during the 1950s, becoming simultaneously voyeuristic and detached.

And guess who was there to capitalize on this space-age tech known as television? Guess who could bond with young people to continue the rebellion once he had conquered radio and live auditoriums almost immediately? Shumway provides the answer:

> No one benefited more from television than Elvis, who appeared on national programs at least twelve times from January 1956 to January 1957.... The controversy he generated had much more to do with what people saw than what they heard. While it is well known that Elvis transgressed racial boundaries that still largely separated

white and black culture in the 1950s, his appearance and behavior on the tube also threatened class hierarchies and reminded people that America's youth were defining themselves against adult norms. Elvis redefined popular music stardom by his failure to conform to accepted conventions of performance decorum, and the most threatening aspect of his performance was his violation of gender codes.[68]

As they say, there is no such thing as bad publicity. Elvis's beaming into homes instantly made him into a household name or perhaps a household god. When he gyrated his hips on *The Ed Sullivan Show* on September 9, 1956, a staggering 82.6 percent of households with televisions were glued to the screen, making for an estimated audience of over 60 million viewers (over a third of Americans), a level not surpassed until the also-historic Apollo 11 moon landing.[69]

Elvis became perhaps the main product marketed to teenagers in the 1950s. Unlike James Dean, who was constrained by the movie screen and theater, Elvis could work his sorcery on younger people in real time, at a more personal level, on more occasions, and in the comfort of their homes. The generational battle between teens and adults would happen immediately and in the living rooms of the suburbs.[70]

A powerful bond was created between Rockabilly Elvis and millions of teens trying to find their footing in a nuclear age of breakneck progress, with money in their pockets and radios in their cars, hoping to commune with a young and talented musician who was like them or reflected how they would like to see themselves: "A misfit and an outcast, Elvis was, in essence, a southern juvenile delinquent."[71] He became the rallying cry and main symbol for the youth and others who would not be marginalized or left behind in this brave new world. As scholar Susan Doll wrote:

The backlash against Elvis revealed a chasm in America between different groups and cultures: young versus old; black versus white; working class versus middle class; and Southern culture versus mainstream culture. The success of Elvis Presley and the popularity of his music proved that regionally based entertainers who appealed to specific groups and subcultures could challenge established entertainment institutions and undermine mainstream tastes. On a deeper level, Elvis and his success showed that beneath the complacency that was generally associated with the 1950s, certain groups—blacks, poor whites, teenagers—were dissatisfied with the norms represented by the status quo. Fearful of the challenge to the mainstream tastes and norms that Elvis, his music, and his in-your-face performing style represented, the status quo criticized, ridiculed, and attacked Elvis, his Southern culture, his ties to black rhythm and blues, and his youthful fans.[72]

But since this is a book about high weirdness, the extraordinary must be included as a possibility for the technological boom. The idea that the USA would come out of decades of unforgiving economic stagnation and a punishing war and move straight into a consumer, industrial, and economic utopia is hard to fathom. The chart below details

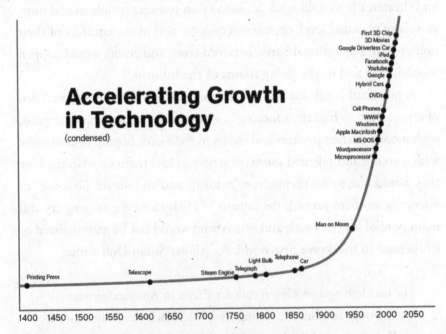

Fig. 2.4. How can we explain this exponential growth of technological advancement? Graph by Muhammad Uzair et al. (CC BY 4.0 DEED)

how, in the 1950s, humanity's technological innovation accelerated like never before, even more than in Sumerian times when a mature civilization seemingly popped out of the ground.

After World War II, the USA became almost sci-fi-like in its ability to create game-changing technology. The machines that rose after technology had remained fundamentally level for millennia. America blinked, and satellites, space exploration, computers, lasers, the internet, and many other advancements sprang ostensibly overnight and didn't slow down until the beginning of the twenty-first century.

Can we speculate on Nazi breakaway or stolen technology being behind these advances? That's always fun, along with watching the camp film *Iron Skies*, but the Nazis had a good ten years of innovation on American scientists, and their advancements pale in comparison to the USA's in the decade after World War II. Anything is possible, and the USA definitely brought ex-Nazis to work for NASA and other organizations. But that fact does not fully account for the skyrocketing developments in science, and neither does the fear of Communists who barely made a blip in the novelty radar beyond their own space program.

An attractive option that Chris Knowles entertains can be found in *The Day After Roswell*, by Colonel Philip J. Corso.[73] The retired colonel released his book in 1997, claiming that the 1950s-era explosion in technological advancement was due to pilfering and reverse-engineering crashed UFO technology from the 1947 crash in Roswell, New Mexico. The main treasure from the site crash and its bounty was the transistor, the chief building block of the American technological revolution. As Corso writes:

> More than one historian of the microcomputer age has written that no one before 1947 foresaw the invention of the transistor or had even dreamed about an entirely new technology that relied upon semiconductors, which were silicon based and not carbon based like the Edison incandescent tube. Bigger than the idea of a calculating machine or an Analytical Engine or any combination of the

components that made up the first computers of the 1930s and 1940s, the invention of the transistor and its natural evolution to the silicon chip of integrated circuitry was beyond what anyone could call a quantum leap of technology.[74]

Aside from seeing alien bodies, Corso claims he retrieved alien artifacts that he disseminated to scientists to develop cutting-edge technologies (this included ex-Nazi and rocket scientist Wernher von Braun). Some of these advancements were:

- Image intensifiers (which ultimately became "night vision")
- Fiber optics, super-tenacity fibers, and lasers
- Molecular alignment metallic alloys
- Integrated circuits and microminiaturization of logic boards
- Research conducted via HARP (High Altitude Research Project)
- The plan for Project Horizon (a proposed moon base)
- Portable atomic generators (ion propulsion drive)
- Irradiated food
- Third brain guidance systems (EBE headbands)
- Particle beams ("Star Wars" antimissile energy weapons)
- Electromagnetic propulsion systems
- Depleted uranium projectiles[75]

According to Corso's book, companies like IBM, Bell Labs, Dow Corning, and Hughes Aircraft benefited from the alien tech, manufacturing advanced technologies that gave the USA an edge militarily and commercially.

The Day After Roswell sold like hotcakes, with plenty of pushback from the military and scientific community, and Corso died a year later. Knowles explains that claims against his reputation and credibility were false and that "big breakthroughs with actual working patents came in the period Corso cites (the 1950s and 1960s) and through the companies he claims were seeded with materials to experiment on."[76]

This conjecture is fascinating, and some readers might think sensationalistic. But it's not much less ridiculous than an unknown young man seemingly coming out of nowhere to take over culture and lead a country to a space age. As you will learn, when it comes to Elvis, it seems that all the stars (including their residents) had to be aligned for his rise to fame and his perfect bonding with a new generation and technology that moved as fast as the King's hips during a concert. One cannot deny that something incredible occurred in America and its collective psyche as it became an empire that defied both the starry and quantum worlds.

These days, along with comic books, UFOs are as mainstream as rock 'n' roll became in the 1950s. And both UFOs and Elvis crossed paths several times, but that's for another chapter. I am merely speculating about the aligned freakshows that both Elvis and America became after the fall of the Nazi regime. Perhaps the revolution was televised after all. Or was it an invasion?

Regardless, we must now give the devil his due.

THE BLUES: A DEAL WITH THE DEVIL

From an early age, Elvis loved a variety of music. This fondness evolved into opera, which fascinated him. "I just loved music," he recalled. "Music period."[77] Music was essential to Elvis for solace and identity. From being eight and performing backup vocals for his idol Mississippi Slim on a weekend radio program to breaking through at nineteen in 1954 with the release of "That's All Right (Mama)," he loved connecting with audiences and blending many genres in the bubbling cauldron that was his alchemical imagination: gospel, rhythm & blues, rockabilly, and country.

Without a doubt, a cornerstone of rock music is the blues. The origin of blues is not well documented; the Southern African-American art form emerged from the post-Civil War era. The genre is believed to have developed from a combination of African musical traditions, such as call-and-response vocals, and European musical styles, such as folk and ballad music. Simple chords characterized early blues music. In the 1920s and 1930s, blues music gained popularity outside of its traditional Black audience due in part to the growth of recorded music and the migration of Southern African-Americans to northern cities. By the 1950s, blues music became mainstream in the USA and Europe, with artists like B.B. King and Muddy Waters achieving commercial success. A case could be made that the blues evolved into rhythm and blues (or "race music" as it was called) and then early rock 'n' roll. However, whether blues or jazz came earlier will remain a chicken-or-egg deliberation.

The devil is in the details when it comes to blues, literally and figuratively, with much of its early days shrouded in mystery, but we'll not lose eyes on the devil—or more like on a specific myth of the devil.

Musician and writer Matthew Frederick explains that it "can be said that the blues came out of Africa but was not born in Africa."[78] Frederick states that the blues can be traced in much of African music, from the Xalam of Mali to the ngoni harp of Western Africa. The genesis of blues comes from the migration of enslaved people to the New World in colonial times. Records are incomplete, yet it has been estimated that between six and seven million people were brought from Africa, either directly or via the Caribbean, and brutally treated until the slave trade was outlawed in 1818 and then totally abolished in 1865 with the conclusion of the American Civil War.[79]

The blues was an ocean where many tributaries of African art, storytelling, spirituality, and mythmaking flowed in. As Frederick writes:

> The blues comes out of pain and sorrow, but also immense joy. Blues is a feeling, as the song goes, but it is also so much more than that. It is the story of a culture, a musical form. It can be a way of talking, a way of dressing, a way of being. It comes from within African American culture; it can't be understood without reference to this culture, yet, as we shall see, it belongs to a subset who sit apart from

this culture, who are defined by their separation. The bluesman is defined as much by who he is not as by who he is.[80]

The blues is an emotional state of melancholy, almost an altered state of mind that draws from a tragic past and eternal pride. Frederick brings up an apocryphal quote by Jimi Hendrix: "The blues are easy to play but hard to feel."[81]

Elvis agreed with all of this, one time saying in response to an assumption that he invented rock 'n' roll:

No way man, no way. It all goes way, way back to the days in the old Deep South when the slaves were working and slaving their lives away. I mean those poor old people knew what real pain an' suffering was all about. They used to sing and pour out their hearts to God just to make it through the day.[82]

This fusion of African traditions in the colonial South also included its animistic spirituality, and it mated with Christianity in time. Voodoo, Hoodoo, and Conjure are perfect examples—magical, ecstatic faiths that linger in the American South even today. As Roman Catholic saints replaced pagan gods, African spirits took on Christian overtones. One of these was the Devil, who became a patron muse for the blues. We are not talking about the "Prince of Hell" aspect of Satan, but a more syncretic figure, combining the attributes of the Biblical Satan with African spirits and gods. This character is not the sadistic bastard of orthodox Christianity nor the debonair antihero of Milton, enlightenment occultists, and modern Satanists. He is more like the trickster deity found in various mythologies worldwide. This "Trickster Devil" is more ambiguous, at times good but often evil, sometimes succeeding in his schemes but at other times outwitted by astute humans. In one story, he can assume the role of a cruel white landlord; in another yarn, he manifests as the cheeky African-American hero. For mortals that he takes a liking to, he is an almost omnipotent ally, but one must always read between the lines of his assurances and expect a plot twist or trick here and there.[83]

In prewar blues, Old Nick was frequently portrayed as a playful mischief-maker who defied social norms. Clara Smith's classic song from 1924, "Done Sold My Soul to the Devil," exemplified this conception by portraying a contract with Satan as an analogy for her place in the blues world, set apart from what was deemed respectable in "polite society."[84]

The themes of sorrow, loss, and social justice are central to the "Trickster Devil" in Black Southern folklore and blues. He was crucial in navigating the American diaspora with wit and guile. But one had to watch out, for this magical force could doom you as much as he could liberate you, perhaps serving as a symbol of the white man and his machinations during the nineteenth century.

One of the most famous accounts of the African-American Devil was that of Robert Johnson, legendary musician and the "last of the great Delta bluesman [sic] and America's first rock star."[85] One day, Robert was walking alone in the forest when he came upon a crossroads. There, he encountered a mysterious man garbed in black who offered to make him a deal—to teach him how to play guitar like no other mortal in exchange for his soul. Robert agreed to the deal, and the Devil taught him how to play the blues like a god. Soon after, Robert became a renowned blues musician, and his haunting melodies were said to have the power to move people to tears. The story was a way to explain how, after a period of vanishing from society, he reappeared with celestial talent.

Any deal with the Devil is a monkey's paw, of course. Johnson dealt with personal demons, including substance abuse and periods of depression. His death is almost as strange as his business with Lucifer. The official cause of death listed on his death certificate is "no doctor," which indicates no medical professional was present at the time of his passing. However, there are several speculations as to how he died. One theory is that Johnson was poisoned by a jealous husband of a woman with whom he had an affair. Another theory suggests that he died from syphilis, a sexually transmitted disease he is believed to have contracted earlier in his life.[86] No record in this world talks about Satan coming to collect a soul.

What is known is that Johnson died on August 16, 1938, exactly thirty-nine years before Elvis succumbed to his own demons.[87] The Devil does have a sense of irony, perhaps.

The Crossroads and the Devil became central themes for the blues. In many cultures, trickster deities like Hermes or Hekate can be found at the Crossroads—that uncanny place where morality and opportunity, tradition and innovation, blur together, where it seems a person may be lost forever. The only way to be found is to transform permanently, in both this existence and sometimes the afterlife. As Frederick states, the Crossroads is not an event or place but a "way of being" for the bluesman and "a way of becoming."[88]

The perceptive Elvis, quiet but ambitious and with one eye on otherworldly realms (a gift from both Gladys and Jesse), must have known that the blues would be part of his transformation out of poverty and into Captain Marvel. As he once said, "Black musicians have more soul in their little fingers than most whites have in their whole bodies."[89]

In fact, devilish blues wizardry might have kickstarted his career. As the story goes, Elvis was auditioning for Sam Phillips at Sun Studios in June of 1955—and the session proceeded poorly. Every genre he performed was underwhelming. At the end of an aggravating day and with everyone in the studio about to call it a night, Elvis allowed the Devil to possess him. The nineteen-year-old let it all out and launched into a wild, unhinged performance, singing a rhythm-and-blues song: Arthur Crudup's "That's All Right (Mama)." Phillips was floored, knowing he had caught lightning in a bottle with a singer tapping directly into Black magic (pun intended on my part, but that's the Crossroads for you). Elvis's career officially started with what would become his first hit single.[90]

Many biographers and music critics agree that something

extraordinary happened that fateful day. Like Johnson, Elvis traveled to the Crossroads with his own pain, agenda, and rebellion. Unlike Johnson, he would seemingly trick the Trickster, as we shall see.

For now, though, it is only essential to see the metaphysical under-pinning of the blues: the idea of Devil-as-Trickster. One could say that most musicians in the 1950s knew nothing of African-American folk-lore. The sound was simply an increasingly popular genre with young people and complemented other forms of music. But that's like telling someone without any idea of what gospel music is that they won't be moved or affected by its essence. The blues was a state of being, a word-less emotion and memory spanning centuries to connect with ancient prankster spirits. Elvis was indeed "the Devil in disguise."

Back to Frederick, who further explains the transgressive character of the blues:

> Blues caters to carnal needs, not spiritual, and while there may be some who barrelhouse on Saturday night before attending the service on Sunday morning, it is not a thing to be accepted or encouraged. You can live a double life for a while, but sooner or later you've got to make a choice. We're back to the crossroads. You can choose to serve the Devil or the Lord, and it is made quite clear that the blues belongs to the Devil. And for those with spiritual needs that were not catered for by the church, there were other options available.[91]

One exception to this dichotomy, though, would be Elvis. The King tapped into a primordial magic of pain, lust, ecstasy, and longing—and it rewarded him with a forbidden Lightbringer power that, as with Robert Johnson, made him superhuman among mere mortals. He was also, at the same time, downloading the powers of Heaven, as we will cover in the next section. This tricking the Trickster Devil kept him far enough from the gates of Hell. Elvis himself confirmed this: "I have the power of heaven and hell in me, and that's what I've got to learn to balance. Because they're dangerous."[92]

GOSPEL MUSIC:
A CONTRACT WITH ANGELS

Now it's time to get off that highway to Hell and up the stairway to Heaven.

It is established that the blues significantly influenced Elvis and his "becoming" in the Crossroads. An even more significant impact came from the other side of the tracks. It is no secret that Black churches disapproved of blues.[93] But in a way typical of cosmic polarities, the sound of churches and blues was interconnected. Indeed, the Crossroads also originates in churches and their spiritual music. An illustration is found in part of William S. Hays's 1875 Jubilee spiritual "Angels Meet Me at the Crossroads":

> *Angels meet me at the crossroads, meet me*
> *Angels meet me at the crossroads, meet me*
> *Angels meet me at the crossroads, meet me*
> *Don't charge a sinner any toll.*[94]

Gospel was Elvis's favorite genre, white or Black. This music enraptured him since he was three, when he would loudly sing during church service. As a teen, he would sneak out of his church to attend a Black church nearby, East Trigg Baptist Church, where he was mesmerized by the music and preaching of Reverend W. Herbert Brewster. At the Sunday night all-Black service, Elvis would have to sit in the back where a segregated row was available for white people. The service was often broadcast on live radio.[95]

Elvis once said:

I came to know the black people, and to appreciate them, to understand their simple faith, and their patient enduring, to love their music, born of their troubles. Their gospel music became my music, and their spirituals my spirituals. I change them only slightly. For they, too, are my people, and I sing of them as well.[96]

His favorite band growing up was The Statesmen Quartet. Their rendition of "In My Father's Kingdom" and "Known Only to Him" inspired him to record a gospel album in 1960. He loved how slower gospel tunes made him contemplative while stronger ones ignited jubilation in his heart. Gospel music altered his consciousness and brought about a state of rapture.[97]

Elvis's three Grammys were for his gospel albums. He boasted that he knew almost every religious song ever written.[98]

When it came to blues and gospel, Elvis loved that they were both experiential music forms that opened the channels of communication to higher states of existence. That is also where blues and gospel meet at the Crossroads: they are shamanistic.

What is shamanism, exactly? In the past section, Frederick explained how the blues drew from African shamanism. Yet shamanism is another polysemous word like "magic" and "pagan," although it does have a concise definition that ties it into blues and gospel and, as I will explain, Pentecostalism.

Shamanism has been called the world's oldest religion, originating in Siberia and Central Asia. However, some experts have surmised that Shamanism is not a true religion but more of a spiritual modality that attaches itself to organized religions. Thus, one can have Buddhist, Mongolian, Persian, or Islamic shamanism.[99]

How shamanism materialized across so many religions throughout the world is formally a scholarly mystery. Still, one can easily see the collective consciousness's intrinsic need for an animistic, mystic, and firsthand spirituality. Shamanism deals with the spiritual health of an individual (typically by union with the Divine or benign spirits). Shamanism is also responsible for the mental and physical well-being of the community. The shaman is a "spiritual troubleshooter" who directly negotiates with the spirit world and often brings back magical solutions for the tribe. While a priest deals with ritualist, exoteric chores like sacrifices, weddings, funerals, and theology, the shaman quests the underworld for information and mentally, physically, and spiritually heals the sick. Ecstatic or altered states of mind, prophecy, elaborate experiential ceremonies, shapeshifting and crossdressing, and entheogen use are part of the shamanic repertoire. And so is music. Music is essential.[100]

There is even Christian shamanism, first manifesting in Egyptian mystery schools via the Christian Gnostics during Greco-Roman times. More than travelers of the spiritual world looking for magical solutions, the Christian Gnostics were more like buccaneers stealing treasures from the gods and rebelling like anarchists against the conventional societal structure.[101] Shamanistic Christianity later evolved into other types like those found in the mystical orders of the Greek Orthodox Church.[102]

Pentecostalism was another Christian movement that incorporated shamanism, according to Karin Horwatt in *The Shamanistic Complex in the Pentecostal*, and did so more ardently in Black Pentecostalism. Horwatt draws on the shamanic research of Claude Lévi-Strauss and Mircea Eliade, among others. The animal totems, potions, and drums were replaced by church altars, faith healing, and pianos (later electric guitars). Yet Pentecostals employed the same oral-formulaic technique that could send a crowd into a trance and provide possible healing. Instead of encountering ecstatic gods like Apollo or Dionysus, Pentecostals asked the Holy Spirit to enter them with her gifts. Both the Pentecostal preacher and the shaman are the "center of magico-religious life." Both the preacher and the shaman require a crowd (or we could say a crowd's soul energy) to heal a patient. We can add "musician" to the role of the public healer.[103]

Elvis was utterly immersed in the Pentecostal Assemblies of God as a youth and visited Black Pentecostal churches. He once said in an interview on the impact of church music:

> We used to go to these religious singins all the time. There were these singers, perfectly fine singers, but nobody responded to 'em. Then there were these other singers—the leader wuz a preacher—and they cut up all over the place, jumpin' on the piano, movin' every which way. The audience liked 'em. I guess I learned from them singers.[104]

As the Black Pentecostal movement informed much of gospel music,[105] gospel would, like the blues, inform rock 'n' roll. As Randall J. Stephens wrote in his article, "God Gave Rock and Roll to You":

> Rock and roll—the soundtrack of rebellion and the music of side-burned delinquents and teenage consumers—owed a surprising debt to Holy Ghost religion. It is true that Pentecostalism formed just one of the tributaries that fed the raging river of rock and roll, but the importance of the spirit-filled faith to the new hybrid genre was significant."[106]

That Egyptian Christian Gnosticism never died away, did it? Its shamanism and rebellious ethos echoed strongly in Elvis's early entertainer persona. And as mentioned in a previous section, gospel is Christian magic.

In Pentecostal churches across the South, the phrase "rocking and rolling" was meant to describe the excitement of the Holy Spirit descending and possessing people. The congregation crowded into the aisles to vent their feelings (the public therapy of the shaman).[107] The first known use of the term "rock 'n' roll" as a music genre was in 1951 when Cleveland disc jockey Alan Freed started employing it on his radio show to describe the rhythm and blues records he was playing.

Bringing back Knowles, in *Secret History of Rock 'n' Roll*, he makes the case that gospel has the same lineage as blues and is more influential than blues in the formation of rock music:

> Although many historians cite blues music and jazz as primary in the development of rock 'n' roll, it is this writer's opinion that by far the greatest—and most direct—influence on what we know as rock is gospel music. Gospel, which began to emerge as a distinct musical form toward the end of the 19th century, traces its roots to traditional African song styles, as well as Diaspora adaptations such as field hollers and voodoo drumming.[108]

Knowles also points out that Elvis and other rock pioneers like Little Richard and Jerry Lee Lewis were first inspired and consumed by the spiritual fire of the gospel genre (and I should add B. B. King and Johnny Cash to that list). It was a "drugless Bacchanalia that provided relief for the marginalized and poor, infecting other denominations including white churches in the south, ultimately being a building block to 'race music' that included the blues."[109]

According to Southern music and art legend Tav Falco: "Gospel and rock 'n' roll were cut from the same cloth, even though one is considered to be the devil's music, and the other sanctified music. It was played by the same people, and appealed to the same audience."[110]

In the 1950s, gospel and the blues, Paradise and Hades, blended to usher in a new age, and Elvis would be the greatest advocate and disseminator of this merged shamanistic tradition, Hell-bent and Heaven-sent. For decades, religious critics claimed that Pentecostals had pushed the boundaries of decency by mixing sex and salvation, and now it was realized in Elvis and his rock music.[111]

It was no secret, and it was ironic that rock 'n' roll and its Pentecostal roots would be condemned by the same people who promoted gospel, as Randall J. Stephens writes:

> Deep in America's Bible belt, rock music lit a raging fire of controversy. The rebellious, loud anthems of black and white teenagers threatened the good order of the white Christian South and stirred the leadership and laity in black churches as well. As rock 'n' roll music hit big in 1955 and 1956, southern ministers and laypeople lined up to condemn the new genre. If rock *did* owe something to pentecostalism, said detractors, it was only a perverted, blasphemous copy. Churchmen had long guarded their Zion from encroaching threats—whether those were in the form of religious rebels, political radicals, or deviants of any stripe.[112]

Rock 'n' roll was church music at its core, and some Pentecostalists

noticed how rock concerts were dead ringers of a Holy Ghost revival—
but they were inversions of the latter, Mephistopheles's call to young
people to take a shamanic trip down into the underworld. Gladys was
vocal about Elvis being a sound, moral person. Yet, at times, it "seemed
impossible to convince half the adult population in the world that
Presley was not the devil incarnate." Elvis's childhood pastor, James
Hamill, turned on him when he became famous, stating that Elvis
was caught in a web spun by Satan and should be prayed for. America's
most famous preacher, Billy Graham, doubted Elvis's faith and rock
music. Elvis remained sensitive to these accusations early in his career,
performing a balancing act in interviews between saying he wasn't a
"holy roller" but a regular Christian and explaining that his music was
detached from his church roots. Being more astute than the Beatles,
who claimed years later they were more famous than Jesus, Elvis tapped
into the persecuted Messiah energy to the press to get the public off his
back: "There were people that didn't like Jesus Christ. They killed him.
And Jesus Christ was a perfect man."[113]

More than a popularizer and spreader of this shamanistic energy,
Elvis *was a shaman*. Seeking the spirits with magical music, embracing an altered state of mind while straddling Heaven and Hell at the
Crossroads, and providing ecstasy to his audience, Elvis took on the
role of a shaman (we will explore magic more deeply in chapter 9,
specifically with regard to his Vegas Elvis manifestation). Elvis didn't
write his music; his only two social songs were "In The Ghetto" and
"If I Can Dream." What he did, instinctually knowing the spiritual
forces underneath any genre, was pull magic from music to affect his
tribe, the American tribe waking up to its new role in history.

Knowles calls him the "original Apollo of 20th-century rock"
(the solar god included shamanic followers in his cult; it's notable
that Elvis first signed with Sun Records). Lastly, Knowles states
what many biographers and rock historians have echoed: "It's
hard to imagine rock 'n' roll becoming the phenomenon it became
without him."[114]

THE GREATEST TRICK(STER)
THE DEVIL EVER PULLED

It can't be stressed enough what an impact rock 'n' roll had on the American psyche. It was almost an overdose of steroids for the culture, sidelining old customs and standards to allow an explorative ethos to couple with postwar America's materialism. As Tillery writes:

> Rock and roll ignited a firestorm. Preachers, teachers, politicians, professors, and worried parents saw in the unbridled emotions it unleashed an express lane to immorality and crime. And lurking in the background—particularly in the South—was a perceived mixing of the races. Many white listeners, hearing Elvis on the radio, assumed he was black. The unrestrained passion in his voice, and the overt sexuality in his stage performance, frightened many white leaders, who feared it could lead to breaking down the barriers of segregation (a well-founded fear, as it turned out).[115]

From allegedly recording a song for his mother (who didn't own a record player) to "Heartbreak Hotel" hitting the top of the charts (the number-one single of 1956), Elvis's rise to the top was nothing short of dominant if not miraculous. He didn't merely get the country's attention but the entire world's. John Lennon once said, "Before there was Elvis, there was nothing." By the end of 1956, Elvis had released five of the best-selling singles in America: "Heartbreak Hotel," "I Want You, I Need You, I Love You," "Hound Dog," "Don't Be Cruel," and "Love Me Tender." He owned the top of the chart for twenty-five weeks of that year—all after May.[116] Elvis kept touring, gaining crowds, appearing on television, making movies, and recording albums. He ruled pop culture like no other artist had or would in history—in just a few years and barely being an adult. Out of the gate, he was the proverbial GOAT. The world soul of the world was forever altered by his glamour.

But it almost *had* to be Elvis, this techno and boundary-eradicating messiah of a new age. As Knowles writes, "The Muses choose broken vessels: that's just the way it's always been."[117] Elvis *had* to be broken, as happens to many artists. The death of Jesse forever kept part of him in the magical underworld. The ecstatic, musical religion he was exposed to before being born endlessly kept him downloading from the spirit lands of Heaven and Hell. The Archon of Poverty kept him rich in the soul but injured in the heart. Gladys provided him with witch blood and her dark spell that kept him in an eternally altering state of manhood. All of this made him the perfect court wizard for a changing era, the pied piper of the Atomic-Age young, and, yes, the chaotic Orpheus who could thrive at the Crossroads.

Those at the margins are known to leverage the most forbidden of magical systems, from folk magic to curses, whether under the shadow of the Roman Empire or the church. The Archon of Poverty, and all other archons, will force those with nothing to lose to seek what should belong to everyone who dreams. As Chaos magician Gordon White writes:

> Magic is always the tactic of last resort for those who refuse to give up hope. You do not summon Cthulhu to help you find the TV remote. You only visit the witch at the edge of the village when all other options have been explored, for she is the loan shark of the gods."[118]

Elvis wanted everything for his family and life, and he took that forbidden magic to the Crossroads, backed with stargazing energy from a young population of dreamers. By balancing dark and light magic, taking the form of an African exile, and pretending to be a superhero, Elvis didn't make a deal or sell his soul at the Crossroads, like Robert Johnson, but *became* the Lord of the Crossroads, the Lord of that liminal, mythic, and imaginal space that divides all dimensions, Earth and dream, the average. Elvis *became* the avatar of the Trickster, the blues Devil incarnate. Like the ancient Gnostics and Siberian shamans, he dominated the "other side" and brought strength, reverie, and magic to a new generation, reflecting his extreme abilities and a new nation. He ruled the Crossroads.

Think about it:

1. **Elvis was the Crossroads of a segregated, multicultural, global society.**

This bridging of people and their cultures didn't come without criticism from preachers and politicians desperate to defend the status quo. For example, Ray Charles, who never particularly liked Elvis, once said in an interview, "I know too many artists that are far greater. He was doing our kind of music. So what the hell am I supposed to get so excited about?" On the other hand, Elvis's friend and another founder of rock 'n' roll, B. B. King, wrote in his autobiography: "Elvis didn't steal any music from anyone. He just had his own interpretation of the music he'd grown up on, same is true for everyone. I think Elvis had integrity."[119]

The issue of Elvis's appropriation has been debated for generations. Still, in a broader context, Ted Harrison contextualizes the King's impact by stating that "Elvis, by crossing the musical Rubicon, represented a new social order that was not to be delineated by race." He allowed a massive shift to take place by being at the vanguard of shattering racial segregation, a shift that directly contributed to a more pluralistic society today. Yet his legacy still remains a controversial topic. Obviously, to some in Western societies, Elvis has been taken on as a representation of antiquated values, even if the poverty-stricken rural communities of the South have looked to Elvis for comfort. He stands as a symbol for the unfortunate in this area, many of whom are disreputably referred to as "white trash."[120]

Even if Elvis stole African-American music and style, what did you expect from a Trickster? Like Hermes thieving cattle from Apollo or Prometheus stealing fire from Olympus, that's what they do. It's a feature, not a bug. Elvis and Chuck Berry helped build a bridge between blues and country music (Tricksters live in bridges as well as at Crossroads, you see).[121]

At his core, Elvis was colorblind but keen in sight for the deeper essence of any individual or art form. For example, he had no problem dating black girls as a teen, and when caught by white officers, he almost got a beating for daring to break the unwritten race code of the time (he escaped by telling the police they were just a gospel choir practicing extra).[122] Thus, we see Elvis accepting people for who they are, empathizing with their core human narratives, not just seeking their magical shamanic roots and melancholic art. He saw the African-American plight as his own, having been born a penniless Southerner in the Great Depression.

One of his childhood heroes was Sister Rosetta Tharpe, a Black gospel singer from Arkansas who was often featured on a radio station with a half-hour of Black gospel. Elvis would rush home from school to listen to her. Tharpe became the perfect role model for the young Elvis: she was an individual who came from agricultural poverty and rose to international fame. Tharpe possessed the gift of turning gospel music into cabaret tunes, being as outrageous and as sexual as she felt. She was flashy in dress and swung a guitar on stage like a warrior. In her, Elvis understood the plight of the marginalized but the potential of a star who wrote their own unique narrative. Tharpe showed that the forgotten in the South could attain social mobility through Christian magic and the Gnostic rage of an artist living in the desert of the real, an inspirational wasteland. Elvis probably imagined he could have what she had, and it could be a damn good time.[123] Nobody had to lose their soul. On the contrary, one's soul grew with the audience's help.

2. Elvis was at the Crossroads of gender identity and sexual roles.

How the sexes behaved would drastically change in the country and worldwide during and after Elvis. Men and women would explore sexual frontiers like never before.

As Knowles writes:

> Elvis Presley projected a kind of ambiguous sexuality in his younger
> days, which he modeled on the rebel archetypes popularized by

(bisexual) screen idols like James Dean and Marlon Brando. But the combination of gender-bending and cathartic, almost shamanic power would become a major force in the spread of rock 'n' roll, particularly in the post hippie era when the glam movement took hold in the UK and Europe.[124]

Supporting Elvis's transformative power, Shumway explains that Elvis challenged conventions of performance etiquette and violated gender codes by calling attention to his body as a sexual object. He was the first male star to do so overtly and consistently. He became sexualized like most women. By doing this, he "both exploited and provoked cultural anxiety over the changing construction of gender."[125]

Because of Elvis, sexual norms in the West would never be the same, with the only normal being constant gender change and realignment. The sexual revolution of the 1960s was primed, at the very least.

3. Even where he lived was a Crossroads.

It has been stated that the Archon of Poverty sent Elvis and his family to Memphis in 1948 when he was thirteen (an auspicious number in itself). The city was a "crossroads where America's South and North met."[126] Black and white music and culture mingled, and in between, Elvis would strike alchemical gold when he signed with Sun Records. When Elvis gyrated like a madman and blew Sam Phillips away with "That's Alright (Mama)," Phillips wasn't only thinking of his bank account. He knew he had reached his dream of promoting a talented white artist who could express African-American music that was becoming popular, as well as record the music of poor Southerners, both Black and white, who had been overlooked by the world.[127]

Memphis became Elvis's home until his death. The city was named after the great ancient Egyptian metropolis. The reasons for its name remain murky, especially in Tennessee, where most cities are named after Cherokee words or former soldiers. A common explanation is that it overlooks a great river (the Mississippi) like the Egyptian city overlooked the Nile. The ancient Egyptian capital was called Ankh-Tawy, which meant "Life of the Two Lands," stressing the city's tactical position between Lower Egypt and Upper Egypt. Like its counterpart in Tennessee, it was a place of Crossroads, and as we will see, much magic.

As noted previously, Elvis was at the Crossroads of traditional media and mass media, industrial technology and the space age, the famous musician and the multichannel superstar. Even as a movie star, Elvis's popularity wasn't due to his (sadly untapped) acting skills or because of a particular director: the draw was always Elvis, the modern box-office star template that would drive much of cinema in the late twentieth century. He was at the Crossroads of two different nations with two different destinies. He was the Lord of the Crossroads, between Heaven and Hell, fueled by the magic of daemons, tricksters, and unusually advanced technology.

We're only getting started.

The ideas of the Trickster, Gladys's influence, and guiding dark and light higher forces will be expanded upon and further contextualized in chapters 8 and 9. First, it's important to see Elvis's further evolution and impact on culture, from Army Elvis to Vegas Elvis, as well as the other arcane influences that shaped him even before he entered the army. His unearthly experiences will bring more context.

The freakshow is over. You are at the Crossroads now.

3
THE KING'S
ESOTERIC STUDIES AND
OCCULT INFLUENCES

A VARIED ESOTERIC STREAM FED ELVIS'S SOUL. Before addressing these streams, a question lingering in the air should be addressed: Was Elvis a Christian?

The answer is yes—at least in Elvis's mind and heart. By outside categorizations, though, he was a specific type of Christian, as will be revealed.

THE LIVING JESUS

Jesus remained the lodestar for Elvis's pilgrimage through *samsara* and his shepherding of a new age. From a small child singing at church to his last years as a hapless workaholic and drug addict, Jesus was the other daemon in his life. From an early age, he felt there was more to spirituality than organized Christianity promised.[1] As he once said:

> I never believed that anything was a coincidence. There's a meaning for everything. There's gotta be. Man, I always knew there was real spiritual life, not the way the church dishes it out, you know, with hellfire and damnation and using fear.[2]

Like with most things in his life, Elvis didn't care about outside pressures or expectations once his mind was aflame with purpose—whether it was the genre of an album he chose to record, how he spent his millions, or the friends he surrounded himself with. For example, when he built an Eastern-style meditation garden at Graceland in the mid-1960s, the place's focal point was a statue of Jesus.[3] As Depeche Mode sang, he was always going for his own "personal Jesus."

One might think of the William Blake quote from "The Everlasting Gospel": "The Vision of Christ that thou dost see is my vision's greatest enemy." And even more relevant to Elvis and the fundamentalist take on Christianity is this section: "Both read the Bible day and night, where thou read black I read white." As will become apparent in the following chapters, beyond Elvis's instinctual tapping into ancient shamanism, his conscious views were unconsciously more in line with the Gnostics and other Christian mystics. Sometimes it *was* conscious, though, like telling his friend and bodyguard, Sonny West, that he believed in reincarnation—but a kind closer to the limited type you find in Gnostic texts like *The Secret Book of John*, in which a person must evolve in a spirit or devolve to remain forever a part of inert matter.[4] During his army service in Germany in the late 1950s, Elvis would often talk to the owner of the hotel he stayed at about his quasi-Gnostic view of reincarnation.[5]

Elvis's view of the Bible was just as unorthodox as his spiritual mentor explained:

> For Elvis, the Bible was sacred, the blueprint of creation in allegorical and metaphoric form. But his interest went beyond the orthodox, extending into Gnostic and esoteric literature.[6]

He contended that the Bible was not meant to be taken literally, as it was composed of "words and stories that were mere symbols and myths that held deeper significance and meaning for those who sought to discover them."[7]

At times, Elvis felt that God had put him on the path of being a superstar to show others the path to higher realms. "I'm not a preacher," he said, "I'm an entertainer, a singer. That's how God and the Brotherhood are helping and usin' me, that's my role, and I love it."[8]

Multiple stories exist of women wanting to worship Elvis, and him countering with a variation of, "Love my music, but don't ever worship anyone but the Lord." There was that fabled interaction when a doting woman approached him on stage during one of his Las Vegas performances. She carried a pillow with a crown and told him passionately, "It's for you. You are the King." Elvis responded, "No, honey, there is only one king, and his name is Jesus Christ. I'm just a singer."[9]

When he said this, few knew that Elvis believed Jesus was one of many salvific avatars. As Elvis said, God chose Buddha, Muhammad, Moses, and others to "serve a purpose."[10]

Again, gospel music charged his heart like no other genre. He enjoyed attending religious services. When fame impeded him from appearing in church, he never wavered in his commitment to prayer and his favorite book, the Bible. A prayer circle with his cast or entourage was common before he went on stage. It wasn't unusual for him to hold Bible studies at his Graceland mansion, and he took on the role of a loud, rapturous clergyman when the Spirit took him. During times of crisis, he turned to the Bible and its wisdom, even as his theology became more eclectic and radical. When fame became empty to him (as it often does with many deep-mind celebrities like John Lennon or Greta Garbo), he still held on to reading the Bible and supplicating God to tell him his true purpose.[11]

But a key theme in Elvis's life, as with any seeker, is that the seeker is never truly satisfied, and the seeking never stops. Neither do the questions. Neither does the doubt. As I always quip on my podcast, "We run with those searching for the truth and avoid those who have found it." Or as Elvis's friend Bill Browder said: "I think Elvis often thought he was a prophet. He was very religious. Everything in his life was connected to spirituality. As Elvis got older, he was seeking and searching, and therefore, in a strange way he became more religious as time went on."[12]

That was the central ethos of Elvis, with Jesus and Jesse as his sea mates on the oceans of the mundane, searching for the farthest shores of meaning. It is a matter of speculation if he met his twin after leaving this world. However, it can be concluded that meeting Christ was the final thing on his mortal mind right before his death on August 16, 1977. Many know the rather tawdry account of Elvis dying while going to the bathroom, his life finally culminating under the effects of drugs and a poor lifestyle, his body found by fiancée Ginger Alden.[13]

What is rarely mentioned is what Elvis was reading before his meatsack failed him: *A Scientific Search for the Face of Jesus*. The book, written by Frank Adams, concerns the authenticity of the Shroud of Turin. Elvis was fascinated by the idea of finding the authentic Jesus of Nazareth and even considered going on a pilgrimage to the Holy Land to see the sites where Jesus lived and preached.[14]

In his last moments, Elvis wanted to be face-to-face with Christ.

THE PROPHET BY KAHLIL GIBRAN

Losing Jesse was a unique but eternally recurring event in his life. The second significant loss in his life was as impactful. At the time, he was only twenty-three and on top of a world he practically owned.

The Lord of the Crossroads transformed from Rockabilly Elvis to Army Elvis in late March 1958. The King had been drafted (some have mused it was all a publicity stunt to sanitize the Gnostic rebel and showcase him as the boy next door). After completing a three-day orientation at Fort Chaffee, Arkansas, he was ordered to complete twenty-two weeks of specialized training at Fort Hood, Texas. He chartered a Greyhound bus that was followed for two hundred miles by a convoy of fans.

Gladys was not doing well before going to meet Elvis. She had never enjoyed her son's meteoric rise to fame, hating their time apart with every ounce of her being. Calling him on the phone was the best way she could connect with him while he toured. But Elvis not answering the phone brought about psychic torment. She turned to alcohol to manage the emotional pain.

Gladys and Vernon were given a trailer near the base to be close to their son. She showed up depressed and tired, suffering from untreated gallstones and abusing diet pills to lose weight. She was at least happy that the army allowed Elvis to move in with Vernon and her. That joy didn't last when she learned that her only son was being deployed to West Germany for eighteen months. Being in the early and aggressive days of the Cold War, the news chilled her heart, and her body took the brunt of the stress.

Shortly after the family was reunited, Gladys contracted hepatitis. She was taken to a family doctor back in Memphis and recuperated for a while, but then took a turn for the worse. Elvis was allowed to leave his base, arriving on the evening of August 12. Thirty-six hours later, Gladys Love Presley was gone. The reason was heart failure. She was only forty-six.

The bond between a twinless child and their mother can be cosmically strong, probably more when the mother can't have more children. Gladys had ensured her son was a surrogate spouse until fame stole him away. Elvis was devastated. He howled like a demon when he found out at Graceland she had died, and at the hospital, he kept "touching the body over and over, until hospital attendants had to ask him to stop."[15] If Jesse had been his unconscious reason for becoming the King, Gladys was his conscious reason. His wealth primarily existed to be shared with his mother. And he knew very consciously that he had struck a Faustian bargain: his absence as a celebrity to give his family a good life was also why her health had deteriorated. Perhaps the Devil that Elvis met at the Crossroads had one deal he could cash in on after all.

At her new gravesite in Graceland, Elvis cried uncontrollably: "I love you so much. I lived my whole life for you. Oh, God, everything I have is gone!"[16]

A broken vessel, Elvis returned to Fort Hood weeks later to finish his training and then was deployed to Europe. He never truly recovered.[17]

Sixty days later, in Friedberg, Germany, as a Jeep driver in

Company D, First Battalion of the Third Armored Division's Thirty-Second Armor, Elvis was still grief-stricken. Because of his fame (fans had even followed him to Germany), he was allowed to stay at a hotel with family and friends a few miles away in Bad Nauheim. Despite the company and attention, he felt utterly alone, staying up at night reading a Bible he kept on his nightstand. The book wasn't working this time, and his mind sought some other relief. He leaned on a book that an old girlfriend, June Juanico, had given him more than two years earlier; he had enjoyed it then, but at the time it was more of a romance-sharing work.[18]

The book was Kahlil Gibran's *The Prophet.*

The Prophet brought immense solace to Elvis, becoming one of his most treasured books. He would often turn to this mystical work when needing soul healing. He loved giving copies of the book to his friends and, in the 1970s, considered making a feature film of the work.[19]

The Prophet is a spiritual fiction work, similar to *The Teachings of Don Juan* by Carlos Castaneda or *Illusions* by Richard Bach. The work is a collection of poetic essays exploring various aspects of life and spirituality. The book comprises twenty-six chapters, each focusing on different life-stage topics like love, marriage, children, work, and death. The story centers on the character of Almustafa, a prophet who has lived in a foreign land for many years and is about to return home. Before leaving the city of Orphalese, he imparts eternal wisdom to the people who loved him one last time.

The Prophet was a vehicle for Gibran to share his insights and wisdom on timeless topics, offering profound and often thought-provoking reflections on the human condition. He was influenced by the Bahá'í faith, Theosophy, Sufism, and C. G. Jung. The book has been widely acclaimed for its beautiful language, deep concepts, and universal appeal—and has become one of the most beloved and enduring works of religious literature of the twentieth century.

One can see how such a work would have carried Elvis's soul through the hurricanes of grief, with passages like, "The deeper that sorrow carves into your being, the more joy you can contain. . . . When you are sorrowful look again in your heart, and you shall see that in truth you are weeping for that which has been your delight."[20] Or when Gibran writes on love, "And when he speaks to you believe in him. Though his voice may shatter your dreams as the north wind lays waste the garden. For even as love crowns you so shall he crucify you. Even as he is for your growth so is he for your pruning."[21]

Without a doubt, the passage on death would have given Elvis a sense of perspective and hope:

You would know the secret of death.

But how shall you find it unless you seek it in the heart of life?

The owl whose night-bound eyes are blind unto the day cannot unveil the mystery of light.

If you would indeed behold the spirit of death, open your heart wide unto the body of life.

For life and death are one, even as the river and the sea are one.

In the depth of your hopes and desires lies your silent knowledge of the beyond;

And like seeds dreaming beneath the snow your heart dreams of spring.

Trust the dreams, for in them is hidden the gate to eternity.

Your fear of death is but the trembling of the shepherd when he stands before the king whose hand is to be laid upon him in honour.

Is the shepherd not joyful beneath his trembling, that he shall wear the mark of the king?

Yet is he not more mindful of his trembling?

For what is it to die but to stand naked in the wind and to melt into the sun?

And what is it to cease breathing, but to free the breath from its restless tides, that it may rise and expand and seek God unencumbered?

Only when you drink from the river of silence shall you indeed sing.

And when you have reached the mountain top, then you shall begin to climb.

And when the earth shall claim your limbs, then shall you truly dance.[22]

The Prophet became the first of many esoteric books that Elvis would read. It is important to note that his hunger for books sometimes matched his thirst to know the Divine. This passion evolved him from being curious "to a more fully realized spiritual seeker, well read, conversant in an eclectic range of religious and Gnostic philosophies."[23] He was a voracious reader. There were times when, wherever he traveled, his staff carried a personal library of two hundred books.[24] He certainly was a man of contradiction who could lose himself in the carnal ecstasy of being a performer, yet switch to an almost sage-like precision when quietly studying a religious or philosophical tradition. As Peter Guralnick writes: "It was never enough for him to simply read a book; he had to absorb it, think about it, question it, link its thoughts and ideas with all he had read before and things he had heard people say."[25]

More than the King of Rock 'n' Roll, Elvis might have been closer to Plato's philosopher king or Marcus Aurelius, the Stoic emperor. Regardless, all learned nobility need a curator of information, just as Alexander the Great needed Aristotle or Jesus needed John the Baptist to come into their purpose.

For Elvis that curator would be Larry Geller.

ELVIS'S GURU

As the saying goes, when the student is ready, the master will appear.

The student was more than ready. He was also bored, empty, and generally dissatisfied with his career and life. Meet Elvis in 1964.

He had transmuted from Rockabilly Elvis to Army Elvis and now was in the depths of his Movie Star Elvis avatar. No longer ruling the charts or even touring, he still earned millions of dollars annually by making movies and their soundtracks. Unfortunately, the films were shallow entertainment, formulaic. Just as tedious was his commuting between

Memphis and Los Angeles (this was a time before Vegas Elvis and his private jets, when the King didn't fly because of personal trepidation and his mother's warning to stay away from planes). Gladys had been repelled by Hollywood the one time she'd set foot in Los Angeles, and Elvis's attitude was just as bad, disliking the "phonies and users" of the movie industry.[26]

To wit, Elvis was disenchanted with the trajectory of his life, wondering if making popular B-movies was the dead end of his run as an impactful entertainer.[27]

It all changed abruptly in April 1964 when Elvis lost his hairdresser, who wanted to open his own salon. His soon-to-be-former hairdresser recommended Larry Geller, who just happened to have spent years studying and practicing alternative spiritual traditions. Plus, Geller was a huge Elvis fan. The hairdresser promptly came to the King's Bel Air house one afternoon. Part of his initiation was negotiating hundreds of female fans who kept permanent vigil outside the gates of the King's abode.[28]

While Geller worked his hair alchemy on Elvis, doing some trimming and tinting, the two exchanged casual conversation for the first hour. Suddenly, Elvis turned to him, stuck his finger in his face, and said, "Larry, let me ask you something. . . . Who are you? Who are you, man? What are you really all about? What are you really into?"

Geller took the fateful bait of the Trickster, at first saying that his job was his job, but his chief passion for years was delving into spirituality that addressed the deeper questions of existence: Why are we here? Where are we going?

Elvis's eyes lit up. "Man, just keep talking, just keep talking."

Geller kept talking about finding a higher purpose in life, and Elvis experienced a profound epiphany. He said:

Whoa, whoa, man. Larry, I don't believe it. I mean, what you're talking about is what I secretly think about *all the time*. . . . I've always known that there had to be a purpose for my life. I've always felt an unseen hand behind me, guiding my life. I mean, there *has* to be a purpose . . . there's got to be a reason . . . why I was chosen to be Elvis Presley.[29]

They spoke for the next four hours in the bathroom, both men admitting they felt alienated in the material world and how a divine destiny was what they craved more than anything. A new friendship began, setting Elvis deep into the path of alternative spirituality and praxis.[30]

A spark like this is what Elvis needed. Ironically, the world that allowed Elvis to reach the top, the culture he had shepherded into its new postwar incarnation of possibility, also constrained him from ever truly being able to express himself, from being free. He was the King of Rock 'n' Roll, one of Hollywood's highest-paid actors, but he was, as he sang, "caught in a trap." He was the Elvis the public expected him to be and had lost his ability to expand. Geller changed all of this, externally and internally, even allowing Elvis to open up, with tears, about his missing Jesse.[31]

Geller also catalyzed Elvis's most extraordinary mystical experience, which will be addressed in chapter 5.

Over the next several years, Geller became Elvis's portal to paranormal books, occult traditions, Eastern practices, and heretical speculations rarely found outside secret society circles in those days. He also became his spiritual coach and constant companion. Elvis began to meditate daily and became more mature, reflective, and giving. As Geller explains:

> If there was no chance of him being taken seriously as an actor, then at least he could be respected as a person. . . . Elvis knew that other people—intelligent people—recognized the value of his studies and liked the changes they saw in him. Elvis was rarely happier than when he was in a position to enlighten someone else. I don't think he was that way because he liked to show off, but because he wanted to try desperately to be seen as an intelligent, thinking person.[32]

One must wonder if this was again the Trickster ushering in and reflecting the change of age, as music and culture were shifting to a more mystic and explorative arena in the mid-1960s, the dawn of the

Age of Aquarius. At some point, as Elvis declared, we must dispense with the idea of coincidences, like Elvis asking Geller what he was into.

Such was the impact Geller had on Elvis that while filming *Harum Scarum* in November 1965, the King told him that he was ready to embrace the nonmaterial life fully and wanted to be initiated into Kriya Yoga (which, in itself, took two years of austere practice). As far as Elvis joining, that will be addressed in the following chapter.

Not everyone was happy with the relationship between Elvis and Geller, and neither their friendship nor Elvis's enlightenment would be a straight, easy road. This was the case with the Memphis Mafia, Elvis's infamous entourage that served as bodyguards, assistants, and daily bros. He was their cult leader of material delights, and they were often his punching bag. When Elvis embraced the occult, the sophomoric horse-playing like shaving cream fights, cherry bomb pranks, and so forth ended.[33] Instead of playing football after a long workday, Elvis would stare at the stars and ask questions about religion. Beyond losing their fraternal identity, some members of the Memphis Mafia, like Joe Esposito, worried that Geller was brainwashing his boss and becoming a de facto guru.[34]

The Memphis Mafia's resentment grew as they gradually lost their beloved party animal and big bro. They lobbed slurs at Geller, calling him Swami, Rasputin, or, for a dose of antisemitism, Lawrence of Israel or the Wandering Jew (never within Elvis's earshot, of course).[35]

The Memphis Mafia members weren't the only people around Elvis who disliked the King's evolution into a savant. Colonel Tom Parker, his notorious Machiavellian manager, and Priscilla Presley, his fiancée at the time, felt similarly. Parker felt that Elvis's "religious kick" was mind control, while Priscilla felt that her betrothed was moving away from her and her role as his soulmate.[36]

Was Geller some con man or deep-stated handler trying to turn Elvis into his personal Manchurian candidate? That is highly doubtful. Geller was an ex-musician, devout seeker, and polymath when it came to alternative spiritualities—a typical L.A. dreamer of the 1950s. He never cared too much about celebrity status, although he often orbited the

Hollywood elite, being friends with legendary producer Phil Spector and singer Ricky Nelson. His life was just fine being a hairdresser of celebrities (in fact, he had been cutting Johnny Rivers's hair when he got a call about hairdressing for Elvis).

Like most young people, Geller was an Elvis fan in the 1950s, and funny enough, their famous encounter wasn't the first time they had met, although only Geller remembered their earlier encounter. In 1957, Elvis was relaxing outside by a stage door before a show at the Los Angeles Pan Pacific Auditorium, foot on the bumper of a car, glowing with his golden lamé jacket. Geller, who had been hunting with his friends for his idol that night, spotted him. He summoned all his courage and went up to the young Elvis, ignoring the two bodyguards, and said, less-than-mystically: "Hi."

"Hi," Elvis said, extending a hand like Larry was just another neighbor. "I'm Elvis Presley."

"Hi," Geller repeated, half-stunned and impressed at the commanding inner aura the Southerner exuded. Geller wouldn't become spiritual until 1960, so he didn't have a chance to astonish Elvis with knowledge of Ascended Masters or Kabbalistic magic. Instead, he followed with, "I'm Larry Geller."

After a few more moments of Geller staring at him dumbfounded, Elvis said politely, "Well, they want me in there." He nodded at the stage door and the thunderous sound of an eager crowd growing inside the auditorium. Then Elvis walked inside.

Geller was transformed after that night, forever high that he had shaken the hand of the most influential person of his generation. Years later, when Larry mentioned their encounter, Elvis gave his patented answer about there being more than meets the eye and the illusion of coincidences.[37]

Between Geller's kind heart and adoration of Elvis, it's implausible he would have ever taken advantage of their friendship. If I were a betting man, I'd take this wager to the Devil at the Crossroads. If Elvis met me there, he probably wouldn't remember me either, even after I won the bet.

But that's not what Elvis's court thought, and Parker eventually managed to create a wedge between the two friends. He was not alone: Elvis's own impatience and personality lent a hand. The King struggled with the labyrinth that is spiritual awakening. One time, when Elvis was frustrated with his evolution, Geller told him not only that it took time and that Elvis was always trying to "crash the gates of heaven"; he also had to drop his ego and allow God in.[38]

During this fluctuating spiritual evolution, Parker worked his own sorcery to plant the seeds of doubt in the mind of his famous client. These machinations included:

- Insisting and demanding that Elvis stop reading so much
- Preventing Elvis and Geller from spending time alone
- Subtly communicating to Elvis that his friend didn't have his best interests in mind, and that he was yet another gold digger[39]

Geller even came home one night with his wife after having dinner with Parker and found that his house had been ransacked. Nothing was missing except for some audiotapes and numerological/astrological charts on Elvis. On another occasion, Parker met Geller alone for dinner and seemed to hit on him by placing a hand on his thigh under the table, inviting him for a private swim later. Parker was likely fishing to see if Geller and Elvis had more than a spiritual bond, but regardless, it unnerved Geller.[40]

The campaign evidently worked in the end; Elvis offhandedly told Geller one day: "Those masters of yours have hidden motives. They want to control others, and use them for their own damn purposes."[41]

Outside of Elvis's impatience, his eternal balance of material desires and metaphysical thirst didn't help. As Geller writes:

Any time Elvis made a gesture toward change, whether small or large and regardless of what it concerned something inside him instinctively resisted. This behavior took its toll, eventually squelching even Elvis's inclination and enthusiasm, until he didn't dare consider change.[42]

Ironically, Elvis knew of this character trait. Geller had introduced Elvis to numerology. The King, on the most basic level, was a perfect 8. This meant he was equally concerned with the spiritual and material (being at the Crossroads), and was an intense, ambitious, misunderstood, and eternally lonely individual.[43]

Between Parker's campaign and Elvis's bipolar essence, Geller was forced to leave the Memphis Mafia cult. The two-and-a-half-year friendship ended poignantly in 1967, during the Summer of Love. When Geller left the King, the latter's spiritual growth decelerated. There must have been plenty of residual magic, for Elvis transformed once again, moving away from Movie Star Elvis into Vegas Elvis, also buoyed by his marriage, the birth of his daughter, and his legendary 1968 Christmas Special that catapulted him once again to be the greatest showman on Earth.

Geller's fall was so hard that he went from being invited to be Elvis's best man at his wedding to having to read the news of the secretive marriage in a newspaper. Priscilla was no innocent bystander. Once Geller was gone and just as she became Mrs. Presley, she convinced Elvis to get rid of his beloved books. To please his new bride, he threw his books and magazines into a deserted well behind Graceland, poured gasoline on them, and set them alight.[44]

Geller and Elvis's friendship, like the books, burned again in 1972. Geller visited Elvis in Las Vegas with Johnny Rivers. The King acknowledged Rivers and invited them both over after the show. Elvis and Geller made up and restarted their close friendship again. The books returned, the conversations continued, and insights were shared—even if it was probably too late.

Years later, Elvis asked Geller to marry Ginger Alden and him, which never happened. A day before his death, he told Geller over the phone, "If you didn't help me on the spiritual path, I would've been dead years ago."[45]

Maybe there's something to John Lennon's remark about Elvis: "The king is always killed by his courtiers. He is overfed, overindulged, overdrunk to keep him tied to the throne. Most people in the position never wake up."

THE IMPERSONAL LIFE

The Key is
"To THINK is to CREATE," or
"As you THINK in your HEART, so is it with you" . . .
You have within you all possibilities.

THE IMPERSONAL LIFE,
JOSEPH BENNER

On his second visit to Elvis, after their hours-long soul-bonding in 1964, Geller brought him a haul of spirituality books. The first book he read was *The Impersonal Life*. Elvis was instantly and deeply moved by its message. As with *The Prophet*, he reread it constantly and carried hundreds of copies (sometimes with passages highlighted) to distribute to friends or colleagues. It was his favorite book. Less than two years after Elvis died in 1977, Vernon asked Geller for a copy of *The Impersonal Life*. He wanted to read it to know his son better.[46]

This was the book that enabled Elvis to truly grasp, for the first time, "the universal Christ . . . embodied in everyone." *The Impersonal Life* also proved to him that all religions were based on a perennial faith and were loyal interpretations of God's message. Other arcane practices could be added into his worldview without losing his connection to Christianity.[47]

The floodgates of mystic speculation had opened.

The Impersonal Life was authored in 1924 by American Joseph Benner. This esoteric Christian and New Thought fusion quickly became a spiritual classic and monster bestseller, touching the lives of millions of readers worldwide. The book focuses on the concept of the "Christ within," which is the true essence of every individual.

By recognizing this inner divinity, individuals can live a life of abundance, fulfillment, and purpose.

The Impersonal Life also teaches that the ego or the individual self is merely an illusion one needs to transcend to discover their true nature. Brenner encouraged readers to let go of their limiting beliefs, fears, and desires—and instead to focus on their divine essence, which he called the "I AM" presence. In doing so, Benner asserted that individuals could connect with the universal consciousness and manifest their highest potential in all areas of their lives. *The Impersonal Life* deals with the famous Pierre Teilhard de Chardin aphorism that each person is a spiritual being having a human experience. An individual's true purpose is to awaken to their divine nature.

For a Gnostic two thousand years ago, a Rosicrucian during the Enlightenment, or the more progressive modern Christian (such as a devotee of *A Course in Miracles*), *The Impersonal Life* is sound and commonsense metaphysics. For Elvis, the book allowed him to fully exorcise the idea of an orthodox Jesus that damned people and died so that churches could be built.

More than being liberated by knowing he housed an inner Christ and shared an essence with the ultimate consciousness, Elvis found himself speculating about all the possibilities of Jesus. What had happened to him when he went to Egypt as a child? Did he travel to India as an adult before his ministry? Did Jesus ever personally teach reincarnation, and when he said, "Aren't ye all gods?" wasn't he speaking to every person, to Elvis himself?

Like many deep thinkers, Elvis had been tormented by his relationship with the Divine for most of his life. The paradox of his life was perplexing. Why had he lived, and his twin brother died? Why had he suffered in squalor but then found himself the wealthiest celebrity in the country? Why had God taken his mother when he needed her the most? What kind of god would do all of this?

The Impersonal Life provided the answers: The world was basically an illusion of separateness, with our daily lives being silly fiction, the authentic reality being the I AM permeating every atom in the cosmos. As Brenner wrote, "You are what you believe you are. Not one thing in your life is Real or has any value to you only as your *thinking* and *believing* has made it such."

Pain occurs when one pulls away from the sacred goal ordained by God and doesn't work for the common good. Elvis felt that everything that happened to him was meant to evolve him into his divine self, the true Elvis. This perfected Elvis could leverage his fame and music to help others wake up to their potential—an endless tapestry of Christs simultaneously saying, "Aren't ye all gods?"[48]

The pain indeed came when Elvis resisted his destiny, as happens with most of us. When Elvis was his true self, entertaining and spiritual simultaneously, peace flowed through him and to those around him. All he had to do, as *The Impersonal Life* states, was first change his "attitude toward all these things you now think are not what they ought to be."

Gary Tillery describes well the core of the book:

The point of view in *The Impersonal Life* is Gnostic, seeking to awaken the individual to an insight that no mediator—i.e., teacher or priest—is necessary since divinity and wisdom lie within. All any person has to do is look within for answers to his or her questions. After all, every person is one with God, a fragment of the deity. The I AM asserts that Jesus was the first individual chosen to awaken and express this great truth, but he was not the only one capable of awakening. By discovering the Christ Consciousness within oneself, any person can join the Great Brotherhood of the Spirit. "For I as the Christ dwell in all men and AM their One and Only Self."

The point is to move beyond the personal point of view. The awakened person learns to live an *impersonal* life and discover *impersonal* love—a love detached from any human or personal interest. The enlightened person feels *selfless* love, an urge to eliminate suffering, heal people, and bring happiness to others, without ulterior motives.[49]

By reading this book in 1964, Elvis had utterly left the fundamentalist church behind.

BLAVATSKY AND THEOSOPHY

Elvis was fascinated by the teachings of Helena Petrovna Blavatsky, the founder of Theosophy, for various metaphysical reasons. She also struck him for a very physical reason: Blavatsky reminded Elvis of Gladys. "Look at the eyes, Larry," he once told Geller, one of many times he made the comparison while they discussed Theosophy, "the shape of the face, the cheekbones. I've never seen anything like it."[50]

The Russian Blavatsky might or might not have reincarnated as the King's mother. But she could be considered the mother of alternative spirituality in the twentieth century. Like Elvis, she was a walking contradiction who made headlines and irritated the establishment— a woman who smoked, cursed, and ate an unhealthy diet but could

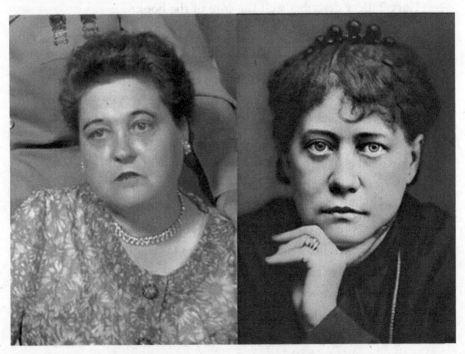

Fig. 3.1. Gladys Presley and Helena Blavatsky.

interpret and express the spirit realm like few individuals of that time. Also, like Elvis, she was forever trapped in her age. In her case, it was the stern and masculine nineteenth century, meaning she was (and still is) often marginalized in patriarchal circles (and sometimes by feminists and occultists because of her political incorrectness). Perhaps she was cursed and gifted like Elvis by being at the Crossroads, as she was a critical bridge between Eastern and Western spiritualities, perennial wisdom and mainstream religiosity. Elvis was the King of Rock 'n' Roll, and according to novelist Kurt Vonnegut, Blavatsky was the "Founding Mother of the Occult in America."[51]

Many today, including seasoned occultists, fail to grasp how revolutionary the Theosophical Society was when it first stormed the religious landscape. The movement was founded in New York City in 1875 and taught occult philosophy openly, the first organization to do so in the Western world since classical paganism. It attracted people interested in mysticism worldwide and became a venue for creative spiritual ventures for decades after. Branches soon sprang up across Europe, India, and Australia.[52]

Despite Blavatsky being overlooked—she was one of the most remarkable women in history, but is virtually unknown by the general public—her movement, Theosophy, became a worldwide phenomenon and had a significant influence on twentieth-century religion. Among her devotees were Thomas Edison, L. Frank Baum, Greta Garbo, Albert Einstein, and Mohandas Gandhi.[53]

Blavatsky was the Elvis of occultism in America, Europe, and India in the nineteenth century. And Elvis, in his thirst for mystical lore, read her works, including *The Secret Doctrine*, along with other key Theosophical books like *The Chakras* by C. W. Leadbeater and *You Are the World* by Jiddu Krishnamurti. Elvis was so enthralled by Blavatsky's *The Voice of the Silence*, containing the purported translation of ancient Tibetan incantations, that on occasion he read from it onstage during his Vegas Elvis period.[54]

Elvis connected to Theosophy's core tenets of philosophically and religiously grasping the mysteries of existence through direct involvement and intuition. He valued how it emphasized the unity and interconnectedness of all things and the possibility of attaining spiritual knowledge beyond the limitations of traditional religion and scientific inquiry.

Perhaps what Elvis loved most about Theosophy was the idea of a universal brotherhood that fought for human equality and happiness, shepherded by benign and unselfish masters (and he strived to become one). That is why he was also profoundly engaged by Vera Stanley Alder's *The Initiation of the World* and its discussion of an enigmatic Great White Brotherhood, a legion of magicians ushering in the healing wisdom of the ages. According to the book, the group included Jesus, Blavatsky, Aleister Crowley, Alice Bailey, and Elizabeth Clare Prophet.[55]

On an interesting note, Elvis believed in the Theosophical idea of telepathy and avoiding communicating with the dead (Blavatsky often warned Spiritualists that trickster spirits were hoodwinking them).[56]

Former religion professor Marla J. Selvidge claims that Elvis's interest was more than utopian or for spiritual enlightenment. He was interested in Alice Bailey—especially after reading her *Esoteric Healing*—the Theosophical writer who covered many New Age subjects in the early twentieth century. He was specifically drawn to her ideas on healing through the mind. Selvidge speculates in her biography of the King, *For the Love of Elvis*, that his health was terrible even at a younger age and that the real cause of his death was bone cancer or leukemia.[57]

Selvidge details in her blog:

> Elvis may have found some relief from his illnesses, as he read Bailey by disassociating his mind and body. Control may have been a way that allowed him to sing longer than most normal people who were ill. Perhaps it helped with his constant pain? Maybe she helped him to understand his purpose in life?[58]

Blavatsky's legacy might have been suppressed, while Elvis's desire to express his occultism might have been repressed, but in the end, both tower as world-changing figures often demonized by the status quo.

Devotees of philosopher and spiritual teacher G. I. Gurdjieff might also be interested to know that Elvis read *Meetings with Remarkable Men* and P. D. Ouspensky's *The Fourth Way*. For those into Freemasonry, Elvis was familiar with "The Craft," having read the works of legendary Freemason Albert Pike. Elvis was immediately drawn to the idea of a benign fraternity that nurtured human progress.[59]

THE GOSPEL OF THOMAS AND OTHER CHRISTIAN MYSTIC WORKS

Elvis must have been stricken by a Jesus who was "something of a Zen Buddhist" in a text he read known as the Gospel of Thomas, dating from the middle of the first century CE to the middle of the second century CE.[60] After all, the apocryphal text doesn't contain any traditional narrative about Jesus, such as his death and resurrection. The work is a collection of 114 wisdom sayings spoken by the "Living Jesus" to Thomas, possibly the apostle himself. Although many of the sayings are verbatim or a variation of ones found in the canonical gospels, some are marked mystical declarations about humans' inner light and transcending an illusionary world.

According to Geller, Elvis revered and employed two passages from the Gospel of Thomas as keystones to his mystical research, emphasizing the central theme of this "Zen Jesus." The first was saying 2:

> *Jesus said, "Those who seek should not stop seeking until they find. When they find, they will be disturbed. When they are disturbed, they will marvel, and will reign over all."*

The second Elvis utilized was saying 3:

> *Jesus said, "If your leaders say to you, 'Look, the (Father's) kingdom is in the sky,' then the birds of the sky will precede*

you. If they say to you, 'It is in the sea,' then the fish will precede you. Rather, the (Father's) kingdom is within you and it is outside you.

"When you know yourselves, then you will be known, and you will understand that you are children of the living Father. But if you do not know yourselves, then you live in poverty, and you are the poverty."[61]

The Gospel of Thomas is arguably Gnostic. Although the scripture doesn't present the edgy ideas of a prison world ruled by fallen angels generally found in Gnosticism, the Jesus of this work is closer to the Cosmic Christ of the Gnostics. This Jesus doesn't save the world by his cross sacrifice but by his teaching and rituals. He doesn't even save but *awakens*. This Jesus also stresses that, as in *The Impersonal Life*, each person houses a shard of the godhead. The reader is presented with a Jesus who provides an enlightenment message (Gnosis) and not dogmatic beliefs (Faith). To grasp the spiritual tech that is Gnosis, we turn to the definition by Gnostic bishop and academic Stephan Hoeller: "Salvific knowing, arrived at intuitively but facilitated by various stimuli, including the teaching and mysteries brought to humans by messengers of divinity from outside the cosmos."[62]

In addition, Elaine Pagels, in her landmark *The Gnostic Gospels*, writes that beyond the ecstatic practices, Gnosis is an inner discovery that leads to an "insight, for Gnosis involves an intuitive process of knowing oneself. Yet to know oneself, at the deepest level is to know God; this is the secret of Gnosis."[63]

An example of Gnosis and its mining for each person's indwelling savior comes when Jesus declares in saying 108 of the Gospel of Thomas: "Whoever drinks from my mouth will become like me; I myself shall become that person, and the hidden things will be revealed to him."[64]

The statement means that sacred (and often secret) information must be passed along for inner transformation.[65] The result is becoming a "Living Jesus" while still in the flesh, or as another Gnostic text, the

Gospel of Philip, states: "You saw Christ, you became Christ."

The Gospel of Thomas surely pleased Elvis like *The Impersonal Life* did, supporting his idea of every person possessing a Christ Consciousness. Elvis told Geller that he thought all people had Christ in them and had the potential to be saviors. "Didn't Jesus say that you could do greater things?" Elvis asked, echoing what Jesus said that his followers could attain. The passage is found in the Gospel of John (14:12), Elvis's favorite Bible scripture because of its lofty mysticism[66] (and a work that the Gnostics used initially before it was appropriated by mainstream Christendom).[67]

An interesting point in the Gospel of Thomas is that the text begins with: "These are the secret sayings that the living Jesus spoke and Didymos Judas Thomas recorded."

Judas refers to Jude, the brother of Jesus in the New Testament (Mark 6:3 and Matthew 13:55). The Greek "Didymos" means twin, and "Thomas" is Aramaic for twin, too. Curiously, the author would twice be named twin. Is the text saying that Thomas is the literal twin of Jesus? Or could it be stated that Jesus and Thomas are spiritual twins, that Jesus, in essence, is Thomas' Daemon or Higher Self (as discussed in chapter 2)?[68]

Elvis was familiar with the Nag Hammadi library (and appreciated the Dead Sea Scrolls as well) but probably never discovered this daemon/divine twin idea, as scholarship was sparse during his lifetime regarding this Gnostic discovery.[69] Yet the theme was there, always close to Elvis, like Jesse and Jesus.

The Cosmic Christ or Living Jesus continued in Elvis's ongoing study of esoteric Christian texts. Here are some more instances—included as they may be obscure for modern seekers—and their summaries:

- *The Aquarian Gospel of Jesus the Christ* by Levi H. Dowling (1908): This book is claimed to have been found in the mystical realm of the Akashic Records and proffers a detailed account of Jesus Christ's life, including his travels to India and teachings on spiritual truths. It also incorporates spiritual traditions from

Hinduism and Buddhism and emphasizes universal love and interconnectedness (here we go again, Elvis). However, don't get too excited about the Akashic Record, as more recent scholarship points to the work plagiarizing Nicolas Notovitch's *The Lost Years of Jesus*.

- *The Mystical Christ* by Manly P. Hall (1951): The book explores the mystical and esoteric aspects of Jesus Christ's life and teachings and examines parallels between Christian mysticism and other traditions. It also delves into the symbolism and hidden meanings in the Bible and Jesus's parables and miracles, offering a distinctive perspective on Christian mysticism and spirituality.

- *Old Testament Wisdom* by Manly P. Hall (1957): The book explores the teachings of the Old Testament's Book of Proverbs and its use of symbolism and metaphors to convey moral and ethical principles. Hall interprets the text practically for daily life and examines the influence of Egyptian and Babylonian wisdom traditions on the Old Testament's development and impact on Western philosophy and spirituality.

- *The Lost Books of the Bible and the Forgotten Books of Eden*, compiled and edited by Rutherford H. Platt (1926): The work discusses heterodox biblical texts like the Book of Enoch, the Book of Jubilees, and the Infancy Gospel of James. These texts offer insights into the beliefs and practices of early Christians and Jews. Platt provides introductions and commentary for each text to provide historical and contextual background. These books were popular among scholars and readers (like Elvis) interested in early Christian history and alternative interpretations of biblical texts.

- *The Hidden Wisdom in the Holy Bible*, volumes I and II, by Geoffrey Hodson (1963): The book explores the spiritual significance of passages in the Bible and draws on Theosophy and other traditions to emphasize the unity of all religions. The author describes his clairvoyant experiences in which he claims to have seen hidden spiritual beings and dimensions.

- *The Rosicrucian Cosmo-Conception*, by Max Heindel (1909): The book explores the universe's spiritual hierarchy and cosmic principles. It discusses the evolution of the soul, the afterlife, and the purpose of human existence. The book also investigates the symbolism and teachings of various religious and esoteric traditions, including Christianity, Hinduism, and astrology. The text has influenced the development of many modern spiritual movements and emphasizes the unity of all religions and a holistic approach to spirituality.

Like any good modern Gnostic, Elvis knew that the Vatican held secrets and texts from humanity that could change the world for the better: "I'm not a prophet, but I'll tell you, some day all that information they're hiding from the masses will become known, and it will be a whole new ballgame," he said.[70] And like any good Gnostic in any era, synthesizing Egyptian mysteries with other traditions was just "all right, mama." In one of his private rituals, Elvis explained to Ginger that to contact one's higher self or Christ Consciousness, a seeker needed to form a pyramid shape with index fingers and thumbs and then place the hands up to their forehead. "Pyramids possess a special energy which help give strength to an individual," he declared. "Pray to the third eye and say, 'Christ light, Christ love, Christ peace.'"

(Elvis wanted to marry Ginger in a pyramid-shaped church, indicating that, like the ankh, he was fond of this Egyptian elemental symbol.)[71]

Lastly, Elvis developed an interest in the mystical elements of two different Christian denominations. His friendship with Ed Parker, a Mormon, instilled his curiosity about the Church of Jesus Christ of Latter-Day Saints. Donny Osmond remembers seeing Elvis in the early 1970s discussing the Book of Mormon with his mother, Olive. In his book *American Religion*, Harold Bloom, renowned literary critic, characterizes Mormonism as a modern Gnostic religion.[72]

Elvis also became attentive to Greek Orthodoxy. This interest grew after Elvis met his doctor's pastor, Father Nicholas Vieron, and engaged in a rewarding theological conversation. Vieron even gave him copies of *The Incarnation* by St. Athanasios, the *Philokalia*, and sermons by the fourth-century mystic St. John Chrysostom.[73]

NUMEROLOGY, GEMATRIA, AND KABBALAH

Elvis generally avoided mainstream astrology, psychics, or fortune-telling, although he was captivated by *New Mansions for New Men* by Dane Rudhyar, who was a groundbreaking astrological innovator of the twentieth century.[74] Numerology didn't engross Elvis as much as the cosmic and transcendental power of numbers.[75] Why did specific numbers like seven or ten appear in the Bible and other sacred texts? Was there a foundational formula to the universe?[76] His main book for this inquiry was the *Book of Numbers* by Cheiro, also known as Count Louis Hamon, one of the most celebrated and colorful metaphysical figures of the early twentieth century. Elvis was fascinated with his life and works. Cheiro's clients included Mark Twain, Mata Hari, Oscar Wilde, President Grover Cleveland, Thomas Edison, King Edward VII of Great Britain, King Leopold l of Belgium, Nicholas II and his wife Alexandra of Russia, Rasputin, Pope Leo XII, and Joseph Chamberlain. Cheiro employed the ancient Chaldean system to zero in on a person's most profound traits, providing insights into one's life and destiny.[77]

Not only did Elvis carry the *Book of Numbers* around to give away or start a conversation with friends, but he also leveraged it when buying his expensive jewelry, matching the gems to some numerical value.[78]

Elvis's interest in numbers extended to other times and places. Together, Geller and Elvis heeded the words of the *Zohar*, "The Universe was created by three forms of expression—Numbers, Letters, and Words," and studied the ancient Greek philosopher Pythagoras and his ideas of gematria and the harmony of the spheres. Both loved the philosopher's dictum of "God geometrizes," and this led them to study the numerology, geometry, and architecture of Islamic and Asian cultures (including that found in the I Ching). Such a rabbit hole logically led Elvis to the Kabbalah and the mystical numerology of the Hebrew Bible.[79]

As Geller, drawing from his religion and studies, told Elvis:

Hebrew letters all have a numerical value, and Gematria uses those values to explore the interrelation of different words and ideas. Each letter also represents an aspect of human experience, ideas about creation, and man's connection to God, to himself and to nature. In times of crisis or crossroads in people's lives, rabbis change their names to change their destiny.[80]

Not surprisingly, since all roads had to lead to Elvis in Elvis's mind, he became fascinated by the esoteric meanings of his name. Geller found that the "El" in "Elvis" perhaps traced back to ancient times, a cross-cultural phoneme meaning light or shining. El was utilized in Hebrew, for instance, to connote God (think of Beth-El, "House of God," and Elohim, the plural of God.) And "Vis" in Latin meant the power of God, Geller further told him.[81]

Elvis's exploration and connection with Hebrew traditions deeply affected his worldview. He never said why until the year of his death and only to Geller—for reasons he wouldn't divulge to anyone until then. Yet soon after the study of Kabbalah, Elvis began to wear a *chai* pendant, the Jewish symbol for living and life, alongside his customary cross (and secretly the ankh, as mentioned). "I don't want to be kept out of heaven on a technicality," he told a reporter when asked why he wore the two symbols. When Elvis donated $12,500 toward a fund to build a Jewish community center in Memphis, it was assumed it was merely Elvis being his legendary philanthropic self. Nevertheless, when they visited his mother's grave site to meditate, Geller found it odd that Elvis declared that he would place a Star of David on her memorial stone one day.

When he told Vernon about this idea, his father was displeased and wondered why a good Christian memorial would need a "Jewish sign."

In 1977, Elvis confessed to Geller that he had Jewish heritage, which made Geller wonder if his religion had been part of his destiny in meeting him. Gladys's maternal great-grandmother had been Jewish. This truth was kept from Vernon and the rest of the world by both Gladys and Elvis. For unspoken reasons, Elvis, even as the King, even as Vernon was on his payroll, was reluctant to let his father know about his Jewish blood. This was the same case with Colonel Parker and his entourage (even if three members of Elvis's inner circle were Jews). As Geller admitted, many around Elvis still believed "Jews had horns."[82]

Elvis mined mountains of research (including gematria) from the scholarship of Manly P. Hall, the august Canadian mystic, philosopher, and author who dedicated his life to esoteric knowledge, best known for his best-selling and classic *The Secret Teachings of All Ages*. Elvis desperately wanted to hear from the sage himself and see Hall lecture at his Philosophical Research Society while filming movies in Los Angeles. Of course, Elvis Presley walking anywhere in public was akin to an alien craft landing on the White House, especially in Tinsel Town.

So, he sent his then-fiancée Priscilla to take notes and return with the Gnosis (the other purpose of the mission, and why Geller didn't go instead, was for Priscilla to elevate her own spiritual awareness so that she would share and grow with Elvis in finding "the answers to the universe"). She did her best but found it all too dense and hard to endure.[83]

Elvis and Hall came close to meeting, though. In the early 1970s, Elvis sent Geller to purchase a deluxe edition of *The Secret Teachings of All Ages* and have Hall sign it. Geller purchased the book at the Philosophical Research Society and asked Hall's secretary to speak with her boss to sign the work for Elvis. Hall was in a meeting but immediately left and signed the book once his secretary informed him of the request. Geller invited Hall to meet Elvis at his hotel, as the King was recording music in town. Hall politely declined due to commitments.

Despite being unable to meet his hero, Elvis was still elated when

Geller presented him with the autographed copy. That night, at the Sunset Boulevard recording studio, he showed the book to band members, proudly flipping through the ornately illustrated pages and decoding many symbols. He urged everyone to delve into the images and myths to uncover life's deeper meaning. The musicians just wanted to play music.[84]

That was the story of the Occult Elvis at any stage of his Trickster transformation: a shining spark of arcane curiosity surrounded by those who cared for him but were primarily interested in the status quo and matters of the flesh.

THE ONE RELIGION ELVIS DISLIKED

Elvis was wise in more ways than deciding not to show up to see Hall orate at the Philosophical Research Center. The pitches were numerous once the Hollywood grapevine discovered that the King was interested in unorthodox spiritual traditions. He never judged any movement as lesser or greater; he simply had his personal tastes. As explained, it wasn't that he adopted any mysticism that came his way and wore it like one of his Las Vegas suits; instead, he carefully built on his peculiar Gnostic Christianity even as fame, drugs, those around him, and his own ego destroyed it at times.

There was one movement, though, about which he was extremely vocal. Fundamentalist Christianity disappointed him to no end, but he still maintained a connection to its values and shamanistic pedigree. He never disliked it, even as many turned against him once he became the chief herald of rock 'n' roll.

The same cannot be said about Scientology. Founded in 1953 by occultist and science fiction author L. Ron Hubbard, this ideology of applying the healing human spirit to the universe and its living forms was making inroads in Los Angeles in the 1970s. Hubbard's book *Dianetics* had already sold millions of copies, and the city's Celebrity Centre was recruiting quickly.

Elvis read up on Scientology and found it no different than the fundamentalist churches he had walked away from as a young adult: mind-controlling, interested merely in money, and perverting actual holy teachings of past masters. Most of all, to him, Scientology was a dangerous organization and a godless religion. "They never mention God," Elvis said. "They just want me. They want my name and my money. That's what they're into. I've got to be extremely careful; I just can't let my name be used for something so important except when it's right."

"He stayed away from Scientology like it was a cobra," Lamar Fike once said about Elvis.[85]

Scientology did get Elvis's name and money many years after his death, however, when both Priscilla and his daughter, Lisa Marie, became involved with the organization.[86]

4
EASTERN INFLUENCES

From Kriya Yoga to Karate

AS COVERED IN THE PREVIOUS CHAPTER, Blavatsky and her Theosophical army brought Eastern religious traditions to Europe and the USA. The American shores, though, didn't have the advantage of varied secrets societies and philosophers who sought alternatives to the dry Victorian and Protestant climate of the nineteenth century—names like Aleister Crowley, Arthur Schopenhauer, Friedrich Nietzsche, Paul Deussen, and Max Muller, to give a few. Beyond Theosophy's impact, Eastern religions, notably Buddhism and Hinduism, trickled in at a steady rate in the USA during that same period, as North American scholars began to take an interest in the philosophy and spirituality of the East.

What helped open the doors to the East in America was the World's Parliament of Religions, held in Chicago in 1893. The event was the first interfaith gathering of its kind, bringing together representatives from varied global religious traditions to share their teachings and insights. Attending were Hindu swamis, including Swami Vivekananda, who delivered a series of lectures on Hindu metaphysics that were widely attended and well received. Vivekananda's message of unity and universality, as well as his emphasis on the importance of spiritual practice and self-realization, resonated with many Americans seeking substitutes for the materialistic and spiritually bankrupt culture of the time.

Some American intellectuals like Ralph Waldo Emerson, Henry David Thoreau, and William James were influenced by Eastern thought and incorporated it into their own literary and philosophical works. This interest in Eastern ideas was further energized by the influx of Asian immigrants from Japan and China. Many great scientists of the atomic age, like Albert Einstein and Richard Feynman, were known to be open to Asian mysticism. In the 1950s, Beat writers like Jack Kerouac, Allen Ginsberg, and Gary Snyder were drawn to Buddhism and infused its themes into their work.

But it wasn't until the 1960s that Eastern religions caught fire with a sizeable amount of the American population. The influential teenagers discussed in chapter 2 continued to search for meaning in an atomic age, and the answers came from other shores as the world shrank with commercial airplanes and mass media. The pivotal point was the counterculture movement that saw superstars like the Beatles advocate for Eastern faiths.

KRIYA YOGA

Elvis was ahead of the hippies and other metaphysical innovators, embracing the East right when he met Geller in 1964. As mentioned in the previous chapter, meditation became a staple of his religious life, whether in his Graceland garden, when visiting cemeteries, or after shows. Elvis himself said, "Meditation is better than any drug I know. I can relax, I can breathe deeper, I'm calmer."[1]

Elvis had three favorite books ironically embraced by the counterculture movement he later disdained.[2] After *The Prophet* and *The Impersonal Life*, his favored work was *Autobiography of a Yogi*, a 1946 spiritual memoir by Indian yogi Paramahansa Yogananda, describing his life experiences and spiritual journey while exploring the teachings of the arcane Kriya Yoga.

Elvis devoured the book while filming *Harum Scarum* in 1965. He was impressed by Yogananda's universal message and supernatural feats, including the legendary story of his body not decomposing for over twenty days after his death. He highly regarded how Kriya Yoga advocated "to prove the practical truth in the immortal teachings of Jesus Christ."

The King wanted that kind of mastery over his body and consciousness (and to still be in good standing with J. C.). He sought to be a master like Yogananda. In the middle of filming, as previously mentioned, he wanted to start the spiritual journey immediately. He looked up at Geller from his book while taking a break and said, "Lawrence, I think I'm ready to be initiated into Kriya Yoga." He then quoted an underlined passage from Yogananda's book: "When (Kriya) is practiced during meditation, it greatly accelerates one's spiritual evolution."

He then asked Geller to get him through the process, as Geller had already been initiated, which entailed two years of demanding training that included clean living, disciplined meditation, and heavy yoga regimens. Geller warned him about the challenging preparation but agreed to take Elvis to the Kriya Yoga headquarters in Los Angeles, the Self-Realization Fellowship (SRF). The head of the organization, Sri Daya Mata (formerly Faye Wright), had been a disciple of Yogananda. She quickly agreed to meet the King of Rock 'n' Roll.

At the scenic ashram on Mount Washington, Elvis and Daya Mata immediately bonded. Daya Mata was magnetic in look and aura, and like Blavatsky, she reminded Elvis of his mother. Elvis confessed that he was ready to turn his back on fame and materiality and join a commune or monastery to make a spiritual example to the entire world. Daya Mata told him that the best path was the gradual path. She gave him two bound volumes containing lessons and instructions for his initiation into Kriya Yoga for the coming year.

Elvis often returned, calling Daya Mata simply "Ma" for mother, as she was known in the ashram. He spent many evenings with her, and, like most who got to know him personally, she grew to love him for the innate goodness and spiritual potential that even he didn't think he possessed. On the other hand, Elvis considered her his "spiritual mother" and a living saint.

Elvis tried to glean some "shortcuts" in his training. Daya Mata would not budge, uncaring about his money, charisma, or power. She told him to relax and enjoy an existence where he could be both a family-loving celebrity in public and an individual benefiting from mystical practices in seclusion. He didn't have to go to extremes. "The inner peace you seek can be yours no matter what your work," she told him. His time with her and that teaching was a central inspiration to build his meditation garden in Graceland. He could have the best of both worlds.

Elvis also loved visiting the SRF's fourteen-acre, monk-tended retreat by the ocean in Pacific Palisades. Yogananda wrote most of his autobiography there, and the location was also famous for the many visits of George Harrison when the "Quiet Beatle" visited Los Angeles. Beyond the beautiful gardens and natural-fed lake, part of Gandhi's ashes were enshrined there.

At the Lake Shrine, Elvis met an old monk, Brother Adolph (I know what you're thinking, conspiracy theorists). The elderly man said he was impressed that a man with Elvis's wealth and status was so eagerly searching for God and that both transcendence and immortality were genuine concepts.

"My search is real," Elvis said. "I'm not playing games, Brother Adolph. But I have a long way to go, that's for sure."

The monk told him the cliché of a journey of a thousand miles beginning with a single step, but that he sensed Elvis was an old soul ready for the final stage of his incarnations. Self-realization was the King's for the taking.

Elvis balked, providing his own cliché: the more he learned, the more he felt he didn't know. The monk chuckled and said self-doubt was healthy while one attempted to understand what could not be understood and experience a sense of the limitless. However, Brother Adolph added, doubt could mean he was presently in the wrong place.

They chatted for a while, the monk insisting that Elvis was sincere in his pursuit and that his ability to inspire people was a blessing. Yet he warned Elvis that reading too many books was like "the blind leading the blind" (a third cliché) since those who wrote books were themselves searching. In the end, a guru could open some doors, but only Elvis could step into the experience of God. "The truth is in you," Brother Adolph said, "and ultimately only you know where to find it." Elvis laughed and agreed, surely recalling those mystical Jesus books that spoke of no intermediary and that Inner Christ, the Living Jesus.[3]

Elvis failed to heed the wise Brother Adolph. The balance formula from Daya Mata didn't work out because of Elvis's usual lack of patience and his eternally being "caught in a trap" of his fanbase and inner circle. As Geller wrote after Elvis connected with "Ma":

> Elvis listened. He had enormous respect for this woman. Part of him understood what she was saying. But part of him—the impatient part—wanted another answer. He did want instant evolution. Accustomed to having everything he wanted when he wanted it, it was emotionally difficult for him to see why this would be any different. At the same time, he was able to be completely honest with Daya Mata. She was perhaps the only one who understood the enormity of Elvis' fears. She understood because he told her. The pressure of staying in the limelight, retaining his popularity and pleasing his fans—not to mention placating the manager who helped establish his fame—was gut wrenching.[4]

Along with his impatience, a part of Elvis was stuck as a child under Gladys, living in an imaginary world and unable to grow in the real world. As Geller noticed, Elvis was a "witty, insightful, impractical man riven with contradictions." At his core, Elvis was shy and didn't trust himself, always afraid people might laugh at him. At the same time, he held a quality of inner calm that permitted him to explore himself thoroughly, without self-consciousness or pride. "When Elvis appreciated something, when he appreciated beauty," Geller said, "he just appreciated it; it was timeless to him. Like a flower—a flower just exists now, it doesn't exist yesterday. It just is. If Elvis loved something, it just was. [That kind of appreciation] is different, perhaps 'abnormal.' But there's something beautiful and interesting about it."

Geller also contended that Elvis possessed an uncanny ability to "read" people. "His intuition was highly developed, and very little escaped his notice," he said. Or as Elvis film documentarian Bob Abel said, "He had incredible native intelligence, the ability to read a human being, to watch someone's eyes and look inside their soul."[5] Sheila Ryan, who dated Elvis in the 1970s, claims that Elvis could read her so well that he "knew things before I knew them. He knew things that I was feeling before I was feeling them."[6]

Simultaneously, Elvis's persuasion and magnetism were reality-bending, almost supernatural, especially when he wanted something. As bodyguard and karate instructor Dave Hebler said:

He can walk into a room without saying a word and fill it with sunshine. I later learned that he could walk into that same room and fill it with black violence that got to be very hard on the nerves. He can manipulate your emotions like no human being I have ever seen. Suddenly you feel you're living your own life in a series of highs and lows dependent on his highs and lows.[7]

Elvis was never initiated in Kriya Yoga, although he retained many of its practices and kept in touch with Daya Mata, frequently calling her for advice. During a period as Vegas Elvis, he tapped into his yoga teaching to meditate himself out of throat and high blood pressure issues, and could reach such strong trances that he would perform in a fog during some of his Las Vegas shows. The influence of drugs was always a possibility, but Elvis had always been halfway in a higher world. As his stepbrother and bodyguard, Richard Stanley, said, "Elvis could be as quiet and reflective as a monk. Within the confines of his isolated life, he remained a deeply spiritual man."

When his marriage to Priscilla officially ended in 1973, he met with Daya Mata privately for advice and medicinal meditation sessions. He was broken, likely to be relatively financially challenged by the divorce settlement, and all his dreams seemed to be falling apart. He told her that his biggest goal remained unchanged, rationalizing that it was why he had returned to live shows and become Vegas Elvis: "I want to feel God's love. I want to give back. I want to awaken in all these young people a closer relationship with God."

Daya Mata assured Elvis that his heart would heal in time. Nonetheless, he was currently on dangerous ground when it came to the way he treated his body. Elvis knew she was right but knew he might be too far along the destructive path. He never spoke to her again.[8]

OTHER EASTERN TRADITIONS AND MEETING THE BEATLES

Via Theosophy, Elvis was exposed by default to Asian mysticism. He was well versed in the chakra systems, knowing that these "wheel centers" channeled "life force, feelings, memories, and thoughts."[9] While studying numerology and gematria, he covered Taoism, even claiming that the Tao was just another word for God.[10] He loved the writings of Lao Tzu, often quoting aloud these sayings for spiritual fortitude:

- A brave soldier is not violent.
- A skilled fighter does not lose his temper.
- A great general wins without a battle.
- A mighty ruler governs through humility.[11]

Elvis read *Siddhartha* by Hermann Hesse, published in 1922, a historical fiction novel about a man named Siddhartha in the era of the Buddha who wrestles with the doctrinal dictates of orthodox religion and the soul's inner prompts, culminating with acceptance of human separateness and discovery of an eternal spirit of divine love. The work is loosely based on the historical Gautama Buddha, a metaphoric journey that draws on both Hindu and Buddhist teachings, all highlighting the importance of personal experience in achieving self-actualization. The book became very influential with the 1960s counterculture movement, along with Hesse's *Steppenwolf* and *Damien*.

Deborah Walley was Elvis's costar in the 1966 film *Spinout*. In that film, Walley, best known for her iconic teen movies *Gidget Goes Hawaiian* and *Beach Blanket Bingo*, played an androgynous drummer vying for Elvis, who played a lead singer for a traveling band and a part-time race car driver. She admitted having no interest in getting acquainted with the King since she was a Beatles fan (the Elvis/Beatles camps tended not to overlap in those days). Nevertheless, she was immediately mesmerized by his presence and became even more fascinated when they began discussing spirituality. "We had a very close relationship, a spiritual relationship," she said. "I really have to say he changed my life."

A lapsed Catholic searching for new meanings, Walley was impressed with Elvis's thirst for learning and sharing knowledge. She had lunch with Elvis in his trailer daily, and he took her for motorcycle rides on his Harley. He once confessed to her: "I'm not a man. I'm not a woman—I'm a soul, a spirit, a force. I have no interest in anything of this world. I want to live in another dimension entirely."

Walley summarized her early days with the King:

"I think Elvis found in me an empty vessel into which he could pour all the knowledge that he had acquired. We talked about Buddhism, Hinduism, and all types of religion. He taught me how to meditate. He took me to the Self-Realization Center and introduced me to [the teachings of Paramahansa Yogananda. We talked a lot at either my house or his house . . . eating big bowls full of ice cream."[12]

Walley admitted she was never the same after Elvis. Their friendship continued until the end of his life, and she claimed his presence was felt often until her passing in 2001.[13]

Oddly enough, the one group of individuals with whom Elvis could have discussed Eastern spirituality was Walley's favorite band, the Beatles, especially since they had already met once in person.

On the night of August 27, 1965, three limousines carrying the Fab Four and their entourage arrived at Elvis Presley's residence in Bel Air. The Beatles were in town to perform their historic Hollywood Bowl concerts. Arriving at the mansion, the band saw their idol lounging on a long sofa in the living room. John and Paul took a seat next to him on one side, with Ringo taking a seat on the other side, while George Harrison made himself comfortable on the floor facing Elvis. Initially, the conversation flowed awkwardly, mainly because the Beatles were stoned on marijuana, which made them even more intimidated at meeting their musical idol.

Elvis broke the tension by saying, "Look, guys, if you're just going to sit there and stare at me, I'm going to bed." The warning led to a conversation about the color television in the room, which hadn't reached the UK yet. Elvis then picked up his bass guitar and began to jam along to "Mohair Sam" by Charlie Rich, followed by the Beatles playing some of their own songs like "You're My World," "Johnny B. Goode," and "I Feel Fine." Paul gave Elvis tips on how to play the bass guitar. The King, who had just started learning that instrument, appreciated the lesson.

Ringo abandoned thumping on the sofa during their jam and went to shoot pool with the Memphis Mafia. George went outside to have a joint. Paul and Elvis shared horror stories of almost being torn apart by fan mobs. Geller went out to search for George, and they discussed Indian religion and philosophy (without Elvis!).

At one point in the evening, Elvis, who had made many dentists rich by his oral obsession, whispered to Geller when they were alone, "Man, what's with these guys, what's with their teeth? Don't they know better? They've got the money."

Finally, Elvis gave the tour of his garage that stored his new Rolls-Royce. Along the way, they were spotted by the throng of fans milling the front gate, chanting "Elvis! Elvis!" and "Beatles! Beatles!" back and forth. The Beatles finally left the King's castle at around two in the morning. The five never met again, though Ringo did visit Elvis during some of his Las Vegas performances, while Lennon shared several phone conversations with Elvis years later regarding his troubles with the American government (Elvis advised him to publicly denounce drugs, which Lennon did).

After the Fab Four left that evening, Elvis remarked to Geller, "I like them. They're good boys."[14]

MARTIAL ARTS

What is so esoteric about karate? When Elvis became a black belt in 1960, he was only one of perhaps one hundred Americans with such an honor—in a country of more than 179 million—and he did so long before the age of Bruce Lee, David Carradine, Chuck Norris, Kareem Abdul Jabbar, and others who popularized martial arts in the West.[15]

Elvis's journey with martial arts started while he was in service in Germany in 1958 (Army Elvis). He took the discipline seriously because of continuous altercations with jealous boyfriends and husbands.

Elvis received personalized lessons three or four times a week at his off-base residence from Jürgen Seydel, otherwise known as "the father of German karate." The two practiced in the living room and other times in the garage on a large carpet. Elvis loved displaying his moves to his entourage and stressing its superiority as a form of self-defense. Seydel regarded Elvis as one of his most gifted pupils and thus allowed him to take lessons from the renowned kenpo Japanese master, Murakami Tetsuji, when Elvis enjoyed a furlough in Paris in 1960.

As mentioned, once he completed his service and resumed training in America, he attained his first-degree black belt in the same year.[16]

Karate became a passion and method of meditation for Elvis for the rest of his life. He even opened a dojo, the Tennessee Karate Institute, in 1974. YouTube houses plenty of videos of Elvis being a student and master in the dojo. He was undoubtedly a pioneer in the 1970s in America's discovery of martial arts. He attained an eigth-degree black belt the same year he opened his dojo, a testament to his dedication and skill set.[17] Through more rigorous training, he earned a sixth-degree black belt from Ed Parker, and a seventh-degree from Kang Rhee in taekwondo.[18]

Martial arts blended into the Elvis Presley public persona, from horse fighting with the Memphis Mafia during downtimes to fight scenes in his zany movies to employing kicks/punches in his Vegas Elvis manifestation. And it extended to the real world in ways that could have come from a 1970s or 1980s martial arts movie. Every Elvis was kung fu fighting, and at the Crossroads, the Trickster never worries about the difference between fantasy and reality. As Peter O. Whitmer wrote, paraphrasing Sigmund Freud, "To live without a dream is foolish, and to live within a dream is insane. However, dreaming of living within a dream was pure Elvis, the actualization of his 'illusion of illusion.'"[19] On a more material level, it was Priscilla who said that "one thing he couldn't pass up was a good fight."[20]

This once happened an afternoon after Elvis left the Self-Realization Fellowship Center. He rode with Priscilla in a limousine on their way home, his mind full of calmness and universal love. That was short-lived. Passing a service station, Elvis spotted two attendants fighting outside the station and told the driver to pull over. "Someone's in trouble," he declared, like Captain Marvel Jr. might have.

The King jumped out of the vehicle, tailed by two bodyguards. He went up to one of the men and informed him that any trouble he had should be directed at him. The man was stunned at who had just challenged him. "Hey man," he stuttered. "I don't have any problem with you. I'm not arguing with you."

"I'll show you something," Elvis said, "if you want to get into an argument."

Elvis delivered a karate kick, incredibly knocking a pack of cigarettes from the man's pockets.

Priscilla felt Elvis was incredibly lucky, but in karate circles, breaking boards with his hands or knocking cigarette packs out of pockets with kicks were feats he did commonly, like magic tricks. Regardless, the strike was what it took to defuse the situation. Elvis warned the alleged villain to stay out of trouble or more of those laser-accurate kicks would strike at something other than cigarettes.

Elvis's recounting of the story grew from one man to a battalion, but Priscilla allowed him to have his "dream within a dream."[21]

A similar situation transpired over a decade later during his Fat Elvis stage. Instead of in Los Angeles, it occurred in Madison, Wisconsin. This time, the limousine was driving Elvis, Vernon, and Ginger. A gas station was the same backdrop for this karate movie, but on this occasion, Elvis spotted two youths harassing the attendant. He ignored the warnings of his father and fiancée not to transform into Captain Marvel Jr., leaping out of the limousine. He struck a warning karate pose and warned loudly he was ready to take out the two young men. The fight broke up without any blows being exchanged as the three men were too stunned at the sight of the King of Rock 'n' Roll standing in the flesh. In fact, it ended with a round of handshakes and Elvis posing for photographs with the three. Everyone left happy.[22]

Then there was that time when rock star Alice Cooper was welcomed to his own nightmare. The surreal experience occurred in 1970 in the Las Vegas Hilton. Cooper had been summoned to meet the King. He rode up an elevator with a group that included Liza Minnelli, Chubby Checker, and adult actress Linda Lovelace. After being searched for guns, they were allowed into Elvis's floor, ironically full of guns casually strewn everywhere.

The first thing Elvis said when meeting Cooper was, "Hey, man. You're that cat with the snake, ain't ya?" Cooper agreed with a yes, and Elvis said, "That's cool, man. I wish I woulda thought that."

Elvis signaled Cooper to follow him into the kitchen. Elvis opened a drawer and took out a loaded .38 snub nose. He placed the weapon in Cooper's hand and told him he would show him how to disarm a person. In a rising state of alarm, Cooper thought that the only way out of this situation safely might be to wound Elvis with the gun. His contemplation was cut short by overwhelming blackness. Suddenly, he was lying on the floor with the King's boot on his throat. Cooper groaned and said, "That's good, Elvis."

Despite the encounter, Cooper was impressed by the King's humor and presence for the rest of the meeting. "He was Elvis" was all he could say, and with awe.[23]

Sometimes Elvis's karate demonstrations didn't go the way they do in the movies, like when he broke a woman's ankle during a karate demonstration at a party in his Vegas suite. This fiasco occurred during his devolving years, as drugs combusted his mind. A personal injury lawsuit came out of that incident.[24]

On one occasion martial arts possibly saved his life, even as his mind at the time was also suffering from increased drug use. In February of 1973, at the midnight show in Vegas, four men positioned themselves next to the stage. One of them abruptly rushed to the stage, coat folded over his arm as if concealing a weapon. One of the bodyguards intercepted the man and placed him in a headlock. The other three men continued towards Elvis. More bodyguards appeared and took down two of the men, leaving one free to attack the King. Elvis nailed the assailant with a powerful karate kick that sent him flying into the audience. Then Elvis went more ballistic, attacking the air with karate moves. Even his father couldn't calm him down. Elvis finally relaxed when the authorities dragged the four men away, telling the audience before resuming the concert, "I'm sorry, ladies and gentlemen. I'm sorry I didn't break his goddamn neck is what I'm sorry about." The crowd went wild because, as the saying goes, if you come at the king, you better not miss.

The authorities never gave a reason for the assault, even if they found that the first man had a sheath for a hidden sword. Elvis had received threats and there had even been assassination attempts before. In this situation, he suspected the mastermind was Mike Stone, Priscilla's martial arts instructor, who later became her lover and had seeded her desire to leave the marriage.

Elvis's outrageous behavior is legion and notorious, from shooting television sets when he didn't like a show to smashing toilets if the color irked his taste. Yet martial arts granted him peace, sobriety, safety, and a sense of immortality that worked out for him when effectively leveraged. It helped him transcend even more into those magical states of being.[25]

The world almost gained an Elvis karate movie. As rock 'n' roll (briefly) left Elvis behind in the middle and late 1960s, karate was leaving him behind in 1973 as the face of martial arts in America. Bruce Lee's *Enter the Dragon* and the *Billy Jack* movies were hits and instant classics, while Davie Carradine's *Kung Fu* series was entertaining television audiences across the country. Elvis loved watching all types of karate movies (and making everyone around him do the same until they prayed he would find another obsession). This interest included the blaxploitation films that leaned on martial arts, like *Cleopatra Jones*, *Black Belt Jones*, and even *Shaft*.

So why not an Elvis karate movie? The idea of a feature film evolved into a documentary titled *The New Gladiators*. Elvis would narrate the film and appear occasionally to instruct. Techniques, karate masters, and tournaments around the world would be featured. Geller was recruited to write the narration, which would include the history of karate and how it could positively transform anyone who immersed himself in the self-defense art.

The project eventually fell apart, with some footage shot and Elvis losing his $125,000 investment. (The film was finally remastered and released in 2002.) This disappointment occurred as Elvis was apparently losing all his magic to his shadow and complexes, which we will discuss in another chapter.[26]

It's probably not surprising at this stage of the Trickster journey, but Priscilla, considering her embracing of Scientology and eventually bonding with Daya Mata for spiritual guidance, also embraced martial arts. She became proficient in her own right, studying with various prominent figures like Chuck Norris and, as mentioned, Mike Stone, who was a former pupil of Bruce Lee.[27]

5

A NATURAL HEALER AND SORCERER

He's the Magic Man

MAGIC AND OTHER HIGH WEIRDNESS soaked Elvis and his family, outside and within. Whether it was genetic, environmental, or destiny is a debate that can last forever. But it was around.

Magic was there the day Elvis was born. In the Presleys' small house rested two identical, small glass bottles on a wooden shelf. As soon as Gladys went into labor, one of them fell to the floor and shattered, a foreshadowing of what would happen to one of the humans in the pair that was arriving that night.[1] At one point that evening, Vernon walked out to have a cigarette. He was stunned to see a blue light from the sky that lit up his house. The wind died, and an eternal silence permeated the area. Vernon was startled, naturally, and ran into the house. Still, the tragedy of Jesse that night, and life in general, made him forget the incident until one day when Elvis, while doing an astrological chart, asked him about the day of his birth.[2]

Elvis was always drawn to the color blue. He felt that the blue light incident at birth represented God's relationship with him and his destined path in this incarnation.[3] Blue materialized as the force of divine energies when he meditated or prayed. The first time Ginger met Elvis in Vegas, he was sitting on a couch in the middle of a suite, dressed in a hooded blue terry-cloth robe, surrounded by bodyguards and Larry Geller (and one of the first things Elvis did was show her his collection of philosophy and religious books, wanting to talk metaphysics).[4] Blue was the color of healing to him, and healing was one of the reasons he believed he had materialized in this world. And healing Elvis did—a gift that ran in his family. As an example, when Elvis was six years old, he developed acute tonsillitis during the day. His fever was high, and his body was near convulsions. The family doctor said there was nothing he could do. Gladys and Vernon decided to join in a healing prayer. By nighttime, Elvis was completely cured.[5]

ELVIS THE HEALER

Healing others became almost a full-time job once Elvis embraced the occult. At Graceland he healed the arthritis and other ailments of his grandmother, Minnie Mae. The ritual involved Larry Geller and him placing their hands on Mae's forehead, praying, and visualizing blue.[6] Priscilla admitted that Elvis's abilities were real, being able to heal even the worst headaches with a touch of his hand.[7] Ginger claimed that during a bout of nausea, Elvis cured her by placing his hand on her abdomen.[8] He once healed the sprained leg of a groupie at his house, all with a bout of meditation, sharing about religious backgrounds, and laying of the hands.[9]

The healing magic wasn't just for the lady loves, mind you.

Jerry Schilling, an inner circle member and childhood friend of Elvis, was once in a hospital in agony after a motorcycle accident. Elvis came to visit him, saying he had a feeling that Jerry wasn't sleeping because of back pain. "I'm afraid so, Elvis," Jerry answered. Elvis placed his hands on Jerry's back and began to pray. Again, he visualized blue light. The following day Schilling woke up without any back pain. "Whatever Elvis did somehow worked," he admitted.[10]

As we've seen, Elvis was never one to avoid jumping out of his limo to join a public fracas. This time it happened in Nashville. Elvis noticed a curbed bus on the side of the road, with the driver on the street staggering about and holding his chest. Elvis rushed the man, put an arm around his shoulder, and placed the other on his heart. The King reassured him everything was going to be fine. And it was! Moments later, the man felt great, the only shock coming from his mind as he realized the magical touch of Elvis Presley had just saved him. Elvis made sure an ambulance arrived before getting back in his vehicle.[11]

Like many in the King's court, bodyguard and friend Sonny West was cynical about Elvis's supernatural powers; however, his skepticism abated when a high fever gripped his infant son. After hearing the news, Elvis requested to come over to pray. When he got to West's house, he donned a turban and laid the child upon a green scarf. Elvis prayed over the boy, making circular motions with his hands. To the amazement of West and his wife, the child's temperature dropped below 100 degrees and remained at a safe level.[12]

A healing transpired in yet another peculiar instance. While going to the movies, girlfriend Linda Thompson mentioned that her brother's wife had just conceived. It didn't matter that it was one in the morning—Elvis insisted on a visit. Despite visitation rules and the late hour, Elvis's appearance turned the hospital into a circus, with nurses "dropping patients everywhere and running to get his autograph."

At one point, Elvis noticed a pregnant woman on a stretcher being wheeled down a hallway toward the delivery room. For unknown reasons, Elvis went to talk to the woman, who was in a mixture of awe and pain as she was deep in labor. Elvis felt sorrow for her and laid his hands on her stomach. Without donning a turban, he started imploring in a trance voice, "Now, there, it won't hurt anymore. It won't hurt anymore. Everything is going to be fine. You're not going to hurt anymore."

Eventually, the woman said, "You're right, the pain is gone, you're right."

The doctors arrived and urged that the soon-to-be mother be taken to the delivery room. Elvis wanted to accompany her. "Can I come to the delivery room? I have never seen a baby born. I want to see life."

The doctors denied his request, even as the woman insisted that Elvis be present for the birth of her child.[13]

According to Sylvia Shemwell, a member of The Sweet Inspirations, Elvis's backup singers in Las Vegas during the 1970s, the King saved her life. Shemwell claimed that Elvis found her one evening despondent in the dressing room alongside the other concerned backup singers. He asked what was wrong, and she answered that she had just returned from the hospital with news of stomach cancer. Elvis fell to his knees in front of Shemwell, put his hands on her stomach, and began praying. The next day, she returned to the hospital and was told that the cancer had vanished.[14]

Another astounding healing session happened while Elvis was on vacation in Colorado. He and his entourage were sledding down a hill. Since it was Elvis in charge, recklessness and bravado were on the agenda, the group plowing and smashing their way down the snowy slope. Everyone made it to the bottom more or less unscathed, except for Dean, the son of Elvis's physician, Dr. Nichopoulos. Dean Nichopoulos hit a fence pole. The group quickly went to the fallen, screaming man. His father unzipped and pulled back the snowsuit, seeing his leg broken. He required hospital attention immediately.

"Let me see him," Elvis ordered, shoving his physician to the side. He knelt over Dean's shattered leg. His face went into deep concentration, and a powerful aura surrounded him. "Hold on there, son," Elvis told Dean with a steady but comforting tone. Elvis then rubbed his hands together quickly as if to bring fire from them. Seconds later, he began to pray and placed his hands on Dean's left broken leg.

Dean's screams and expression of pain vanished. Elvis stood up and backed away, allowing Dr. Nichopoulos to check his son. The leg was broken no more. Dean got up in disbelief, and they all walked back to the house in shock—except for Elvis, who continued enjoying his vacation even though he was treated more as a ghost than a monarch for a while.[15]

Sometimes the healing didn't work, as happened with another

bodyguard and friend, Red West. West suffered chronic pain from his youthful days of playing football. He would avoid mentioning this to Elvis because he knew what would inevitably happen if he did: If Elvis got wind of his friend's pain, he would make him sit down and get the obligatory laying of the hands. As in other instances, Elvis would command the pain to go away. West would tell his boss that the pain had vanished, though it was a lie to set him free. The pain was still there, but at least West appreciated Elvis's intentions and character.[16]

Could these successful instances mean there was a placebo effect going on? Some people might have believed in healing, and that was enough. Was West, like most in the Memphis Mafia, too resistant to Elvis's constant occult behavior? The placebo explanation doesn't quite satisfy the situations with the bus driver, Dean's broken leg, and other cases. Perhaps it is more like Gordon White once told me: "Magic is about probability." Even medical treatment or your average ibuprofen doesn't bat .1000. In the end, Elvis was batting pretty high, and, at the very least, his successful healings are a testament to the magic of the mind when it believes in something and trusts a magician's abilities.

We may never get the complete statistics of Elvis's healing. Beyond so many anecdotes and cases, it wasn't uncommon for a mother to bring their sick children to his Vegas shows for healing.[17] These shows were truly religious festivals, as were all of Elvis's performances. There will be more on the shamanistic festival and Elvis being the healer of his tribe in chapter 9.

As Peter O. Whitmer argues in *Inner Elvis*, in a way, Elvis was healing himself or at least took on the responsibility for healing because of his own pain. Elvis carried the trauma of his twin, the lashes of the Archon of Poverty, and his dysfunctional relationship with his mother (and her subsequent loss). He could channel all of it mystically and artistically by tapping into the magic of Pentecostalism, occultism, the blues, gospel, and constant rock shows where he bonded with his audience.

This brings us to the idea of the "wounded healer," a figure astoundingly found across various diverse cultures, displaying similar emotional needs. Whether in Mongolia, Nigeria, Belize, India, Malaysia, Hong Kong, the Russian Arctic, or North America, this type of shaman lives a life that evolves from suffering to strength. Trauma is not just a way to open the channels to the mystical world but a *training* tool for shamans across history. Generally, an initial experience of psychological trauma is followed by an ecstatic, divine revelation that propels them into their life mission as healers.[18]

Elvis was set in his role as a healer in a specific tribe of believers (that often didn't include much of his vampiric inner circle). Ironically, perhaps he couldn't or dared not heal himself fully because his psychic injuries were the source of his magical power.

Or was there ever a choice for Elvis? Such is the way with muses and their broken vessels. Such is the way of the Gnostic who wants to experience, as Paul writes in Corinthians, "what no eye has seen, nor ear heard, nor human heart conceived . . ."

An argument can be made about Elvis's music's emotional and mental healing powers. But could his music heal physically?

We know the impact on the psyche of America, and in one recorded instant, it saved a life. Geller relates a story in which he walked through a hotel lobby in St. Petersburg, Florida. Elvis was due to give a concert. Geller heard someone say hello and turned to see a woman in her mid-twenties whom he recognized as a fan who traveled from city to city following Elvis on his tours. He asked why she was so passionate about Elvis.

She answered, "That's simple: he saved my life. And now it's his."

Geller was startled. Now more curious, he asked her to join him for coffee at a shop. He learned that she had epilepsy. During one attack, she fell down a flight of stairs, injuring her lower back. The back pain was chronic and unbearable, and no medicine or medical treatment worked. She decided one night that the pain wasn't worth it. She wrote a suicide note to her family and spread sleeping pills on a nightstand. Glancing around her room before taking the pills, the woman noticed the radio was still on. She reached over to turn it off. Just then, Elvis came on the radio with a gospel tune. Her body was filled with light.

"It was the way he sang it," she said. "All the love of God seemed to come through him. . . . I felt the courage flow back through my body, and with it the will to live. . . . There and then, I vowed to dedicate my life to Elvis, to help and protect him."[19]

PROPHECY, INTUITION, AND ASTRAL TRAVEL

Another high weirdness aspect of Vernon, Gladys, and Elvis since their days in Tupelo was their collective and continuous bouts of sleepwalking (or, as Gladys's cousin Leona Richards called it, "action nightmares"). Elvis was hit hardest: his eternal inner storm and daemon call were always active. Once, he walked out of an apartment in his underwear, only to be woken up by a female neighbor (which led to him running back inside, full of terror). On another occasion, he wandered asleep to the top floor of the Lauderdale Courts in Memphis where he lived. Something jolted him out of his trance. He was standing in his underwear, feeling the freezing cold, unable to reenter the building because a young woman and her date were in his way, busy in a conversation that might have been the trigger that brought him back to consciousness. Due to his sleepwalking, Elvis often slept with his parents well into his teens. At other times, Gladys removed the inner doorknob from his bedroom.

While filming one of his first movies, *Loving You*, in 1957, he almost stepped out of an eleventh-story window at the Beverly Wilshire Hotel. At the last moment, his cousin Gene Smith caught him. Sleepwalking became a reason Elvis was terrified of sleeping alone as an adult.[20]

In the aforementioned *The Daemon*, Peake presents evidence that sleepwalking is a sort of trance state in which the daemon or a dissociative disorder personality is allowed to enter the operating system called the material mind. Jesse might have been taking over the wheel for mysterious reasons or simply to unconsciously interact with his brother as he once did in the womb.[21]

The dreamworld was also a source of perils and opportunities for Elvis and his family. Sonny and Red West contended that much of Elvis's mystic abilities started with Gladys and Vernon's dreams. As Sonny West said:

> Like his mother, who dreamed that his car was on fire and was right, Elvis told us about his dad, who also had these weird dreams and would walk in his sleep, like Elvis did. He told us of a time that his dad had this dream that the house was on fire. So his dad jumped up and ran toward where Elvis, who was three years old at the time, was sleeping. He grabbed little Elvis, and he thought he was throwing him out of a window to escape the flames. Of course, the house wasn't on fire. He threw Elvis out of his cot, and Elvis landed butt first against the wall.[22]

As a child, Elvis was known to have constant bad dreams.[23] After he broke out as the world's greatest pop star in the 1950s, he was asked if he dreamed. He answered he only had nightmares: "I'm about to fight somebody or to be in a car wreck or . . . I'm breaking things."[24]

During the filming of *Loving You*, strange dreaming also accompanied Elvis's sleepwalking. He stood over a casket in one dream, which was more like a nightmare. A dead infant was inside it, and this image brought immense sorrow to Elvis.[25]

After communing with his audience in an immersive 1974 show, a recurring dream began to haunt Elvis. He was on stage in front of a packed crowd that worshipped him like the Lord of the Crossroads he was. However, his "dream" performance was not solo; he had been singing with Jesse. When he woke up, he felt depressed and crushed, feeling that he should be sharing his earthly adulation with Jesse.

His twin, his daemon, was indeed reaching out to him in a way beyond that voice in his head which urged him to do the right thing.

Elvis's own intuition and psychic abilities extended beyond the dream world. As we are here at the Crossroads, you won't be surprised there exists plenty of evidence that he knew in advance of his death. In the summer of 1956, during his relationship with June Juanico, he admitted to her that his fate would be similar to that of James Dean: death at a young age. "He didn't say this with fear," June said. "He just would say, 'I'm not going to be here long.'" Shortly later, and after a concert in New Orleans, Elvis woke up trembling and sweating. He called out to June, who was sleeping in the next room. When she came to him, he said, "I had a horrible dream. I was in a coffin, and my mother was looking down, crying over me. I can't leave my mother. My mother needs me. She really needs me."[26]

During his friendship with and tutoring of Deborah Walley in the 1960s, Elvis spoke about a truncated life. "He told me that he wasn't going to be around for very long," Walley said. "He was very clear about what he was saying. He said he wasn't going to live a full life, that he was going to exit early. He was done."[27]

A few months before his death, Elvis and Geller met in Georgia to review some legal documents. Elvis stated that his Los Angeles attorney would prepare them soon. "I'll sign them when they are ready," he said, "but it'll all turn out different from what you think." Geller felt a chill at the tone of his friend. "He knew it was coming," Geller said, "My very first thought was he's gonna die. It was one of the strangest moments of my life."[28] It didn't help that the last thing Elvis ever told Geller was, "Don't forget, angels fly because they take themselves so lightly."[29]

Around that time, Elvis began driving to his birthplace in Tupelo with a friend. After parking his vehicle, Elvis would tour the small, restored house, lighting the way with his official Memphis Police flashlight. At one point, he shone the beam under the house and told his friend he was looking for a marble lost while playing as a child. He then turned off the flashlight and stood there in silence, after a while saying, "It's always important to visit the place where your Mama birthed you."[30]

Elvis made other predictions about an untimely exit of samsara. An argument can be made that some declarations were the melancholic histrionics of a young and famous person living a frenetic existence. Another argument could be—in the case of Geller and the visit to his home in Mississippi—that these predictions occurred during a time when Elvis's drug addiction was severe and his faculties were failing. The writing was on the wall—not that Elvis would have cared, once saying, "I'm not afraid of death. Only the ignorant, the unenlightened person is afraid of death."[31]

Yet the most eerie instance might be when Elvis predicted his death three days before it happened. This event occurred when David Stanley came to chat with Elvis on the evening of August 14, 1977 while he read the Bible. It was the day before Stanley was scheduled to travel from Memphis to Nashville to try and mend matters with his estranged wife. They chatted about the issue, and then Elvis asked a similar question he had asked Larry Geller, but about himself: "Who am I?"

Stanley bumbled the usual bromide about Elvis being the King, and Elvis shot back with his standard response about Jesus being the only king. Elvis told his stepbrother how much he loved him, and Stanley asked if everything was okay.

"I just wanted you to know that when you see me next," Elvis said, "I'll be on a higher plane."

Elvis motioned to his bedside, littered with spirituality-themed books. Stanley wasn't going to get into yet another metaphysical discussion with his stepbrother and retorted, "Sure, Elvis. The only plane I wanna see you on is the plane to Portland on the sixteenth."

Elvis smiled and gave out a chuckle. Stanley pressed Elvis about being okay. But the King said simply, "Goodbye, David."[32]

Elvis was gone on the sixteenth, never making it to Portland.

Stanley coming to Elvis for advice was a common theme: this monarch, perhaps drawing from Captain Marvel's Solomonic powers, was approachable to anyone when it came to heart-to-heart or general advice, even in the latter stage of his life when he and reality were no longer getting along. His highly developed intuition and, as mentioned earlier, his "surrogate-spouse" spectrum of his lethal enmeshments (that is, naturally assuming the role of caretaker) were likely reasons. Again, Elvis can be seen as the philosopher king—of America.

Elvis noticed and visited realms beyond the material, as he confessed to June. One night, after a visit to a hospital to see a girl June knew who was suffering from leukemia, the couple went to a pier to watch the water. Elvis told her to look up at the moon, totally relax, and not think at all—to allow herself to float in the space between the moon and the stars. He said that one could stand next to these celestial bodies.

"How long have you been doing this?" she asked him.

"Since I was a little boy," he answered. He never mentioned this gift, except to his mother, as people wouldn't understand such an ability and would accuse him of being crazy.[33] This deception would be a constant theme in his life: searching and evaluating a mystical experience while hiding it from a society that scorned such Gnosis. Gnostic bishop Stephan Hoeller once told me, "The difference between a mystic and a madman is that the mystic knows whom NOT to tell."

Elvis's astral traveling must have continued for most of his life. As detailed, there were those bouts of Zen silence and aloofness, even during concerts. It was common knowledge in his inner circles that he liked to be outside in the middle of the night—spending hours gazing at the movement of the planets. He believed cosmic waves of energy moved planets across the universe; with proper attunement, a magus like him could witness the heavenly bodies and their paths.[34]

It is said that William Blake could see angels daily. What about Elvis? On one occasion, Elvis, Priscilla, and his entourage stood outside his Bel Air home, overlooking the country club busy with fanlike sprinklers. Elvis blurted out, "Do you see them?" Priscilla asked what he was looking at so intently on the course. "The angels, out there," he responded.

"Angels?" Priscilla looked intently at the sprinklers, hoping it was true.

"You stay here," Elvis said. "They're trying to tell me something." He wandered off onto the course as if in a trance, followed by a worried bodyguard. Years later and after his death, Priscilla and others mused that Elvis was either having a pill-induced nervous breakdown, taking his mystical side too seriously, or just pulling one of his usual pranks.[35]

Sometimes his gifts weren't for transcendence and mysticism—nor any greater good. After the onstage attack in Vegas, Elvis was convinced that Priscilla's lover, Mike Stone, had hired the four men to kill him. He wanted retribution at all costs. He wanted Stone dead. During an emotional outburst the morning after the attack, alone with Sonny and Red West, he grabbed Sonny and said, "Look into my eyes, Sonny, look into my eyes. The man has to die. You know the man has to die. . . . There is too much pain in me, and he did it. Do you hear me? I am right. You know I'm right. Mike Stone has to die."

Sonny recoiled, feeling Elvis attempting to control his mind with some recondite sorcery. When the hypnotism didn't work, Elvis grabbed an M-16 from his closet and went on a tirade about killing Stone himself. His obsession grew to the point he almost hired a killer, but in the end, he let spirituality or Jesse's voice take over him and overlooked the whole situation.[36]

HE'S THE MAGIC MAN

A true magician can alter reality, the *goeteia* mentioned in the introduction of this book. Never mind that Elvis was the Trickster, the Lord of the Crossroads, a man busy changing history, fortune's fool and healer of the sick, or that he transformed millions of souls who listened to his music or saw him live. Never mind that so many prophecies and portents followed him like a messiah. Reality is still that persistent illusion, to paraphrase Albert Einstein, and the crowds always want more proof that the shaman can manipulate that illusion.

George Klein was a recipient of some of Elvis's eldritch abilities. While they were alone on the grounds of Graceland, Elvis told him to focus on some bushes they had come upon. The King hovered his hand over them. The bushes began to shake. If Klein wasn't stunned enough,

Elvis then told him to gaze up at a lonely cloud and then began to gesture wildly with his hands. The cloud suddenly moved at an impressive speed.[37]

On another occasion at Graceland (the day of his death), Elvis walked early in the morning on a concrete walkway with two visiting friends. Rain nagged the group as they neared Elvis's private court for an impromptu game of racquetball. One friend mentioned it was a pity about the weather.

Elvis said, "Ain't no problem. I'll take care of it."

The King raised his hands toward the sky. The rain immediately stopped.

"See, I told you," Elvis said calmly.[38]

Another incident in which the King turned out to be the kind of person you would want present at outdoor activities (except weddings) happened during a Hawaiian vacation in 1977. This time, Elvis had just read a book about how individuals across history could manipulate clouds with only their stares. He decided to test the knowledge. After meditating with Geller in the backyard of the beach house, the two eyeballed a cloud formation. A group of young women was present and wore skeptical half smiles. Within minutes, the clouds parted like a curtain to reveal a patch of blue sky.

"Just to prove this was no fluke," Elvis said, "we're going to bring the clouds back." The clouds came together to drown the blue sky. Everyone, including Elvis, was amazed.[39]

Had enough of weather manipulation? One more.

During a heavy group reading of spiritual books in Elvis's Palm Springs residence, Ginger's sister, Rosemary Alden, felt nauseated. Predictably, Elvis called a healing circle. Part of the ad hoc ritual was Elvis lifting his hand high, shaking it, apparently trying to shoo away her ailment. The ceremony worked, and Rosemary was stunned at feeling better. Elvis explained the innate power of the human mind, leading Rosemary and the group outside in the backyard. He attempted to move a nearby shrub with his abilities, but nothing happened. Not to be dissuaded by the illusion that is matter, he raised his arms and turned his palms upward, focusing on some overhead clouds. Seconds later, the clouds began to part. Elvis offered Rosemary a small but satisfied smile, and she exclaimed, "That's wild!"[40]

Just as wild but closer to a comic-book hero than a cloud bully, Elvis claimed to Ginger that he had finally tapped into an ancient martial art skill that could summon a force field created by the very aggression of an attacker. To prove to his fiancée that he was one of the few individuals with this skill, he called over his friend Charlie Hodges. Elvis placed his hands in front of him, intensely focused as if calling upon some arcane energy (but no turban this time!). After a few breaths, he asked Hodges to rush him. Hodges obeyed and charged his friend at full speed, abruptly hitting some invisible object and falling down. Ginger laughed, suspecting it was some act, but Elvis and Charlie were serious about the occurrence. Ginger had to try, try, try to understand—he's the magic man.[41]

The most humorous occurrence (in an edgy way) might have been with Linda Thompson. Separate from shooting televisions out of boredom or anger, Elvis underwent a one-way shootout with a brand-new Pantera car. The vehicle wouldn't start, so he got out and casually shot the engine five times. The car magically started. "It's like he even scared the hell out of the car," Thompson remarked.[42]

It's mind boggling to speculate how many of these illusion-piercing acts Elvis might have performed, considering how guarded and selective he could be about the arcane or supernatural. But with powers like that, who needs fame? That's a valid question, actually.

As previously mentioned, Elvis felt his fame was a way to facilitate others experiencing the godhead in their own way. Moreover, like Yogananda and the many masters he studied, supernatural powers meant an individual was on the right track to self-actualization. A seeker is closer to transcending the world when its seeming laws are less resistant to their will. Magical powers were not for personal gain or attention-seeking with the masses.

This attitude is perfectly illustrated in Elvis's beloved Gospel of

John. In this scripture, Jesus performs his usual miracles, but he calls them signs. Thus, Christ is not a wonder-worker for impressing the crowds; he reveals that his reality-bending feats indicate God is manifest due to his presence.

The Bible also says Jesus's family thought he was mad. Jesus himself said that a prophet only lacks honor in his hometown. With Elvis, America was his hometown, and millions were his children. A messiah always needs to tread carefully, lest the crowds turn on you if the Archons of this aeon don't crucify you first.

But shouldn't a master commune with the divine?

Elvis did that, too, but first, let's briefly cover psychedelics and whether they did the magic trick.

LSD ENCOUNTER

During the 1960s, it's unsurprising that the book-devouring Elvis would have come across Aldous Huxley's *The Doors of Perception* and Timothy Leary's *The Psychedelic Experience*. In that case, why not delve into the mystic drug known as LSD? At first, he coaxed some in his inner circle, including Geller, to give the entheogen a ride to ensure it was safe. Elvis watched them during their entire trip (often urging them to try to see and experience God). Then he took the psychedelic himself, roping Priscilla in as well, at Graceland during Christmas break. Geller and others joined in, too.

The ritual began with around half a tab of LSD and a discussion on Leary, the group sitting at a conference table in Elvis's upstairs office. The psychedelic safari predictably started with the typical bouts of laughter and distortions of reality. Priscilla saw her fiancé's multicolored shirt expand and almost burst. Also standard with acid trips, they spent time intently staring at colored fish in an aquarium, with Priscilla unsure about the number of fish. At one point, she burst into a "you don't love me" melodrama and called herself ugly, later ending up in Elvis's walk-in closet purring like a kitten. The group eventually watched a film (*The Time Machine*). Elvis was mesmerized by the movie, eating pizza and feeling amused by the expressions of the others.

At sunrise the trippers went outside and were dazzled by the colors of the morning. They also marveled at the breathing grass that seemed to have concise veins. Hugs and love declarations followed.[43]

The experience was rewarding, but neither Elvis nor Priscilla ever tried LSD again. Marijuana was also a drug the couple tried together, in brownie form, but you can file the two under the "gave them the munchies / made them sleepy" category of stoners. They never went back to marijuana, either.[44]

MYSTICAL EXPERIENCES

All the reading, drugs, miracles, and theological banter don't matter unless a magician, a shaman, or a Gnostic has that direct experience with the Divine. The experience varies for everyone: sometimes, it is a constant occurrence, like with Socrates, William Blake, or Teresa of Ávila; sometimes, it is less regular but still monumentally life-changing, as with Paul of Tarsus or C. G. Jung.

Elvis fell in the latter camp.

Remember the lady saved from self-harm and physically invigorated by an Elvis song on the radio? The song was "How Great Thou Art" from the 1967 album of the same name. Stuck in a liminal space between Movie Star Elvis and Vegas Elvis, the King was invigorated when he got a chance to perform a gospel album. Recall that this genre was his favorite for its deep roots in Black and Southern wizardry. He was directly involved in the album process, selecting every song, backup singer, and quartet (put together by his childhood idol, gospel singer Jake Hess). This project was a rare opportunity for Elvis to put his entire heart and soul into a project, a perfect mystery religion experience to share with the world.

It was a mystic experience recording the songs, especially "How Great Thou Art." Astral energies swept away Elvis. Jerry Schilling said he was shaken to the core by the voice of Elvis. It seemed like a spirit had possessed his friend. Elvis's face turned white during the performance of the song, and he nearly passed out when he finished. For Elvis and those listening in the booth, something had broken open in the fabric of reality.[45]

Before the recording session, Elvis had prepared for an experience that would bring his faith and vitality back, granting him the strength for his future metamorphosis into Vegas Elvis. At his hotel room before going to the studio, while his crew was loading instruments downstairs, he asked Geller to meditate with him in the dark. He wasn't going anywhere until God allowed him because he didn't want this project to be driven by his ego. After twenty minutes, Geller turned on the lights. Elvis said that since he was three years old, jumping off Gladys's lap in church to join the choir, he wanted to sing and make others happy. He was on the right path, then, especially with the opportunity to perform a gospel album so late in his career.[46]

Years later, after the breakup and reunion of the two friends, Geller told him about the effects of "How Great Thou Art" on the woman he had met. Elvis pondered the message and said, "God works in His own ways, that's for sure. I thank Him for the life that was saved, and for using me that way. All I ever wanted was to help people; lift them up, spread some joy."[47]

Dear reader, with me at the Crossroads, I would humbly suggest you listen to "How Great Art Though" in the dark or alone in nature, and let me know your experience. But first, let's discuss Elvis's other mystical experience, two years earlier. This unearthly event was more powerful, and it stayed with Elvis all his life and ensured he never gave up on the quest to serve astral forces and his fellow man.

Backtrack to 1965. Elvis was driving his luxurious Dodge motor home across Texas. He and his entourage had left Memphis late, and getting to Los Angeles in time for his next film was in question.

To put it bluntly, Elvis didn't give a shit about the situation. Two issues seemed constant: his stagnant career and a snail's pace spiritual growth.

In Amarillo, he abruptly pulled the motor home into a motel parking lot. As Elvis exited the vehicle, the worried entourage in the motor home and two accompanying cars poured out to surround him. They were already running behind, and Colonel Parker would bring his wrath upon them and not his precious client! Elvis assured them he merely needed a short break. He grabbed a room and immediately summoned Geller. Then, he poured his frustration out to his spiritual mentor.

"All right, all right, Larry," Elvis cried. "Just tell me the damn truth, man. What am I doin' wrong, uh? Maybe God doesn't love me or something, because I read for hours every day, every night, ever since you got me started. I haven't stopped. I've been like a damn fiend or something." He paused in anguish and continued. "All I want to know is the truth, to know and experience God. I'm a searcher, that's what I'm all about. You work that up in me. And ever since I started I haven't had one experience—nothing. I believe, only nothing happens, and I want it to. Oh, man, I want it so bad. What the hell is wrong?"[48]

Geller understood his friend's passion and hasty nature (he obviously hadn't listened to Brother Adolph and Daya Mata from the ashram). His only answer to Elvis's frustration was to relate a centuries-old story of a discouraged Zen student. Here is a version:

Once upon a parable, the pupil came to the master and poured out his heart. His years of intense study had seemingly come to naught. He was just as non-enlightened as he was years ago when he began his journey of seeking. The master only listened silently but, at one point, picked up the pot and poured the tea for his student. The tea began to spill over the rim, but the master continued. The student asked alarmedly why he was creating a mess on the table. The master replied, "Exactly. And like the cup, *you* are running over."

That was Elvis's problem, Geller explained. His head was too full of knowledge, desire, and goals. He needed to empty himself to be filled with something from above.

Elvis composed himself, and they were back on the road minutes later. In time, the convoy was crossing the Arizona desert on Route 66, entering the vicinity of the sacred Hopi mountains. Geller rested in the passenger seat while Elvis took the wheel with bodyguards Billy Smith, Red West, and Jerry Schilling lounging somewhere in the back of the motor home.

Elvis and Geller sat quietly and thoughtfully, enjoying the beauty of the scenery. Suddenly, a lonely cloud materialized above the horizon.

"Whoa!" Elvis blurted out, sitting up and tightening the grip on the wheel. Geller followed his gaze to the odd cloud in the sky.

"Do you see what I see?" Elvis asked excitedly.

Both saw that the cloud had turned into the image of Joseph Stalin.

"Why Stalin? Why Stalin?" Elvis asked, eyes locked on the visage of evil and his voice nothing more than a mumble. "Of all people, what's his face doin' up there?"

Geller was speechless, even as the visage of Stalin melted away and the cloud became like any normal one.

Elvis's terror suddenly shifted to excitement. His eyes brightened. He abruptly hit the brakes and pulled over to stop at the shoulder of the road. "Just follow me!" he shouted at Geller before jumping out and running across the desert like a madman. Eventually, Elvis stopped, and Geller reached him. Elvis's face was flushed with emotion, and his cheeks glistened with tears. He embraced Geller passionately and cried, "I love you, I love you. Oh, God is real. It's all true. I'm filled with divine love. I've finally seen what you were tryin' to tell me, and you were right, and so are all those books. It's beyond words and beyond the ego. Now I know, now I know. God loves me; God is love itself. I thank you from the bottom of my heart. You got me here. I'll never forget, man, never."

Elvis explained that he had perceived not only pure evil from a face that represented all that was wrong with the world, but that it also symbolized the darkness inside Elvis. In his mind, Elvis had asked that God destroy him if that's what he had become. Destroy him and fill him with something new.

Elvis had become the empty cup of the Zen parable.

"And then it happened!" Elvis exclaimed. "It exploded inside me. The face of Stalin turned right into the face of Jesus, and he smiled at me, piercing my heart and every fiber of my being with his light. For the first time in my life, I know the truth. I'll never have to doubt again. God and Christ are a living reality."

Elvis then joked about what fans would think of him. Geller, who hadn't seen the face of Christ, told him they would love him even more if he shared. "Yeah? Well, I hope that's true," he said quietly. Geller knew Elvis expected the world would think he was insane, that this was just another aspect of himself he had to hide, as he once told June by the pier—a madman and a mystic at once. He later mentioned how it was amazing that one could have a vision of both the Antichrist and Christ simultaneously.

His bodyguards showed up. Elvis said everything was fine, and for the rest of the trip, he beamed at the experience. The journey to Hollywood continued, not without more magic.

Nearing the California border, the bus caught fire and had to be abandoned. Elvis viewed the accident as a sign verifying his vision. Geller tried to rent a car using a credit card in the name of "Elvis A. Presley." The rental office threw him out because it had to be a fraud! Finally, an incredulous taxi driver took them in his car. Elvis sprawled in the back with arms out the window and gasped for air while Geller gave the driver directions. Geller repeatedly commanded the man to focus on the road, not the famous rock singer who looked like he had recently seen the ghost of Stalin. Once they arrived at Elvis's Bel-Air mansion, he again brought up the idea of retiring forever to serve God, this time in a Christian monastery. Geller talked him out of it, insisting that God had already appeared to him and that there was no reason to walk away from his earthly responsibilities, including Priscilla.

Nine years later, in 1974, Elvis finally found the courage to reveal more to his spiritual mentor. It happened while they were stargazing at Elvis's Palm Springs home. Elvis began with stutters and embarrassment and finally admitted more about the vision. He blurted out that he hadn't merely seen Christ in the cloud but that "Jesus Christ literally exploded inside me. Larry, it was me. I was Christ."

We're back to the Gospel of Philip: "You saw Christ. You became Christ."

However, Elvis explained with as much regret as he could muster that it was a missed opportunity. Soon after, Elvis allowed Colonel Parker, Priscilla, and the Memphis Mafia to place a wedge between the two seekers. The studying, the intense meditation, and the search all went by the wayside to an extent, and precious time was lost.

Just as peculiar about that entire story is that Geller experienced his defining experience near that same location in the Arizona desert five years earlier. Instead of the classic Gnostic dualism of Christ versus the Archons, Geller had received an engulfing, nondual download in his mind. He had been driving with a similar confusion that had tormented Elvis, specifically about the great questions of life and why they weren't being answered. Geller pulled over too because of a peculiar cloud, this time a towering cloud rising above the horizon, forming a white pillar with wisps at the edges detaching themselves. The cloud emitted a ray that struck Geller, filling his body with sublime energy. Behind it a cosmic, loving, and infinite intelligence informed him that once the mind is free from the fiction of the material world, enlightenment is there for the taking. Like Elvis, Geller was enlightened and in a state of pure euphoria for a moment.

The next morning after the Stalin/Christ vision, he told Elvis about his desert experience while they were in the motor home.

"Good God," Elvis said. "I suppose they'd call this a coincidence or something. But how can you possibly explain this? How is it even remotely possible that we both had our first spiritual initiation from God on the very same road and on the exact same mountain? This goes way beyond, and much deeper than we're both probably aware of. We'd better keep this to ourselves, 'cause they'd try putting us both away if we tried to explain this one."

A possible explanation might come from Geller, who recalled that in some Native American tribal beliefs, an individual's soul transforms into a cloud after death. Moreover, an ancient woman called Cloud Gatherer watches over these departed souls.[49] For those always in the liminal places—like perhaps you, reader, or a Trickster at the crossroads of life and death—certain souls always visit with messages, opening the sky to heaven itself. And guess who was really talented at working with cloud formations?

We're not done with clouds and faces in the sky, as we shall see in our discussion of Philip K. Dick.

ACTS OF KINDNESS

Before beaming up to Elvis's encounters with and beliefs in extraterrestrials, it should be mentioned that his innate kindheartedness was one of his greatest magical abilities. He would exemplify another Gospel of Philip passage: "Faith receives, love gives. No one can receive without faith, nor can anyone give without love."

Elvis spent money like a drunken sailor or sober Pentagon general, without a doubt—on fleets of cars, jewelry, airplanes, and guns. He was just as unrestrained when it involved expensive gifts for friends, girlfriends, and sometimes total strangers. He loved animals dearly, making Graceland a de facto zoo of both exotic and banal animals. Vernon was often aghast as his son frequently brought them close to bankruptcy. Elvis just didn't care: if he had his cult, tribe, and America itself to engage with, all would work out.

Beyond constant philanthropy for Memphis and beyond, it was natural for Elvis to help the "least of his brothers." Here are a few instances:

- At a show in South Bend, Indiana, Elvis tossed a $20,000 diamond ring into the crowd—his response when asked why was simply that it would give someone in the audience the "thrill of a lifetime."

- The King got wind of a record producer who needed a kidney transplant. Since the man's funds were too limited to afford it, Elvis stepped in and offered to cover the entire cost of $100,000.
- Elvis provided $40,000 for Jackie Wilson, a singer who was nearly bankrupt and suffering from a recent heart attack on stage, for care in a nursing home as he lingered in a comatose state.
- Elvis's old army buddy had been diagnosed with cerebral palsy. Elvis underwrote a $400-a-month nurse to care for his friend, purchased a special Chevrolet Impala, and even hired the man's father as the gate guard at Graceland.
- Elvis was also moved when he heard of an elderly Black woman in Memphis with no legs who used boards with roller skates on the bottom. In response, he bought her the most advanced electric wheelchair on the market and personally delivered it to her home without warning.
- At the gates of Graceland, Elvis noticed a young man hunched over and unable to move, suffering from cerebral palsy. "Who is he?" he asked his aide. "Who takes care of him?" When the aide said the man was on his own, Elvis said, "Well, I know who is going to take care of him." He put the man on his payroll, placing him in charge of his foreign mail and later making him a coordinator of his fan clubs abroad.
- Elvis heard from Vernon that a nine-year-old girl was dying in a Memphis hospital, and her last wish was to see him. He postponed all his plans and rushed to the hospital. The girl weakly smiled when she saw the King enter her room. Elvis placed her head on his chest, kissed her forehead, and said, "You'll be all right. God will watch over you." Weeks later, when he heard of the child's passing, he broke down in tears and meditated with Geller in her honor and memory.
- Jerry Schilling, who had been living with Elvis in Beverly Hills, was having trouble procuring financing for a house for himself and his girlfriend (part of the Sweet Inspirations). Elvis phoned

the owner at three in the morning and offered to pay the total amount. Once the owner accepted, he wrote a check to his child-hood friend and said that it was because he never had a home growing up. Elvis had always wanted to be the person to give him his first home.[50]

These examples just scratch the surface and are not the type of kindness we typically see with modern celebrities. The archons punish us, but they also hold the keys to our greatness, even the Archon of Poverty. And any magician's most incredible magical feat is caring for the seem-ingly endless poor and powerless, providing food and meaning, healing and hope.

6

CLOSE ENCOUNTERS AND
THE ALIEN BLUE LIGHT

THE STALIN/JESUS FACE IN THE SKY was far from the only celestial phenomena Elvis witnessed. We shall explore others that would commonly fall in the UFO category, as they comport more with the modern extraterrestrial encounter than traditional mystical, transformative experience. However, as modern scholars and occultists are revealing, the line that has historically separated alien visitations and religious visions is blurring to the point of nonexistence. Parallels between the two are becoming clearer by the day. And yet, those parallels were already being grokked by Elvis and Geller in the 1960s, as will be seen. Beyond good scholarship, the necessary context to connecting extraterrestrials to supernal beings was a more secular society where information was more accessible to share due to mass media and higher literacy rates. Add to this the availability of books—lots of books.

As academic Diana Pasulka wrote in *American Cosmic*, institutions inevitably establish interpretations that define the course of history after a contact event occurs. We see this obviously in Christianity, where otherworldly visitations are given final interpretation by church authorities. These same results are also observed in a secular world with UFO-related events. Various organizations and entities will take an interest in UFO experiences and apply their own understandings and narratives to them, with the collective mythology always superceding the meaning or transformation of the individual. These narratives may be scientific, but their overarching agenda is to promote a safe and unified explanation for the masses, no different than the church in medieval times. These organizational entities can be anything from government agencies to social media groups to international scientific bodies, and the massive amounts of energy they spend on information control can make medieval priesthoods seem insightful.[1]

Hence, the days of discriminating between angel and extraterrestrial are over. No longer are these beings relegated to different sections of the bookstore or esoteric conversation. The book *The Super Natural*, co-written by Whitley Strieber and Jeff Kripal, explains how "the modern experience of the alien coming down from the sky can be compared to the ancient experience of the god descending from the heavens."[2]

Again, Elvis and Geller would have been perfectly fine with the ideas of Pasulka, Strieber, and Kripal. Before *Chariots of the Gods* or *Ancient Aliens* on The History Channel, Elvis had already concluded that the imagery in Ezekiel had to be alien technology. He even sketched the prophet's vision one time.[3]

As mentioned, Elvis was familiar with the *Book of Enoch* and had also read *The Urantia Book*.[4] Both works are perennial favorites when it comes to blurring the lines between extraterrestrials and angelic tourists.

Like me, he would disagree with the constant push for human institutions to control the narrative and have VIP access to any heavenly visitors. As a modern Gnostic, the total relationship is between a person and the visitation. Recall Hoeller's definition of Gnosis that says it's "intuitively arrived," meaning it's an inner process; and in *A Dictionary of Gnosticism*, Andrew Phillip Smith explains that Gnosis is a "direct knowledge of the divine."[5] Like rock 'n' roll, UFOs have migrated from the fringe to the mainstream of the twentieth century, from *Coast to Coast AM* to news stories on CNN or in *The New York Times*. Yet it seems governments control the official narrative and access, reminding us of the *X-Files'* famous dictum that "the truth is out there." Like the ancient priests of Jerusalem or the pope in medieval times, a belief exists that only a few can be gatekeepers to starry domains.

At the same time, Elvis might agree with Strieber's remark in his landmark book *Communion*: "But the visitors are not only real and here. In fact, I don't think they are visitors at all. I think that the truth is that we are embedded in their world in the same way that animal species are embedded in ours."[6]

But—as Elvis found during his encounter in the desert—the knowledge of these forces is available to the seeker able to rise above the machinations of shaved monkeys trying to control the narrative of a busy cosmos.

As we've seen so far, whether it was Jesus or an alien, Elvis was never going to let anything get in the way of his seeking, having, and interpreting a direct experience.

THE ALIEN BLUE LIGHT

Recall that Vernon witnessed a blue glow the day Elvis lived and Jesse died. Could this have been some alien visitation? Did Elvis leave the alien planet to be dropped on Earth? Was the American population embedded in his world and not vice versa?

First, it should be noted that the idea of celestial entities introducing a history-changing individual is a timeless story. The most famous example is the Star of Bethlehem (which, despite the average Christmas story, wasn't static but guided the Persian magi right to the location where Jesus was born). According to the Roman historian Suetonius, a comet appeared in the sky shortly after the birth of Julius Caesar. Comets allegedly heralded the births of Emperor Nero, Genghis Khan, and William the Conqueror, to name a few historical A-listers. In the Far East, similar scenes occurred around the births of Emperor Cheng of Han, Ashoka the Great, and even Gautama Buddha.

Whether this is religious propaganda or the gods didn't bother consulting the ruling powers of the time before their light show remains debatable.

Also, as discussed, blue became an essential color in the metaphysics of Elvis. Blue is also a prevalent color in extraterrestrial lore, as detailed by Jason Reza Jorjani in his opus, *Closer Encounters*. One interesting fact is that in alien craft–encounter analysis we commonly find the shift from a red-orange luminosity (at low-power operation) to a blue-white color (at high power) in the plasma cloud of ionization that ensconces UFOs—*and this makes it difficult to take clear and crisp photographs of a craft's contours.*

Here are some examples:

The Rendlesham Forest incident in 1980: In this close encounter of the second kind, an officer of the RAF met a landing of a UFO—a triangular-shaped craft, with blue and yellow lights—up close.

The alien abduction of José Benedito Bogea in Brazil: Bogea was chased by a "bright greenish-blue UFO" for more than 600 feet. He was captured and taken to an extraterrestrial city for what seemed a long time, returning far away from his home city seven hours later in Earth time.

Blue-glowing UFOs terrorizing the island of Colares, also in Brazil, from July 1977 through November 1978: Witnesses claim the aliens wore turquoise blue suits, though their hair was blond (unlike Elvis, they were not fans of Captain Marvel Jr.). The Brazilian Air Force was called in to calm the hysterical population, and to this day, the government secretly guards against details of this incident coming out.

Skinwalker Ranch: Vortexes, the bending of time and space into circular hurricane-like shapes, have appeared near the infamous Skinwalker Ranch in Utah with clear skies even as the incidents happened at night. Luminescent, blue orbs crackle with a sound comparable to that of static electricity.

UFOs possibly behind contagions such as the black plague: Much evidence shows that when people died of this (nano-created?) disease, they would exhale a blue mist; the same blue mists would be seen collecting toward the ceilings of tall rooms found under the roof of the chapel in churches.

We can also count several instances of little gray aliens dressed in blue suits from Georgia to New York.[7]

And we may wonder why Captain Edward J. Ruppelt called his UFO investigation mission Project Blue Book. Regardless, Jorjani provides more cases where the color blue accompanies alien encounters.

Could Elvis have been an alien? That's the case Michael Luckman makes in *Alien Rock*. He records an Elvis fan of fifteen years, Wanda June Hill, who states that one night, when they were alone chatting outside, Elvis divulged he was not from this planet. He might have adopted the context from the Gnostic-leaning Jesus of the Gospel of John, who declares he is not an earthly being. However, Elvis also admitted to meeting a pair of "light form" men who assisted him and revealed his future—like adopting karate and wearing white suits in Las Vegas. Keeping in theme with this book, these men might have been a prophetic projection of his two daemons: Jesus and Jesse. Yet Hill states that toward the end of his life, Elvis spoke of a (here comes the color) "blue star planet." He was referring to Jupiter, a planet of higher learning whose moons, he claimed, housed advanced civilizations. He described a different galaxy as well, in stark detail. Could we file this under Elvis's astral travels?[8]

We can go back to Elvis telling his *Spinout* costar Deborah Walley about his being neither a man nor a woman, that he didn't belong in this dimension. Luckman utilizes this as evidence for the King being an extraterrestrial, but it could easily be Elvis feeling that he was "not of this world," like Jesus. Moreover, Gnostic texts often speak of feeling alienated in the world, a stranger in a strange land, and some sects even called the supreme consciousness the Alien God. Elvis could have easily been talking about spiritual ascension rather than planetary ascension (although many modern mystics would argue they are the same).

Still, Elvis, according to Wanda June Hill's own words in her unpublished book, was very detailed in prophecy:

> He went on telling that people on earth would soon know about other races on planets outside our galaxy and commented that he would like to be around when that happened but guessed not—"in this body" he added. "People will live longer and longer, as they learn from those coming to earth from outer space—they'll practice the oldest forms of medicine, mixing mystical with more conventional methods." He explained something called "Ayurveda" which he said was centuries old and was "medical knowledge taught by God's chosen people and written in Sanskrit. It deals with Bible teachings as well," he continued. "They'll be able to cure many incurable diseases."

Elvis then admitted he specifically was from Jupiter's ninth moon. When Hill wondered why he looked human and didn't have blue skin, she said his eyes glowed and an aura surrounded his form.[9]

Was Hill scandalmongering or deluded? Was Elvis serious at all? Metaphoric? He was a notorious prankster, alone or with the boys of the Memphis Mafia. Ayurveda is an Indian holistic medicine that he easily could have picked up while studying yoga. And with artists of Elvis's magnitude, fiction and reality are often blurred in their feverish lives of mythmaking—that "illusion of illusion" vibe. Luckman even brings Stanley Kubrick into the scene for more evidence of the King tapping into the alien motif—from his fascination and endless viewings of *2001: A Space Odyssey* to adopting the resonant theme of the film ("Also sprach Zarathustra") when making a triumphant entrance on his live shows.[10]

For the record, Elvis was a big fan of Erich von Däniken's *Chariots of the Gods?*, so we return to the idea of alien technology supporting human civilization.[11] Ed Parker said, "Stories of contact with alien beings held a fascination for Elvis."[12]

Should the Elvis-is-an-alien idea be taken with a grain of salt? Perhaps. And maybe the same grain of salt will be needed the next time the evening news broadcasts a story about the military being outwitted or outgunned by a UFO.

What doesn't require salt, though, were his UFO encounters that didn't happen alone.

CLOSE ENCOUNTERS OF THE ELVIS KIND

One night in 1966, at his Bel Air mansion, Elvis was hanging out with Sonny West. Suddenly, Elvis blurted out, "Do you see that?" Sonny glanced up and saw potent light coming through the trees.

"It's a flying saucer!" Elvis said excitedly. West wasn't convinced, expecting the sound or silhouette of a plane or helicopter to join the flooding illumination. The light continued to grow, though, piercing the trees and irradiating the top of the house. The light then shifted to the front of the mansion, leaving the two in the dark. Elvis told West to go into the house and get Jerry West and Jerry Schilling. His friend obeyed, but when he came out to the front moments later with Schilling, the King was gone. The two men shouted for their boss, but received no reply. Had Elvis been taken to the "blue light planet"?

Finally, a voice shouted back, "I'm down here!"

West and Schilling ran toward the voice and found Elvis in a driveway two doors down. He was casually gazing at the sky.

Believing he had seen something not of this world, West said with desperation and half-jest, "Jesus, that light thing scared the hell out of me. I thought they had got you."

"They will come but they won't hurt us," Elvis said with a small grin. "If they make contact, we can't be afraid, because they are not going to hurt us."[13]

Famous last words for a human, Mulder and Scully of *The X-Files* might say—but wise words for a hybrid extraterrestrial who enjoyed alien tech, Luckman and Hill would say. We can't forget Strieber's words: "We're embedded with them."

The second encounter with aliens happened around the same time and again on Route 66. On this occasion, Elvis and his entourage were driving through New Mexico. They all witnessed a bright disk streaking across the dark sky. The UFO was descending but abruptly halted, made a right-angle turn, and accelerated until it vanished from their eyesight.

"That was definitely not a shooting star or a meteor," Elvis said. "It was clearly something different."

"We don't make anything that moves like that," Schilling said, referring to the American government.

Geller went to the only other possible conclusion. "That object maneuvered like a flying saucer."[14]

Later, Elvis would declare to Geller, "It's ridiculous to think we're the only life with millions of planets in the universe."

Geller responded with a counter: "If they want to tell us something, why don't they land on the White House lawn or the Pentagon and contact our leaders instead of visiting an occasional individual out in the boondocks in the middle of the night?"

"I've thought about that," said Elvis. "Maybe they don't want to cause panic, plus they want us to evolve spiritually by giving us a chance to make our own decisions. They'll work quietly behind the scenes, influencing us without appearing to."

"And how will they do that?" Geller asked.

"By the power of their minds," Elvis answered, giving credence to both Hill and Luckman, "which must be vastly superior to ours, or they couldn't be flying across the sky. They wouldn't let us blow ourselves up."[15]

The third and last encounter happened later, this time in Graceland. Only Vernon accompanied Elvis outside. The father and son witnessed a blue flying saucer hovering above the backyard for five minutes. In another version, this incident sparked Vernon's recollection of blue light when Elvis was born, back in Tupelo, and as mentioned, started Elvis on his quest to find more about the mystical side of that color.[16]

There was so much blue in Elvis's life, whether from another planet or dimension. The significance of blue is echoed by Strieber himself, who claimed that when the visitors came to him and he didn't resist, he was allowed to leave his body and float into the ether, seeing the material world shimmering with blue light and that this light "was alive."[17]

The color continued to appear in many other parts of the King's life. As Geller said, Elvis wore a blue jumpsuit to perform when he was feeling down. Here are more examples:

- Early hit songs included "Blue Moon of Kentucky," "Blue Suede Shoes," "Blue Christmas," "Blue River," and "Indescribably Blue."
- He also sang "Blueberry Hill," "Mean Woman Blues," "Blue Moon," "Milk Cow Blues Boogie," "A Mess of Blues," "Something Blue," "Steamroller Blues," and "When My Blue Moon Turns to Gold Again."
- His final album was *Moody Blue*.
- Two of his most popular films were *Blue Hawaii* and *G.I. Blues*.

On the day of his death, Elvis played his last song on the piano in Graceland, just hours before exploring the face of Jesus. The song was: "Blue Eyes Crying in the Rain."[18]

Had the mothership called Elvis that day? File this under conspiracy theory if you want, but as a friend once said, at some point "coincidence theory" seems more absurd.

Something extraterrestrial might have visited Elvis that evening he healed Dean Nichopoulos's leg at the bottom of a Colorado slope. After the group returned to the house and assembled on the back porch, they quietly tried to make sense of what had happened to Dean and the magic of Elvis (everyone except for the magician himself, who chilled). Everyone was gazing at the majestic view of the snow-capped mountains, visible in the cloudless evening.

Suddenly, a flash of light ignited the scenic view. Elvis's entourage was shocked for a second time that night. A massive meteor crossed the sky, vanishing behind a mountain, only to appear on the other side and explode brightly.

Needless to say, the meteor tail was bright *blue* as it blazed across the atmosphere.

Nobody could move. Nobody could talk. Well, almost no one.

"Wow, that's pretty cool," Elvis said with a smile at the end of the meteor's pyrotechnic explosion. He then casually left the stupefied group and went to his bedroom for the night.[19]

7
ELVIS AND PHILIP K. DICK
Lost Twins and Gnostic Seekers

READING THIS CHAPTER'S HEADER, one might wonder how on Earth any similarities could exist between Elvis and a science fiction author. That's already been answered: Elvis's fascination with extraterrestrials and other space civilizations was analogous to Phil's, one of the pioneers of pulp speculative fiction and cyberpunk. That's only scratching the surface (of Jupiter's ninth moon). In the end, connecting these two figures helps us better understand Elvis on many levels and hopefully induces some introspection in many of you reading this.

First, let's establish who Phil was. Another loud member of the Silent Generation, Philip Kindred Dick was born in Chicago in 1928 and grew up in California, where he began writing short stories in the 1950s. Phil's early work was heavily influenced by the pulp magazines of the time, and he later developed a highly original style famous for mining the nature of reality, identity, and consciousness.

Dick published more than 44 novels and 121 short stories in his life. His writing often dealt with themes of dystopia, alternate realities, and technology's (primarily adverse) effects on society. Frequently, different religious and philosophical ideas soaked his futurist landscapes. He wrote some literary novels, but only one was published, *Confession of a Crap Artist*. He died from a stroke in 1982 at the age of 54.

Unlike Elvis, he never reached Olympian echelons in his profession or came close to achieving the cultural status of contemporaneous best-selling science fiction authors like Ray Bradbury, Arthur C. Clarke, Robert A. Heinlein, or Ursula Le Guin (she and Phil attended the same high school). Phil was respected in his field, but that never translated to monetary success; for much of his career, he was tormented by the Archon of Poverty (even having to buy horse meat for food at one point). Phil's reputation did rise to transcendental levels after his death, and he became one of the most influential writers of modern times. His works were adapted into culture-changing films, including *Blade Runner*, *Minority Report*, *Total Recall*, *The Adjustment Bureau*, and *A Scanner Darkly*. His Hugo Award—winning novel, *The Man in the High Castle*, became a popular television series. His work informed a baby-boomer and gen-X generation of science fiction authors and Hollywood directors. Adam Gopnik in *The New Yorker* wrote that films "from Terry Gilliam's 'Brazil' to the 'Matrix' series—owe a defining debt to [Dick's] mixture of mordant comedy and wild metaphysics."[1]

Without a doubt, Phil's DNA is found in *The Matrix*, arguably the greatest popular myth of the last generation. In 1977 Phil gave a speech at a science fiction convention in Metz, France, describing, in essence, the storyline of *The Matrix*:

> We are living in a computer-programmed reality, and the only clue we have to it is when some variable is changed, and some alteration in our reality occurs. We would have the overwhelming impression that we were reliving the present—déjà vu—perhaps in precisely the same way: hearing the same words, saying the same words.[2]

To summarize Phil, we turn to biographer Erik Davis:

> Since his death in 1982, Philip K. Dick has posthumously achieved a dream that remained painfully unfulfilled in his life: to step beyond the ghetto of genre fiction into the ranks of the most important novelists of postwar America. Dick's funny, absurd, and night-

marish science fictions—sometimes hastily written, and sometimes crushingly bleak—have now spawned a dozen or so films, a vibrant critical discourse, and a global cult following not unmarked with the cryptic mania conjured, in the history of religions anyway, by the term *cult*."[3]

Dick's life is a case study of high weirdness, even when detaching from the parallels with Elvis. Here we will discuss their connection and offer a compelling lesson at the end.

LOST TWIN

Like Elvis and Jesse, Dick and his sister Jane were born at home. The Archon of Poverty wasn't precisely the cause of the twins arriving at a poorly heated apartment on Emerald Avenue, in Chicago, on December 16, 1928. The reason was Dick's mother, Dorothy, who, as a rare feminist, wanted her children born at home and delivered by a woman. Dick's father, Ted, agreed but questioned the idea when the twins arrived six weeks early and the doctor was late once labor began.

Unlike Gladys, who knew who she was carrying, the young parents were surprised when two babies came out, the blond Jane and the dark-haired Phil. The twins were tiny but relatively healthy, though they were taken to a hospital and spent time in an incubator.

The situation worsened rather quickly weeks later in January, during a brutal winter. It was apparent that Dorothy, frail and sickly, was not producing enough milk for two children, even for undersized twins. The babies were allergic to any variation of baby formula. Making matters worse, a flu pandemic was harassing the city, and the apartment was constantly freezing due to the harsh weather. At some point, nurses and a doctor arrived with a heated crib. Still, it was apparent the situation was dire: the twins were malnourished and generally in bad condition, particularly Jane. An ambulance was called to rush the babies to Chicago's Michael Reese Hospital.

Only Phil made it to the hospital alive. Jesse came into the world dead, and Jane lived for six weeks.[4]

Phil survived, but like Elvis, he was "haunted for the rest of his life by his missing Other."[5] And like Elvis, the most monumental event of his life happened very early—including the damage that came with it, the nagging, eternal guilt of surviving. As Phil said: "I felt guilty—somehow I got all the milk."[6]

Biographer Lawrence Sutin writes in *Divine Invasions* that the trauma of losing Jane remained the central event in Phil's mental and emotional life. Like so many other twinless survivors, the event tormented him, manifesting as toxic relationships with women, addictive/manic behavior, and an obsession with immersing himself in the dualities of life, philosophically, metaphysically, and physically (in other words, fixating on safety and health or, contrarily, placing himself in dangerous circumstances)."[7]

The death of Jane did not super-bond Dorothy and Phil as it did with Elvis and Gladys. It did the opposite. Dorothy withdrew emotionally from the world, becoming a cold and distant parent. Her marriage to Ted eventually failed, and Dorothy and Phil moved around the country. Phil began to resent his mother and even blamed her for the death of his sister.[8]

In Phil's novels, Jane is objectified in various ways—like in *Flow My Tears The Policeman Said* as Alys Buckman, a bisexual leather queen. Phil was convinced Jane would have been a lesbian. She sometimes was a "voice" that guided him.[9]

Like Jesse to Elvis, Jane was eternally part of Phil, his daemon. Toward the end of his life, Phil wrote:

> She (Jane) fights for my life & I for hers, eternally. . . . My sister is everything to me. I am damned always to be separated from her/& with her, in an oscillation. Very fast. Both: I have her in me, and often outside me, but I have lost her; 2 realities at once yin/yang."[10]

Unlike Elvis, Phil was unabashedly open about the impact and meaning of losing his twin. Yet both men left an incredible, matchless body of work in their fields while leaving a path of broken relationships, psychosis, and drug abuse.

THE FACE IN THE SKY

Duality was part of Elvis's metaphysics, highlighted by the Stalin/Jesus face in the sky he beheld in the Arizona desert. This type of immense vision is rare for seekers, especially in modernity, if you exclude UFO sightings or the mass visions of the moving sun at Fátima or the Virgin Mary at Medjugorje in Bosnia-Herzegovina. So it's remarkable that Phil experienced his specific one.

The vision didn't transpire in the desert but in Point Reyes Station, California. Nevertheless, it did occur during a time of crisis, and not too far apart from Elvis's vision, in the fall of 1963. His marriage to Anne, his third wife, was collapsing in a mess of two-way emotional abuse and amphetamine misuse. While walking to an isolated shack he had rented to write undisturbed, he glanced up and beheld a malevolent face with metallic teeth in the sky. As Phil describes it:

> I looked up at the sky and saw a face. I didn't really see it but the face was there, and it was not a human face; it was a vast visage of perfect evil. . . . It had empty slots for eyes—it was metal and cruel and, worst of all, it was God.[11]

The apparition deeply disturbed Phil so much that he shared it with his shrink and a priest, the latter who identified the image with Satan and gave Dick holy unction (a special sacrament to heal the sick). Soon after, Phil joined the Episcopal Church, and the "vast visage of perfect evil" appeared as the titular character in his terrifying 1965 novel *The Three Stigmata of Palmer Eldritch*. His interpretation changed through the years, as happens with the inexplicability of such an experience, going from "an actual mystic experience . . . I saw the face of evil" to "I didn't really see it, but the face was there" to being understood as

144 ✦ Elvis and Philip K. Dick

a hallucination. He also leaned on Freud, associating the face with a World War I gas mask his father wore when telling Phil war stories.

But as with Elvis, the theophanic apparition stayed with him, and there was a duality to it. Although the image was pure evil, it brought Phil to the Episcopal Church, which brought serenity and meaning to his life. Why the face? As noted, this was Phil's first encounter with Gnosticism, a philosophy in which some sects contended that the universe was ruled by a mechanistic and cruel being sometimes associated with Jehovah in the Old Testament or Kronos in Hellenistic myths. The Gnostics had many names for this cosmic tyrant, including the Demiurge, Yaldabaoth, or Samael.

What's more, Phil joining the church led him to become fascinated by the transubstantiation of the Catholic rite, which then led him to read Carl Jung's "Transformation Symbols in the Mass," which then led down the path of Christian Gnosticism (Jung was deeply influenced by Gnostic thought).[12]

Phil paralleled Elvis as an avid researcher of the mystical and occult, often eclectic in his interpretations and expression. Also, like Elvis, he practiced what he researched, or as the saying goes, he did eat his own dog food (or, I guess, horse meat). Phil didn't merely write about extraterrestrials but considered them real and even encountered them. Before the evil visage in 1962, he had been gardening outside when he saw "a great streak of black sweeping across the sky. For a moment there was utter nothingness dividing the sky in half." He was convinced he had just witnessed something paranormal.[13] He once admitted he was "one of the 'star people.' These are people who have had extra-terrestrial experiences, people who are waking up to their extra-terrestrial memories; in effect 'star seeds.'"[14]

The high weirdness is only getting weirder.

As with Elvis and his blue light planet and other ideas, Phil would develop his personal system as more information was downloaded into him. The most famous was his 2-3-74 experience, where due to a series of events involving sparkling lights, a toothache, and the Christian symbol of the fish, the veil of reality parted momentarily to reveal a more authentic physical dimension. He saw that the world was a hologram hiding a nefarious "Empire" that enslaved all of humanity. A few chosen ones, the Christian Gnostics, battled to bring the truth to the world (echoing Elvis's trust in a White Brotherhood or Ascended Masters). During that mystic experience, Phil realized he was the Apostle Thomas, as time had stopped after the destruction of the Second Temple in Jerusalem in 70 CE—the same Thomas who was part of the syzygy involved in writing the Gospel of Thomas.

In Phil's novel *VALIS*, time begins again in 1974 when President Richard Nixon falls from grace due to Watergate. Elvis was indifferent to American presidents (versus Communist dictators), never having voted, but to Phil, the dishonored Nixon represented the suppressing archon forces on Earth.

Strangely, though, Nixon was a positive and pivotal figure in both of their lives.

NIXON AND DRUGS

Without a doubt, Elvis meeting Nixon is one the most outlandish of many outlandish Elvis stories in the material world.

The story began on December 19, 1970, with Elvis arguing with Vernon and Priscilla. The topic was Elvis's extreme spending habits. The quarrel ended when Elvis stormed out of Graceland. Not only did he leave the building, but he also flew the coop. He vanished for a few days—driving alone and taking commercial airlines across the country, seeing a doctor, retrieving Jerry Schilling from California, and ending up in Washington, D.C. in front of the White House with a handwritten note about his usefulness in the War on Drugs. One staffer contact led to another, and Elvis found himself meeting President Nixon in the Oval Office.

The King and the President, household names but lonely and isolated rulers of their fiefdoms, posed for photos and exchanged small talk, and then Elvis went on a rant about how suspicious the Beatles were considering their money and anti-American comments. He offered his services

Fig. 7.1. President Richard Nixon and Elvis shaking hands in the
White House Oval Office. Photo by Ollie Atkins,
chief White House photographer at the time.

to reach young people with an anti-drug message. To warrant his "mission," he requested Nixon give him a badge from the Bureau of Narcotics and Dangerous Drugs. Nixon agreed, and Elvis gave him a huge bro hug. Shortly after, Elvis received his badge. It was not an official one.[15]

Elvis never realized the inauthenticity of the badge. It didn't stop him from playing the role of a law enforcement agent, especially since he already owned several honorary badges from different police forces. He obtained a police radio and a revolving blue light to put on top of one of his luxury cars. This monarch did not need a Sheriff of Nottingham, for he began to patrol the streets of Memphis. At a crime scene, it wasn't uncommon to see Elvis directing traffic. Sometimes, someone speeding might be pulled over by Elvis himself; instead of a ticket, the individual would receive an autograph if they promised to obey the law.

After he found that one of his employees had stolen from him, he rushed to the airport where the man was already on a plane. Elvis ran on the tarmac and flashed his badge to the taxing airplane. Once the gobsmacked captain opened the doors, he ran inside to find the thief. Embarrassingly, he got on the bloody wrong plane. But Sonny West had already captured the fugitive at the airport and had taken him to a hotel suite to be interrogated. Elvis got his money back (including a $20,000 stolen ring), chewed the man out, and told him never to come close to him. He botched the Miranda rights during the arrest, though.[16]

Rick Stanley, Elvis's other stepbrother who worked for him at the time, provides a different but more poignant ending to the heist. In his version, the thieving employee began crying and apologizing once Elvis had finished his tongue-lashing in the hotel suite. The scars of the Archon of Poverty or Vernon being taken to jail must have possessed Elvis because he suddenly joined the man in weeping. Elvis fell to his knees, repeating, "Why didn't you let me know if you needed money? Why didn't you let me know if you wanted to go back to Memphis? I would have given you money. You didn't have to steal from me." The two men connected for a long time, and Elvis told the thief he could stay and keep his job.[17]

Just as curious but far less touching, Elvis joined a narcotics raid. As bodyguard Dave Abler recalls:

> One night he tells me that a Memphis narc cop is taking us on a drug bust. Presley says he has to go in disguise. First he takes his .22 caliber Savage revolver. Then he puts on a jumpsuit. Then over the jumpsuit he dons a snowsuit. Over his face he puts on a ski mask that had holes for the mouth and eyes. On top of this, he puts on a hat. To cap off the vision of the masked marvel, he then sticks a cigar in his mouth.

They arrived late to the drug bust, but later Elvis impressed everyone at the police station with his superhero attire.[18]

The underlying theme in all these stories is the badge and its symbolism. Elvis loved badges and obsessively collected them. He loved how they pseudo-transformed him into a figure of authority, an agent of order that could reverse growing American decay. As he wrote to Nixon, his two enemies were drugs and communism (the Stalin Demiurge), and that included the drug culture, hippie elements, Students for a Democratic Society, and the Black Panthers. In 1970, as Gary Tillery writes, the country was collapsing into cynicism with the failing Vietnam War and the many deaths of societal exemplars and rock stars in the 1960s.[19]

Elvis, the Trickster who marshaled this new postwar America, would fight to keep the country's innocence and goodness alive. That was always part of his ethos, regardless of stumbles or distractions. One can make a good argument, too, that as someone who received a fair amount of death threats and extortion attempts, the law enforcement abilities offered an extra layer of protection for his family and loved ones. He would always be Captain Marvel Jr., a poor, lonely, and disabled boy who could instantly turn into a protector of the needy.

Some arguments are less kind. The badge was simply a way for Elvis to stay armed to the teeth wherever he went, another rich man's status symbol.[20] Priscilla claims that Elvis coveted a federal narcotics badge more than any other because it would have given Elvis the power to carry weapons and drugs without question wherever he traveled, even outside the USA.[21] According to Peter O. Whitmer, this desire to be an influential law enforcement figure went back to his younger days under the Archon of Poverty in Tupelo. Elvis's wanting to become a law enforcement officer "can be seen as his wish to again usurp his father's power by putting himself in a position of greater authority than Vernon. Additionally, Elvis could have been expressing a wish to punish Vernon for his prolonged absences, and the hardships caused."[22] Recall that Elvis's quest to find Nixon and be knighted with a badge started with his argument with Vernon over money.

Elvis's drive to acquire objects was a way of dealing with the lasting effects of his traumatic experiences. He acquired items such as guns and badges for the permanent security and assurance they offered. He viewed the police badge as representing authority, validation, and strength."[23]

If you're thinking of men and their projection of phallic power instead of introspection on emotional issues, I can't disagree with you there. Dick energy and all that.

Phil's story about Nixon is much shorter and merely involves a letter. In 1973, Phil wrote the Department of Justice and offered assistance in the War on Drugs. He did it because "drug-abuse is the greatest problem I know of, and I hope with all my heart to accomplish something in this novel in the fight against it."[24]

Here lies the paradox of Elvis and Phil, which was part of Elvis's doom and harmed much of Phil's existence: the odd idea that street drugs were nefarious, yet anything prescribed by a doctor was safe and effective.

Elvis abhorred alcohol abuse and recreational drug intake, often citing how weird it was that someone as intelligent and successful as Hank Williams would overdose in his car—and, of course, this was coupled with the alpha-male delusion that all it took was willpower to stop using mind-altering substances (proven to him with his experiences with LSD and marijuana).[25] In the army he was introduced to amphetamines and took them regularly in the 1960s to keep his edge as Movie Star Elvis. Gradually, more narcotics entered his daily routine—Placidyl, Seconal, Quaalude, and Tuinal—all to deal with his fear of insomnia and his everyday use of Dexedrine to maintain his energy and keep his weight down. In his role of Hermes, the Trickster became an alchemist of pharmaceuticals, reading up on the subject and experimenting with his own body.[26]

The spiraling continued for years until his death. After he died, Dr. Nichopoulos provided an itemization of what he prescribed Elvis only from the period January 1975 through August 16, 1977:

- 5,458 amphetamines
- 9,567 sedatives
- 3,988 narcotics[27]

This list didn't even include other doctors Elvis utilized or illegal sources.

Phil also delved into amphetamines for most of his professional life. He was strung out on the drug when he beheld his face in the sky. He often took the stimulant Semoxydrine and, as an alchemist of pharmaceuticals, various other medications for his constant self-diagnoses of myriad ailments he believed he suffered from.[28]

The similarities between Elvis and Phil are evident in this respect, especially when you add hypochondria and rank hypocrisy, as well as the mentioned twinless survivor extremes of self-care and self-abuse.

Elvis obtained pills from nonmedical sources and was known to abuse cocaine for a while.[29] His heavy usage often made him no better than a street junkie: he was lifeless, paranoid, illogical, and violently desperate if his stash ran low. Phil was also known to mix his drugs to the point of psychosis and found himself in a treatment center more than once.[30] Unlike Elvis and Priscilla, at times in his life, LSD and marijuana became part of his drug diet.[31]

Despite both men seeming to never develop an interest in heroin, both were hospitalized for mistreating their bodies, found periods of sobriety, and sometimes got help. But at the end of the twinless day, they simultaneously self-medicated their trauma and sought to optimize their artistry.

We will deal with the esoteric reasons for addiction in the next chapter.

CHRISTIAN WITH THE LIVING JESUS

Like Elvis, Phil was well-read and self-educated—and was syncretic, a throw-everything-and-the-kitchen-sink kind of person when it came to spiritual pursuits. He loved discussing metaphysics, sometimes to the point of annoyance, which parallels Elvis's badgering Priscilla, the Memphis Mafia, or anyone within earshot. Phil took church seriously, practiced meditation, and employed the I Ching (in fact, much of *The Man in the High Castle*, his alternative myth where Japan and Germany win World War II, was written with the consultation of the Oracle).[32]

Unlike Elvis, who never expressed his alternative spirituality in his music, Phil's works adopt various religions and philosophies in futuristic settings—whether Zoroastrianism (*Galactic Pot-Healer*), the Tibetan Book of the Dead and the Catholic Eucharist (*The Three Stigmata of Palmer Eldritch*), or Buddhism (*Ubik*), to name a few examples.

Like Elvis, Phil was a seeker who believed in an experience that would lift all veils. However, he tended to immerse himself in the speculative aspects of technology (think of *Blade Runner*) and was more philosophical. As he wrote:

> The two basic topics which fascinate me are "What is reality?" and "What constitutes the authentic human being?" Over the twenty-seven years in which I have published novels and stories I have investigated these two interrelated topics over and over again."[33]

Most of all, though, Phil considered himself a Christian. Like Elvis, he was an extremely independent Christian who sought that "Living Jesus" or inner Christ (in other words, the Christ that the ancient Gnostics advocated for, this cosmic presence that dwelled inside us; we could become him while still in the flesh).

Phil openly adopted Gnostic ideas, but should we say the same about Elvis, even if not as explicitly? Elvis believed in a direct experience with God and some sort of Christ Consciousness. He embraced reincarnation and understood that ontological evil could declare itself real even if it did not appear in the heavens. But what about the idea of a simulation or a mass hologram that the Gnostics and Phil entertained? We must only look at the views of Yogananda that Elvis loyally followed, who declared that the universe was a "materialization of the thought of God," "a cosmic dream," and "structurally evanescent."[34]

Just like a hologram.

Phil went much deeper than Elvis into the rabbit hole of Gnosticism. Beyond his face-in-the-sky vision and 2-3-74 experience, both very Gnostic, his speculation on the illusionary nature of reality and a cosmic control system set up by astral beings made it inevitable that this deepening would happen. As Phil himself wrote: "I am too far into Gnosticism to back out."[35]

Most of Phil's Gnostic explorations are found during the mid- and late-1970s in his novels *VALIS* (Christian Gnosticism) and *The Divine Invasion* (Jewish Gnosticism or Kabbalah), and in *The Exegesis of Philip K. Dick*, a posthumously published work that catalogs his personal journal entries, essays, letters, and speculations around supernatural incidents.

Although Phil's Gnostic ideas tended to be extreme, Stuart Douglas, in his book, *The Apocalypse of the Reluctant Gnostics*, views Dick's cosmology as softer, calling it "*acosmic* panentheism." The term means God is both beyond and within everything, transcendent and immanent simultaneously. This metaphysics is central to the Gospel of Thomas and claims that God is the illusion *and* the divine reality behind it.[36]

This view would be at home in *The Impersonal Life* and other mystic Christian texts that Elvis had read, even apart from the Gospel of Thomas.

For both Elvis and Phil, Jesus was *the* man—or more like a guiding force in their inner worlds that allowed them to pierce the chimera that was the real world and attain salvation. As a historical figure Jesus was, to them, one of a few enlightened figures who had changed the world through mystic and often cryptic teachings. The Trickster, whether it's Loki or Hermes, must often disguise himself while bringing his gifts into the world.

As Phil wrote in *VALIS*, Earth is at the center of a great battle between dark (the Empire) and light (Christ or the Holy Spirit). Every human contains an element of both principles (like Elvis believing Stalin and Jesus could be both in him). It's a matter of each person to decide what force should guide them, and choosing the light is facilitated by awakened saviors like Zoroaster and others.[37]

Interestingly, ancient Gnostic groups mostly self-identified as Christians, even the more eclectic ones like the Manicheans. They likely did so both because they had no problem with being identified as followers of Jesus—even if it was a very exotic Jesus—and because doing so allowed them to survive in a world that required dogmatic assimilation to orthodox ideals. Elvis and Phil would have been right at home: two figures who often had to fly under the radar of their communities, families, and fans. Yes, the Trickster wears disguises and shrouds his teachings.

PROPHECIES AND OTHER SIMILARITIES

In the previous chapter, I described Elvis's visions, prescient dreams, and psychic skills. These included his prophecies of an early death, which he shared with June Juanico, Deborah Walley, and David Stanley.

Phil was no slouch in these supernatural arenas, albeit without the ability to manipulate reality or heal that Elvis casually wielded. It would take an entire book to safari through Phil's paranormal experiences and declarations and another to separate reliable ones from psychotic expressions.

A few remarkable prophecies should be considered, though. Phil predicting his death is one. But first, let's review the circumstances of his actual passing. At the time, early in 1982, his health was not the best, and he suffered from diabetes and hypertension. He was living in Santa Ana, California. He was finalizing his divorce from his fifth wife, Tessa, but he was in relatively good spirits as director Ridley Scott had shown him some early screenings of *Blade Runner*, based on his novel *Do Android Dream of Electric Sheep?* Yet a sense of dread had settled on Phil, and his eyesight was troubling him, something he shared with his therapist on February 17, 1982. The following day, a neighbor noticed him picking up his newspaper. That would be the last time he was seen conscious. His friend Mary Wilson called him several times that day and became concerned.

Finally, a group of neighbors noticed Phil's door open and thought nobody was home until they saw his feet sticking out from the coffee table next to the couch.

Phil was taken to a hospital, having had a stroke. Although partially paralyzed, he was conscious and communicative with his smile and eyes to Tessa and others. More strokes arrived the following days, and on March 2, he passed away. According to Tessa, he had predicted his death two months earlier, even if he was talking in a "cryptic way."[38]

Even more startling, Phil had written a letter to researcher and biographer Claudia Krenz on February 25, 1975. In one section, he states:

> I was up to 5 a.m. on this last night. I did something I never did before; I commanded the entity to show itself to me—the entity which has been guiding me internally since March. A sort of dream-like period passed, then, of hypnogogic images of underwater cities, very nice, and then a stark single horrifying scene, inert but not still; a man lay dead, on his face, in a living room between the coffee table and the couch.[39]

Phil had been visited by his daemon, obviously, and been shown exactly how he would be found. He finally joined his sister, Jane, and was buried beside her in Riverside Cemetery, Fort Morgan, Colorado.

Regarding psychic abilities, the most famous instance happened when Phil predicted a medical issue with his toddler son in 1974. While listening to the Beatles' "Strawberry Fields Forever" with his eyes closed in his apartment, a strawberry ice cream pink illumination covered his senses, and he received a specific message from beyond: his son Christopher was very sick. He rushed to the bedroom where Tessa was changing the child's diapers. In a trance-like voice, he explained that Christopher had an inguinal hernia and was in danger of dying if it strangulated. Tessa took him to a medical professional, and Phil was spot on with his diagnosis. The child's life was saved.[40]

While Elvis rode the wave of scientific advancements like television, the jukebox, the transistor, and the satellite into a new era, Phil warned of the mushrooming danger of technology. Before they became part of modern society, Phil had written about facial recognition, 3D printing, spray-on clothing, driverless cars, predictive crime prevention, and more.

We can almost envision Elvis and Phil as a sort of two-headed god, like Janus, one looking backward and one looking forward in their views of technology and how it affected the population. The two men had their differences. Phil called himself a "Berkeley beatnik" who migrated from liberal-left to traditional libertarianism.[41] Conversely, Elvis was a Southern boy who championed traditional values when not acting as a reckless rock star. Nevertheless, both were open-minded about complex issues when not struggling with drugs or mental disorders. Returning to Janus, both were dualists, individuals of extremes, always at the intersection of traditional family life and Dionysian morality exploration. Both were explorers of the temptations of the material world and the gifts of the spiritual realms, trying to negotiate the fundamental role of a human male and pushing the limits of the next evolution of humankind.

The salient lesson in this chapter might be that both Elvis and Phil were "caught in a trap." As much as they studied and explored, they couldn't notice their blind spots, like drugs, dysfunctional relationships, and tunnel vision on specific issues. They were "caught in a trap" of their culture, believing pharmaceuticals were safe, wars were a necessary part of the civic order, and being alone was the great failure of the male sex. The trap was fate, and from early on, their fortune was sealed because of a lost sibling, abusive mothers, irresolute fathers, economic hardship, and a society lacking mental health support for children. All the theophanies and therapies couldn't build back their Humpty-Dumpy psyches, and this gave them a life of shattered relationships and mental breakdowns.

It's a grim lesson, as Elvis and Phil were culture-changing figures because of their art, and were often able to see behind the veil of reality and into the numinous. What does it mean for the rest of us, mere mortals? What blind spots will we never see, and what difference does the next breakthrough with our therapists even make? If Jesus or evil incarnate appears, will we forever hold on to our Inner Christ? These are essential questions for a culture full of presentism—a tendency to judge by modern-day standards. If we traveled back in time, would we not make the same mistakes as previous generations? In reality, few of us would condemn slavery in the eighteenth century, just as we wouldn't shake off the constant dread of knowing that we're already in some cemetery and being judged by a culture that has its own blind spots and collective sins.

Moreover, Hermes the Trickster is the god of the roads and not finish lines, or as Gary Lachman writes, "Hermes, we remember, is the god of travelers, not of destinations or arrivals, and as the world is infinite, so too is the knowledge of it."[42] And as Egyptian writer Naguib Mahfouz once famously wrote: "Home is not where you were born; home is where all your attempts to escape cease." The seeker never stops searching and is always trying to escape for the simple reason that they are seeking.

Ultimately, the best we can do is help others "caught in a trap," because perhaps that is true bliss—if we can entertain them and bring a smile to their faces, as Elvis and Phil did. Elvis sang "In the Ghetto," and Oscar Wilde said, in his play *Lady Windermere's Fan*, "We are all in the gutter, but some of us are looking at the stars."

Was Phil a Beatles person while in the gutter that is this world? He did listened to one of the band's songs while getting a download from a higher realm.

Was Phil an Elvis person? We don't really know, as the author enjoyed all manner of popular music. The only crossover between the two men is very tangential: Elvis appears as a hologram in the sequel to *Blade Runner*, *Blade Runner 2049*.

But oddly, Elvis was there to save Phil's legacy.

While Phil lay dying in the hospital, his friend Tim Powers went to his apartment. He didn't find a book on the Shroud of Turin but did come across thousands of loose pages from Phil's *Exegesis*. Powers thought the writing was "crazy" and might reflect negatively on his friend later, regardless of what happened. He began to chuck many of the papers in a large ashtray. Emblazoned in the ashtray was the phrase:
Elvis is King.[43]

8

WHY ELVIS FELL

Shadow Dancing with Addiction

> *Every man has a black star*
> *A black star over his shoulder*
> *And when a man sees his black star*
> *He knows his time, his time has come*
>
> ELVIS PRESLEY, "BLACK STAR"

FATE IS A HARSH MISTRESS, as we've recently seen. She tends to load the dice from the start. The Greeks dreaded her, the Gnostics went to war with her, and the Stoics told us to embrace her with dignity with their *amor fati* (love of fate) dictum.

What other theories or forces from an unconventional perspective can explain Elvis's Icarian fall? There are many to consider, and they should be considered, as it is so confounding to understand how Elvis went from a happy child who happily gave away his Christmas presents to a middle-aged man hopelessly lost in a maze of self-harm. In the Gospel of Mark, Jesus warns about gaining the world at the cost of one's soul, but Elvis never lost his soul even after the world was in the palm of his hand. We may never know the exact cause of why Elvis fell, for at the bardo that is the Crossroads, we all fall under the probability field of magic.

To start, let us psychoanalyze America's Magician through the ideas of the Swiss Magician, a colloquial title often given to psychotherapist and esoteric exemplar, C. G. Jung.

THE UNBEARABLE LIGHTNESS
OF ARCHETYPES

After the term synchronicity, archetypes might be the most misused Jungian term. It doesn't help that Jung's view of them evolved through his long and distinguished career or that his writing tended to be on the dense side. But a workable definition can be gathered here, especially once couched with the truth that the Mother and Trickster archetypes dominated Elvis.

First, one needs to understand the structure of the psyche. What we think is our "I" is truly merely the tip of the iceberg of being. The "I" we know in our daily lives is the personal consciousness, which includes our ego and personas (in other words, the aspects of us that navigate reality). What encompasses most of what we are is the personal unconscious, a vast, mysterious lagoon of psychic currents that include the Shadow, complexes, the Anima/Animus, and some noetic debris. These phenomena always communicate with the personal consciousness but tend to do so in symbols, imagery, dreams, synchronicities, or by some manifested disorder. The ego will often not listen, content to exist in linear time and language.

More on the personal unconscious will be addressed before we go deeper. Below the personal unconscious is the collective unconscious, an even vaster pool of information, memories, and energies that includes the psychic forces of our ancestors, cultures, and even species. For all practical purposes, the collective unconscious is timeless, akin to the Akashic Records or the Pleroma (fullness) of the Gnostics. The building blocks of the collective unconscious are archetypes. They are the foundation of reality as understood by the mind, human or otherwise.

In *Inner Voices*, Robin Robertson writes: "Jung gradually came to consider an archetype to be a formless pattern which underlay both instinctual behaviors and primordial images."[1] Jung cataloged some archetypes like the Mother, the Father, the Child, the Sage, the Trickster, the Hero, the Witch, and a few others. His acolytes and other Jungian luminaries added more in time. Regardless of the number, archetypes are essential for managing reality. Perception starts with projecting archetypal contents onto the physical world, and the unconscious processes and stores these perceptions. Humans learn to recognize family members, food preferences, and even their favorite toys.[2] Archetypes are fundamental patterns of psychic activity that influence emotions, beliefs, thoughts, and behaviors—they are innate and dictate our actions unconsciously.[3]

If instincts or Plato's concept of Ideas comes to mind, then you are in the right arena. Or, as Jungian scholar Becca Tarnas once told me, "An archetype is a universal that manifests as a particular."

Thus, we find an archetype of a Mother that is static and unshapen, yet this archetype manifests in an image or projection that depends on the culture and life-form. Robertson details the Nobel Prize-winning studies of Konrad Lorenz. While studying geese, he was present for the hatching of goslings. The baby birds were instinctually programmed to accept the first living creature they saw as a manifestation of the Mother archetype. They projected or imprinted this archetype on Lorenz, even if he didn't look like Mother Goose. The goslings followed Lorenz around and adopted him as their primary caretaker (and he proudly did the work of raising them).[4]

Much like in astrology or tarot, it can be conducive to our understanding to determine when certain archetypes manifest, drive, or push us. Suppose we identify or tap into the Hero archetype. In that case, it is crucial to understand how that dynamism appears in our family and society and trace it back through history and even mythology (a critical arena where archetypal images communicate vividly). To fully experience the primordial force of an archetype can mean success and liberation. Also, one must understand how archetypes, like the Mother and Child, play with each other, and how we project their images onto others in our daily lives.

A COMPLEX OF COMPLEXES

The problem arises with complexes. In short, complexes, according to Jung, are "clusters of emotionally loaded concepts." You might say they are shards of trauma, defense mechanisms, and unsolved childhood events that revolve around (and obfuscate) an archetype. Jung's mentor, Sigmund Freud, also accepted the idea of complexes. However (and predictably), he claimed they revolved around sexually significant events and could be solved with personal associations that eventually led to a "sexually charged event in childhood." Once this root event was deciphered, the complex would automatically dissipate, and the patient would theoretically be cured.[5]

As Jungian Rachel Conerly said on my podcast, a complex is one of those "moods" that comes over you. A feeling of abandonment or being overwhelmed triggers complexes.[6] Road rage is a perfect example. A person may be level-headed in real life, but suddenly, in traffic, they morph into a screaming beast, almost like a demon possessed them. Once out of the car, the individual returns to their normal personality. The truth is that they were indeed possessed! The locust storm of a complex rose, perhaps triggered by the overwhelming idea they might be late, and took over their ego. They became a being reliving past trauma and conditioning. They might think that the archetype of the Hero or Warrior took over, but it could be that of the Child, masking some pain about being tardy to school or about the father striking the mother during a fight on a car ride. Complexes are complex, requiring a great deal of introspection. Think of a sudden fight with a spouse or a sudden bout of anxiety that seems recurring and almost surreal. Later, calmness returns, and one wonders how the situation escalated.

Most people have heard of a superiority complex, a condition characterized by a person's exaggerated feelings of self-importance, grandiosity, and dominance over others. It's usually assumed to be a temporal disorder that anyone can succumb to under the right circumstances. This is a good understanding of how present complexes can be.

Let's get to Elvis and his main complex.

As mentioned several times, Elvis was dysfunctional in relationships with women. He was never faithful, whether to Priscilla or long-term girlfriends. According to Priscilla, he could be verbally and emotionally abusive.[7] Despite his patriarchal, protective side, he was forever trapped in that "illusion of illusion" that kept him in a childlike state, often feeding his irresponsibility and naiveness.[8] Like any male rock star of that era, he loved female attention and there never was a shortage of it.

At first glance, one might say that Elvis poorly embodied the archetype of the "Husband" or "Prince." He wasn't tapping into tradition, family, myth, or the responsibility of the human species. That's not the case, though. Instead, we must examine the archetype he should have been veering toward when dealing with women. At various stages, it could have been "the Princess," "the Lover," or for non-romantic encounters, "the Sage" feminine archetype. The problem was that his trauma and upbringing had created a misty complex that formed around one specific archetype and clouded his ego when it came to many female relationships.

The archetype was that of the Mother. Recall in previous chapters that Elvis was drawn to women who looked like Gladys, whether it was Blavatsky or Daya Mata. Joe Esposito said Elvis was very open about Priscilla reminding him of Gladys.[9]

The pattern is evident, especially considering that Elvis couldn't have sex with Priscilla once she gave birth to Lisa Marie. Elvis had a hang-up about sex with a woman who had conceived, a neurosis that made him unconsciously believe he was making love to his mother."[10] One must also consider that Elvis met Priscilla in the army serving in Germany—while he still mourned the death of Gladys. She was fourteen years old, while he was twenty-four. Both claimed they waited until marriage to have sex, so it's possible they made love for less than nine months in a relationship spanning many years.

Elvis projected or imprinted the Mother archetype on Gladys, but her manifestation was prickly with trauma. Her warped image came from losing Jesse, the Oedipal weirdness of their relationship, her oce-anic anxiety, and her overprotectiveness—all of which didn't allow Elvis to explore himself and break through boundaries, building men-tal disorders in his psyche. The mental and emotional pain fragments whirled around the Mother archetype, fashioning a complex that sabo-taged long-term relationships. Remember that complexes are triggered by abandonment and overwhelm, and these notions are always present in budding relationships. Complexes are like tornadoes that draw in more trauma and pain, staying longer and thus creating more psychic wounds. With Elvis, the complex set him on a path of self-medicating and anguish. Moreover, without a direct line to the archetypes in the collective unconscious, those foundations of the personal unconscious, the personal consciousness becomes unstable and may suffer severe glitches.

Once again, fate condemned Elvis from the start. After Gladys's untimely death, Elvis was still ruled by the Mother archetype, which was surrounded by a complex, and continued to project that warped image onto other women. This made the prospect of a healthy marriage impossible. One wishes that Larry Geller had handed him a book on Jung in the early days of his spiritual quest.

Elvis's liaison with Ann-Margret, his costar in the 1964 film *Viva Las Vegas*, predictably ignited many conflicts between Elvis and Priscilla, as the two were living together but were not married then. On one occasion, in their Los Angeles home, the couple fought over Elvis's skulking around with Ann-Margret. Priscilla desperately threw a flower vase across the room, shattering it against the wall.

"I hate her!" she cried. "Why doesn't she keep her ass in Sweden where she belongs?" Elvis grabbed her and threw her on the bed. In a menacing tone, he said, "Look, goddamn it! I didn't know this was going to get out of hand. I want a woman who's going to understand that things like this might just happen. Are you going to be her—or not?"

Was he talking to Priscilla or the ghost of Gladys, who was known to be critical of her son's girlfriends?

A few weeks later, in Memphis, the fight started up again. This time, Elvis swore the affair was over. It was a mere lapse of judgment on his part! Elvis regressed to his childhood self, perhaps in which he knew he was always protected by the Mother archetype, and said, "I guess the devil made me do it!"[11]

No, King, it was a complex you couldn't understand, even as Priscilla's heart continued to break with your other affairs. Unlike Elvis, someone who does understand complexes is renowned Jungian analyst James Hollis. In fact, in his book *Under Saturn's Shadow*, Hollis illustrates a specific complex that describes the one that often afflicted Elvis:

> The ghost of the mother may assert itself in the so-called virgin-whore complex, where the man can only be enthusiastically sexual with the 'dark' side of the feminine, while he assigns his wife the role of an unapproachable Madonna. Some men are active sexually until their partners become pregnant, or mothers, and then their inner traffic is suddenly too intense. Their eros is sucked down and into the mother complex; they become asexual with their wives, their eros is projected outward in fantasies about other women or acted out in affairs. The romantic Other, for whom one once yearned, is now 'domesticated,' contaminated with unconscious mother material. The sexual infantility evidenced in men's magazines and beauty pageants is a symptom of the need to place eros on a pedestal, for the world of concrete women demands too much. The playboy is literally a boy at play; he can never be a man until he has wrested his eros from the powerful mother-world within.[12]

Complexes are temporal. Without a doubt, there were times when Elvis's ego was in charge and other archetypes were accessed. In these moments we witness the caring, loving, and friendly Elvis that many women spoke about, including Priscilla. This persona was the honorable man who acknowledged the goddess within each woman and defended their honor.

Complexes can create poisonous alter egos, and are hard to detect—except for one. It is the most potent complex, though. With Elvis, it was even more predominant.

SHADOW DANCING

The Shadow is considered both an archetype and a complex in Jungian ideology. We shall approach it as a complex when dealing with Elvis.

As Robertson explains, the Shadow, according to Jung, is a specific complex from the unconscious. Jung called it the "Shadow" because, as with a physical shadow, it emerges when a person is seen in too great a light. Robertson further explains:

> The Shadow seems to represent everything we regard as vile and despicable, everything which we deny and avoid. So a desire for too much light, too much spirituality, creates darkness, or instinctuality.[13]

There is the personal and collective Shadow, and both are often projected upon others. Understanding how we project our Shadow onto others is critical to integrating the Shadow complex. It's the old saying that what we criticize in others is what we must learn to look at in ourselves. This dictum goes back to ancient times with even Jesus declaring in Matthew 7:1–5:

> Judge not, that you be not judged. For with the judgment you pronounce you will be judged, and with the measure you use it will be measured to you. Why do you see the speck that is in your brother's eye, but do not notice the log that is in your own eye?

Robertson states, "Projection is thus a creative attempt by the psyche to resolve the tension created by the shadow problem (or any other stalemated situation between conscious and unconscious)." The collective Shadow might be easier to illustrate as it leaves a more significant footprint: mass-scale bigotry, racism, sexism, and violence throughout history. The classic example is when a population blames all its woes on a minority group or another culture (I'm looking at you, National Socialism).[14]

Not all Shadow material is traumatic or even harmful. Jung said the Shadow is "the thing a person has no wish to be," while Jungian analyst Ann Casement said the Shadow is "everything I don't know about myself and don't want to know."[15] For example, a child might have developed an aptitude for singing but sidelined that pursuit for a normative education and, subsequently, a traditional profession. That person may project their Shadow by feeling anxious at a live music show or dreaming of being Orpheus taming the animals. The Shadow is communicating that perhaps the skill of singing should be addressed, resurrected, or maybe officially shelved for good (which is usually solved with active imagination or some other inner dialogue).

At this point, it's easy to see how Elvis cast a large Shadow, growing more prominent as he grew into a figure of light to the world. The obvious Shadow source was not entirely dealing with the loss of Jesse. Peter O. Whitmer agrees, saying, "Jesse remained a constant, the shadow that would forever haunt him."[16] Not listening to the Shadow or daemon (in Elvis's case, the role Jesse played) can cause mental and even physical disorders. With regard to Jesse, Elvis's lack of integration was projected in the many dysfunctional behaviors discussed in chapter 2 (lethal enmeshment, impostor syndrome, the inability to commit to relationships, an intense if introverted personality, and so on). The Archon of Poverty was a Shadow projected in the form of Elvis's irresponsible spending sprees, from his gun collections to fleets of luxury cars, as well as in his manic workaholism. Vernon being detached might have created a Shadow projected in his obsession with badges, or may have even been why he allowed his father to control his finances. Perhaps Colonel Parker was a Shadow projection of Elvis not having a strong male figure, and that's why he was allowed to have so much power (but we'll get more into Parker at the end of this chapter).

Again, it's a pity Elvis didn't possess these analytical tools. Someone with so much brightness not only cast a massive shadow projected to so many people and situations—he also manifested it with beauty in his voice and performances (artists are great at presenting their Shadow in their work, but not that great at recognizing it). Maybe it wasn't the Devil, and from a Jungian perspective, it might not have even been exactly fate. As Jung himself wrote:

> The psychological rule says that when an inner situation is not made conscious, it happens outside, as fate. That is to say, when the individual remains undivided and does not become conscious of his inner opposite, the world must perforce act out the conflict and be torn into opposing halves.[17]

What is the Jungian solution to Elvis's Shadow and complex issues? It's always about the integration of these forces. Ultimately, the Shadow and complexes want to be heard and understood, whether to revisit an unresolved issue or heal some trauma. A crucial element of Jungian depth psychology is listening to the personal unconscious. Our inner demons have gifts that can turn them into angels. Through a prescription of dream interpretation, speaking therapy, active imagination, and other tools, Elvis could have dialogued with his childhood self, understood his parents, and integrated the many parts of himself until they were all unified in working for a greater purpose. He could have hugged his younger self, telling him it wasn't his fault, and forgiven his mother and father, who were struggling with their own Shadows, knowing they loved him more than anything. He wouldn't need badges and guns to unconsciously keep recreating a scenario in which his father would not be arrested and leave him and Gladys on the streets. The personal and collective unconscious do not follow linear time; everything occurs simultaneously in a timeless state. As William Faulkner wrote: "The past is never dead. It's not even past." Our ghosts and forgotten dreams want a seat at the table. Time doesn't heal all wounds, or really any at all. Time makes no difference in psychic trauma except to make it stronger. Time hides the Shadow and complexes that grow stronger. Elvis once said, "I swear to God, no one knows how lonely I get. And how empty I feel."

Can a Jungian approach reveal a deeper dimension to Elvis's addiction? Yes, it can, as Jungian analyst David Schoen reveals in his book *The War of the Gods in Addiction*, bringing archetypes and the Shadow together into an even more alarming reality.

KALI ADDICTION

As someone who has struggled with addiction much of my life, I'm often in the Alcoholics Anonymous (A.A.) camp of it being "cunning, baffling, and powerful," as the "Big Book" (*Alcoholics Anonymous*) states. This said, I have personally found vast amounts of recovery drawing on a Jungian (esoteric) viewpoint. As you'll discover, Jung and A.A. are connected.

In his book, Schoen presents a two-component definition of true addiction:

1. The addiction takes complete control of a person's personality and life.
2. The addiction is a death sentence.

It's as simple as that. An addiction is like a mind virus that completely colonizes every aspect of a person's intellect: thoughts, judgments, decisions, emotions, actions, and behaviors. Addiction, that feeding of the beast, takes precedence over all other aspects of a person's existence in a life-threatening, destructive manner. This terrible devastation can ruin an addict's career, family, marriage, sanity, body, and spirit.[18]

For those of you out there, struggling or in remission, I'm sure you can understand. It reminds me of a saying I heard in A.A.: "Addiction is suicide in installments." Elvis could have also related to this aphorism. He was a constant drug user in the second half of his life, plunging sharply around 1975 and finalizing his suicidal self-destruction in 1977. Some people will abuse substances or habits like gambling, including for self-medicating purposes, but their egos can flip a switch and alter their behavior before it's too late. For an addict, it's different: he is a dead man walking, heading to a self-created execution.

But not all addicts end up in the gallows. Why is that?

One reason might be found in the correspondence between Jung and Bill Wilson, the cofounder of Alcoholics Anonymous. The two esoteric giants wrote to each other at the sunsets of their lives in 1961. Wilson (or Bill W. as he's known in A.A. circles) wrote Jung an appreciative letter. He stated that the psychologist's work indirectly helped him sober up and start his movement.

The story goes that Jung had once told a patient of his, Rowland Hazard, that his alcoholism couldn't be cured by any material or scientific means. When Hazard asked if there was any hope, Jung replied, "there might be, provided he could become the subject of a spiritual or religious experience—in short, a genuine conversion."

As harsh as it sounded, Jung's ideas worked for Hazard. He sobered up and, later, through a mutual friend, this epiphany reached Bill W. and helped him turn his life around. The notions of surrender, transformation, and a higher call worked on Bill W., too, and even more effectively as they set him on a historic journey. Bill W. admitted that the first three steps of A.A. were directly influenced by the exchange between Jung and Hazard:

1. We admitted we were powerless over alcohol—that our lives had become unmanageable.
2. We came to believe that a Power greater than ourselves could restore us to sanity.
3. We made a decision to turn our will and our lives over to the care of God as we understood Him.[19]

In short, addiction could be tamed with a combination of abstinence and a mystical experience.

With his own gratitude and kindness, Jung answered that a "union with God," leaning on good friendship, and studying material beyond the "mere" rational was undoubtedly part of being sober. Jung wrote about the "protective wall of human community." Then came a startling remark, as Jung stated that without that higher force or a supportive society, an addict "cannot resist the power of evil, which is called very aptly the Devil."[20]

This is not the traditional Satan. For Jung, there existed an archetype of destruction, that bleak force that seeks to consume entirely. This archetype has no moral judgment; creation needs annihilation to have a canvas for its tasks. It manifests in the image of Kali or Shiva in Hindu dispensations, the Norse Ragnarök, or the Persian Ahriman. Schoen states that this is different from the Shadow, for it is eternal and static and cannot be integrated once it possesses a person.

The Destruction archetype must be avoided or wholly rejected.[21] Jung called it "the Devil," while Schoen names it "Archetypal Shadow/ Archetypal Evil."[22]

Schoen goes on to provide a model of addiction from a Jungian perspective:

Stage 1: The Ego/Persona identification alignment with the false self
Stage 2: The development of the Personal Shadow
Stage 3: The introduction of the Potentially Addictive Behavior
Stage 4: The creation of the Addiction-Shadow-Complex
Stage 5: The Addiction-Shadow-Complex taking over the psyche[23]

As "woo woo" as this may sound, we can trace Elvis traveling down this hellish rabbit hole.

In stage 1, Elvis was not allowed to build a healthy ego due to the loss of Jesse, his mother's crushing boundaries that didn't allow him to explore himself, and suffocating poverty. A false self was created through escapism in comic books and music; in other words, a fragmented ego arose due to serious difficulties handling reality.

In stage 2, Elvis's Shadow was created and grew as his ego grew, and past issues and pain were rarely addressed or recognized. Schoen provides more context:

> Our personal shadow is all of the incompatible thoughts, feelings, desires, fantasies, and actions that we have suppressed and repressed into the personal unconscious, along with our more primitive, undifferentiated impulses and instincts. . . . It is what I like to describe as the personal psychological garbage can of our psyches.[24]

As Elvis discovered, not facing the Shadow requires vast energy, distraction, and denial, progressively draining the psyche.

In stage 3 the force of the Shadow begins to take its toll on the body and mind: depression, anxiety, exhaustion, and compulsive disorders balloon. The body feels it. Toward the end of his life, Elvis suffered from glaucoma, diabetes, insomnia, bowel issues, and other disorders. Elvis's solution was to lean into more drugs and stay in denial about the lousy road he had traveled down.

In stage 4, a new Frankenstein entity arose in Elvis, forcing him into dangerous situations and bad decisions. Recall Elvis wanting to take out a hit on Priscilla's lover. A Dr. Jekyll and Mr. Hyde are created, and with Elvis, it was his terrible, increasing mood swings and erratic behavior as his addiction progressed. This is what Schoen also calls the "Addiction-Shadow-Complex."[25]

In stage 5 the possession is complete. The addictive behavior, personal shadow, and archetypal Shadow/Evil become a ruling "entity" that replaces the ego—that dead man walking.[26]

The primordial force of destruction conquered Elvis's psyche, and he could no longer leave the building. This pseudo-entity was now almost a full-time self that sought one ultimate goal: the end of everything at any cost. It didn't matter whom Elvis dragged down into the abyss to get there. A Dark King now ruled the King. As Lamar Fike said, "Those last five years . . . he was just a tormented person. . . . He didn't know how to stop the drugs. And he didn't want to."[27]

Like many addicts, there were times when Elvis abstained for a short period or was so dependent that he was more lucid on drugs than off them (I can relate, remembering my days before hitting rock bottom when I needed cocaine just to pick up the newspaper on the sidewalk and read it). On January 8, 1975, he devoted his fortieth birthday to self-imposed seclusion. Linda Thompson, dating him at the time, characterized Elvis as "a man suffering from severe depression, someone who seemed a willing partner in his self-immolation."[28]

Dead man walking.

This changes the context of Elvis telling Priscilla, "I guess the devil made me do it!" The invasion was already happening in the mid-1960s. Priscilla herself said that even if Elvis had survived his death, he wouldn't have been able to survive his demons. And his demons were part of his family dynamic, a family covered in "sadness."[29] When asked once what his biggest character flaw was, Elvis responded, "I'm self-destructive. But there's not a lot I can do about it."[30]

Schoen gives a final warning of these stages, and for those of you struggling with this mind virus, please take heed:

> I cannot state strongly enough that to describe this core of addiction as a killer is not a dramatic overstatement to get your attention or an alarmist exaggeration; it is the stone-cold truth and reality of addiction. Jung's comments in his letter to Bill W. certainly support this idea, and so does the experience of millions of alcoholic and addicted individuals, their families and friends, and all the therapists and addiction counselors who have gotten into hand-to-hand mortal combat with this awesome, psychological, spiritual monster.[31]

I return to the "cunning, baffling, and powerful" line and how Jung talked about grace. It's a mystery why I was spared while Elvis was not (so far, mind you; I've miles and miles to go before I sleep). My brother was the same age as Elvis when his addiction took him out. To repeat: the Destruction archetype must be vetoed and avoided at all costs. There is no middle path or negotiation. One can call this objective evil personified Stalin or the metal face laughing mockingly in the sky, but the meaning is the same: anti-life.

Jung said, "It is quite within the bounds of possibility for a man to recognize the relative evil of his nature, but it is a rare and shattering experience for him to gaze into the face of absolute evil."[32] (It seems Elvis and Phil more or less survived, though.)

It's important to understand that archetypes are dynamic and active, unlike Plato's world of Ideas. Jung said they "continually influence our thoughts and feelings and actions."[33] If someone discovers the archetype of a Chair, it won't merely sit there but will influence their mind in some mysterious way. Jung said archetypes are "relatively autonomous" and require an inner dialogue to be integrated into the psyche (just as with the Shadow or various complexes).[34] Thus, one can interact with an archetype. Schoen writes that one can even be tempted to be overcome by an archetype for "the fantasy and possibility that we might become gods."[35] Archetypes are the elemental cores of the psyche and perhaps even reality itself. The Archetypal Shadow/Archetypal Evil might unconsciously draw people like Faustus to Mephistopheles for the promise of material fortune. Jung sounded the alarm against identifying too closely with archetypes, which can lead to negative consequences such as madness or destruction. History is full of foolish mortals seeking to become godlike for its seductive (and addictive) power, and the solution is to stay grounded and humble."[36]

Schoen provides the example of Marilyn Monroe, who overidentified with the archetype of the Lover/Maiden in her primary image of the goddess Aphrodite. Tapping into this force was a recipe for destruction, for it meant impossible standards, whirlwind relationships, endless expectations, and other features of being *the* symbol of sex. Monroe eventually descended into depression and drugs, much like Elvis.

Not surprisingly, Schoen uses a second example: Elvis.

Elvis likewise represents the threat of linking excessively with mythical forces. With talent and sex appeal galore, he was the "Adonis of his time," the perfect Greek archetypal and masculine counterpart to Aphrodite. The world "adored him and wanted, literally and figuratively, a piece of him. It ultimately killed him."[37]

I don't entirely agree that Elvis overidentified with the archetype of the King/Ruler or that, at some point, he sold his soul to the Archetypal Shadow/Archetypal Evil like Robert Johnson at the Crossroads (discussed in chapter 2). Elvis may have been the Lord of the Crossroads, but he was overcome by a different archetype: the Trickster. Even his sexuality fits the Trickster archetype better, which will be discussed in chapter 9 when his effects on the public are considered. The reasons for his identification with the Trickster might never be fully known. Destiny? Did the death of Jesse and his witch blood from Gladys open a portal? Was there enough trauma in his childhood psyche that doorways allowed his soul to meet the Trickster at the Crossroads? Was there a program from the mothership and her blue light? So many alternative explanations exist in magic's probability field.

As for why some addicts are spared from "the Devil" and some are not, it's ultimately a mystery, but there is a solution, as I and millions of others have found. Perhaps it's best to lean on the words of Jungian analyst Joel Kroeker: "The ego wants an answer. The Self doesn't care about answers, it just keeps living into the larger question. Always, always, always."

Now, let us revisit the Trickster from chapter 2 in his archetypal form.

THE TRICKSTER ARCHETYPE

A commonality in many Native American myths is the idea of the Changer, an expression of the Trickster archetype. The Changer can appear as a coyote, beaver, dragonfly, or even the moon. It is a herald

174 ⚡ Why Elvis Fell

and agent of massive change. John Michael Greer writes about the Changer in *The King in Orange*, here focusing on the Moon of the Puget Sound version:

> Moon leaves the land of the salmon people under the sea and starts walking up the Snoqualmie River toward the mountains. All the beings who live in that country know that he's coming, and they prepare weapons and traps to stop him, because they don't want him to change the world and make it ready for the people when they come. So he meets a man who's sitting at the water's edge carving a board out of wood. "What are you doing?" Moon asks him, and the man says, "There's someone coming who's going to change things, and I'm going to hit him over the head with this board and kill him." Moon takes the board, sticks it onto the man's rump, and says, "From now on your name is Beaver. When the people come they'll hunt you for your fur."[38]

Moon follows this pattern with other mortals resistant to an epochal shift, altering every one into animals with their own tools. He eventually returns to his divine home, leaving the world completely altered. This story appears in other Native American myths with similar themes.

Permanent change is a central feature of the Trickster Archetype. That's what Elvis did as he embodied the archetype when he exploded on the cultural scene in the mid-1950s, mainlining the Heaven-and-Hell, shamanistic magic of the blues and gospel, guided by the twin daemons of Jesus and Jesse. Rock music was coming. Mass media was coming. Consumerism was coming. Teenage relevance was coming. Alternative spirituality was coming. Multiculturalism was coming. New frontiers of sexuality were coming. Maybe nuclear bombs and aliens were coming! And there was nothing that could be done by those who resisted. Many would be left behind in history or become afterthoughts of American civilization. Those stewards of traditional cultural and artistic power became no better than a beaver in a hunter's world.

As Jungian analyst Dennis Merritt said, speaking of the Trickster Archetype in his Greco-Roman apparition, "Hermes is the god of transitions: dawn and dusk, birth and death . . . the door hinges belong to Hermes."[39]

Elvis was at the Crossroads and became the Lord of the Crossroads, embodying the Trickster archetype to lead America into its postwar incarnation, for better or worse. Change always happens; sometimes, it's monumental and pervasive. It's always magical, even extraterrestrial, as it's prevalent, transforming, and seemingly organic. Hermes, in his aspect of Thoth, was essential for the rise of the Greco-Egyptian world since he patronized magic, astrology, and philosophy. In his role as Hermes Trismegistus during the Renaissance, when Hermetic texts reached Florence, he ushered in a new era of humanities, art, and science. Hermes, in his form as mercury, is the critical element to the Gnosis of any alchemist. In other places, times, and manifestations, the Trickster is always present to conduct change beyond our understanding or desire. His deception is our opportunity for innovation.

In *Mythical Trickster Figures*, William J. Hynes and William G. Doty provide a working list of Trickster traits (I add Elvis to each characteristic):

1. **A fundamentally ambiguous and anomalous personality** (Elvis was a unique personality even as he showed a way of "blending" different dualities in this new American culture; his extreme moods always kept those around him on their heels).

2. **A shapeshifting nature** (Elvis was a comic book character come to life, an exceedingly rare music star who successfully reinvented himself and could appear pleasingly depending on the situation and interview; his costumes represented different animals or themes, like the Changer, and he wore many disguises in his movies).

3. **A tendency to invert situations** (Elvis was a disruption on a mass and personal scale, challenging past orthodoxies and societal standards; he made the liminal into the mainstream and

pioneered exotic disciplines, art forms, and religions for a gentri-
fied population).

4. **A messenger/imitator of the gods** (Elvis believed he was sent
   by a higher authority to change people's lives and had a direct
   line with divine realms; he spent so much of his energy and time
   trying to hear the missives of Heaven . . . and even Hell).

5. **A sacred/lewd bricoleur** (Elvis was worshipped by so many, seen
   as holy by some while representing immoral and even diabolical
   values to others).[40]

In *The Trickster Gods and Their Influence on the Development
of Human Culture*, Jeffrey Lang lists other features of the Trickster
archetype. For starters, the Trickster is not part of and is opposed to
the natural order of things.[41] He urges one to eat from the apple or
accept the stolen fire of the gods, not belonging in Eden or Olympus
(and not belonging to the world, even when changing everything). The
boy from the invisible, poor South rose to entice millions into a new
Dionysian-Epicurean way of living and experiencing reality.

Lang also writes that the Trickster is the doorway between the mysterious ("primal chaos") and our five senses, as well as the "universe's
creative consultant to the living art of creation." It's well-established the
barriers Elvis shattered and how he inspired a generation of musicians
and other artists. As Bruce Springsteen said about the King, "It's like
he came along and whispered some dream in everybody's ear, and somehow we all dreamed it."

In *The Death and Resurrection of Elvis Presley*, Ted Harrison writes
that Elvis "represents the American Dream. This is the most immediately recognized archetype." Little excites Americans more than hearing
a rags-to-riches story, learning about an individual who overcomes and
attains his or her dreams and potential. Harrison further writes that
"perhaps the Elvis story resonates because it promises the potential for
greatness in this life."[42]

I would argue that the American Dream is not an archetype, so

Harrison is off the mark. Nevertheless, he is not wrong that the American Dream matters and can be deciphered as another esoteric concept. This force can be just as powerful as an archetype or fate herself. That, too, is for the next chapter.

Jung detailed another Archetype, similar to the Trickster, as gods like Hermes sometimes encompassed its qualities: *Puer Aeternus* (Eternal Boy). This archetype was a force of boundless instinct, chaos, intoxication, and desire. You can think of the sweet child full of potential, or on the other hand, the man-child who refuses to grow up or take responsibility. From a Peter Pan complex to Heracles being an infantile lout, there are perils and opportunities for the *Puer Aeternus*.

Balancing the *Puer Aeternus* is the *Senex* (Old Man), and this force is composed of pure order, discipline, reason, and control. The god Kronos is an apt image of the *Senex*.[43] In his "illusion of illusion" and other qualities, Elvis was taken by the *Puer Aeternus*.

But who would be his *Senex*?

Let us attend to an elephant in the room, Colonel Parker.

COLONEL PARKER AND SATURN RISING

As Jerry Seinfeld might have said in some standup routine in a parallel universe, "What's the deal with Colonel Parker?"

Before dealing with the deal, let's provide some biography. Colonel Tom Parker was really Andreas Cornelis van Kuijk, a Dutch-born American music manager. He was born on June 26, 1909, in Breda, Netherlands, and immigrated to America in 1929. He began his career as a carnival worker and became a music promoter. He managed Elvis Presley's career from 1956 until his death, and it can't be denied that his management style and tactics contributed to Elvis's success (even if Parker skimmed mightily off the top).

Although Elvis and his inner circle knew of Parker's vampiric habits and tried at times to break away, biographer Alanna Nash sees the relationship between star and manager as analogous to a healthy marriage that rots with time. She compares Elvis to a battered wife who won't leave the marriage because it's the only life she knows, ending up believing she is not worth much.[44]

Although some have speculated Parker held some blackmail over Elvis, Gary Tillery dismisses such allegations and provides a simple, sober reason for their long relationship: loyalty. Elvis was already a rising star before meeting Parker. Yet after signing with Parker in March of 1956, within twelve months he had crossed galaxies no celebrity had come close to reaching. Parker had the connections and guile to navigate the entertainment industry. He could move mountains and break heads simultaneously, though his brutality never extended to his one and essential client.[45]

Peter Guralnick, straying from dry land history and into esoteric pastures, speculates that Parker was Elvis's "talisman" and that "part of Elvis, the part that continued to pore over astrological and numerological charts and place his faith in the role of fate, believed that if he ever left the Colonel, his luck just might run out."[46]

I mentioned *Forrest Gump* at the beginning of this book. In the film *Elvis*, Tom Hanks appears again, playing Parker himself (and with the oddest accent, I must admit). The film does a fine job deciphering Parker, especially at certain pivotal turns in Elvis's life. One of these moments occurs at the death of Gladys, as Parker consoles Elvis and stands in as a stable force. As always, Vernon is sidelined due to his lack of insight and backbone, and Parker is able to convince Elvis to have a service for Gladys at a funeral parlor instead of doing the traditional church celebration. Parker became the central parent figure of Elvis from 1958 onward. Whitmer writes that Parker, in essence, "assumed [Elvis's] mother's soul." Parker stole Gladys's role and powers over Elvis.

Strangely enough, within weeks of Gladys's death, Parker's mother also died. This coincidence could have bonded the two even closer and acted to "free [Elvis] even further in his quest to invent himself as the greatest showman on earth," since Gladys had never enjoyed her son being away making mounds of cash and getting a literal world of attention.[47]

As discussed, a twisted image of the Mother archetype was something Elvis was drawn to, like a moth to a flame, so he may have partly imprinted the archetype upon Parker. Or perhaps Elvis viewed Parker as the symbol of the wizard who grants Captain Marvel his powers. As Geller writes, Elvis kept giving Parker his power instead of the other way around.[48]

The only time that Parker worried about his influence was when Elvis was rising spiritually with his studies, practices, and visions. Then the Colonel had to surgically remove Geller from Elvis's life.

It may seem like Elvis made a deal with the Devil, and he did, but likely closer to the Trickster aspect of the Devil we've covered. Parker was originally a carny, and the title "colonel" was an honorary title bestowed by the governor of Louisiana because of Parker's service to the Louisiana National Guard.[48] He was an illegal alien who flew under the radar even when representing the biggest star in the world for decades. He could wax folky like Elvis, creating an entertaining persona to "snow" the world (a term he loved, referring to taking money). Elvis represented Hermes, but Parker was closer to his Roman version of Mercury, who leaned more on commerce, money, and even thievery. Tricksters sometimes work together in mythology, like Hermes and Hekate assisting Odysseus. Thor and Odin are sometimes considered tricksters, and they enjoy adventures with Loki.

Recall Parker shapeshifting into a gay man while sizing up Geller. Recall Parker manipulating Priscilla and others, as Loki could do, to isolate Elvis from the world of alternative spirituality. Without a doubt, Parker was always there to facilitate Elvis's transformations, although he could never blunt his client's self-destruction. Like Elvis, he was an "8" in numerology.

Summing up the two Changers starting a joke on the world, Geller wrote: "[Elvis] and Parker each loved and hated the other, sometimes simultaneously. But they both loved power even more."[50]

Another occult theory on the relationship between Elvis and Parker can be drawn from Rudolf Steiner, the ex-Theosophist, Austrian philosopher, spiritual guru, and founder of Anthroposophy—and a polymath known for his contributions to education, agriculture, medicine, and the arts.

In various books and lectures, Steiner explained that humanity's spiritual evolution, from Lemuria to Atlantis to today, is influenced by two tectonic metaphysical forces that are always in opposition: Lucifer and Ahriman. These beings rebelled against primordial spiritual hierarchies, and their agendas in the material plane brought about the possibility of free will. Lucifer represents light and artistry, but his dark side is overwhelming pride. Ahriman represents order and reason; his shadow side is soulless, reductionistic materialism. For a healthy human civilization and human psyche, Lucifer and Ahriman must coexist in balance.[51]

It doesn't take an Ascended Master to see that Elvis and Parker were earthly avatars of Lucifer and Ahriman. Elvis was the consummate and consuming creative hellion, while Parker was the saturnine boundary keeper with his ledgers and business plans. As powerful as their essences were, without each other, neither figure would have succeeded in shaping the evolution of the American soul. As Tiller writes, Parker "stayed in his own domain—the business side—and didn't interfere with Elvis's music or stagecraft."[52]

In some works, Steiner contended a mediator must stand between Lucifer and Ahriman, which he called "the Representative of Humanity." Gary Lachman writes, "Left to themselves, the energies represented by Ahriman and Lucifer lead mankind astray, but if their influence can be absorbed and reconciled through the mediating work of the Christ, they can lead to spiritual freedom."[53]

Ultimately, Elvis could not hold on to this Christ power, his Jesus daemon burning out in his hubristic heart. Parker did not fare much better and allowed Jung's "Devil" archetype into his psyche—instead of drugs, Parker suffered from a gambling addiction that drained his massive earnings from Elvis and broke him at the end of his life. The *Elvis* movie portrays him accurately as a lonely, disheveled, and bankrupt old man walking around an empty casino in his pajamas, throwing coins into slot machines.

In alchemy, the forces of Lucifer and Ahriman appear but are named Hermes (or Mercury) and Saturn (also known as Kronos, bringing back the previous *Puer Aeternus/Senex* archetypal polarity). Hermes as Elvis has been solidly established, and Saturn serves a similar role to Steiner's Ahriman, imposing boundaries, limits, and order. Nicolas Flamel, the famous alchemist who appeared in the *Harry Potter* series, represented Hermes and Saturn in his work *The Book of Abraham the Jew*, showing that mercury (Hermes) added to lead helps extract the essence of gold. In her book *Money Grows on the Tree of Knowledge*, researcher Tracy Twyman takes the alchemical-transformation relationship to the next step: Hermes represents youth/money in America. In turn, Saturn is the time/banking system. Money doesn't come out of thin air, but is produced by human labor. An orderly and elderly force consistently exploits those with the energy and talent to make that money. The youth (represented by sprightly, winged Mercury) is sacrificed to Father Time (represented by the scythe-wielding Saturn) to create gold, which ultimately restricts the freedom and idealism of the younger generation.[54]

Fig 8.1 From *The Book of Abraham the Jew* by Nicolas Flamel (1612).

Elvis, the bright spirit of innovation, wealth, and youthful energy—the light side of the American Dream—was Hermes, while Parker was Saturn, representing boundaries, regulations, and greed, the dark side of the American Dream. The image above from Flamel depicts this tragic dichotomy, and perhaps you can see Elvis and Parker.

As above, so below, said Hermes Trismegistus. Hermes is sacrificed, and the game of archetypes never ends. The last time Elvis sang was Parker's birthday on June 26, 1977. Elvis was first called to the Sun Records office on June 26, 1954. On June 26, 1957, he spent his first night at Graceland. On June 26, 1979, Vernon died of heart failure. Elvis's last concert, on Parker's birthday, was at Market Square Arena in Indianapolis. He wore his iconic white and gold jumpsuit and, at one point, sang Simon and Garfunkel's "Bridge Over Troubled Waters." He brought Vernon onstage to wave at the crowd.[55] The spirit of Ahriman/Saturn was around to limit Elvis and his legacy.

Elvis was larger than life and a tool of the gods. But he should take some responsibility, shouldn't he? Shouldn't we all take responsibility for our actions and decisions? Jung seemed to think so. He wrote severely: "The unconscious has a thousand ways of snuffing out a meaningless existence with surprising swiftness."

Jung gives the example of a rock climber who has not followed his destiny, and the unconscious, in conjunction with fate, causes the individual to not step correctly on a ledge, and they fall to their death.

Every person is on a mission, part of a mysterious quest tasked by inner and outer forces beyond meatsack understanding. To not even get close to that mission can lead to an avatar being taken out of the video game, getting called up by the mothership, or whatever metaphor you desire.

Jung further states: "If the demand for self-knowledge is willed by Fate and refused, this negative attitude may end in real death."[56]

Perhaps Elvis was tasked with a titanic pursuit, and he knew about his destiny of employing Gnosis and experiencing the Living Jesus of the Gospel of Thomas, spreading this divine message to the world even as he shepherded America to a place of power and prosperity. As discussed, he was a person of duality who turned away too long from his sacred mission, especially after his divorce and other destructive decisions in the early 1970s. His personal and collective unconscious perhaps decided it was time to exit stage left.

There was no sudden death, no "accident" that ended Elvis's life. Indeed, fate is a harsh mistress, and you never know when it will be your last fried peanut-butter-and-banana sandwich or song onstage. The archetypes or extraterrestrials don't follow human morality, and in Gnostic thought, sadism can be expected if one falls to Steiner's Lucifer. As the heathen proverb goes, "Those whom the gods wish to destroy they first make mad."

Perhaps we are all dead men walking. Fate is a harsh mistress.

9

THE LIVE SHAMAN

An American Egregore in Memphis

"Elvis Presley," [Leonard] Bernstein said, "is the greatest cultural force in the 20th century." . . .

"What about Picasso?" . . .

"No, it's Elvis," Bernstein insisted. "He introduced the beat to everything and he changed everything—music, language, clothes, it's a whole new social revolution—the '60s come from it."

JON MEACHAM,
"ELVIS IN THE HEART OF AMERICA,"
TIME MAGAZINE

ELVIS IS AMERICA'S MAGICIAN. He was the spirit-elected shaman needed to lead the republic into its postwar economic, military, and innovation-centered existence. His daemons, Jesse and Jesus, were like winged sandals at each foot, lifting the American soul to heights no other nation had experienced. But like a wild Icarus, we just witnessed his encounter with the black sun that is Saturn, and he was ultimately crushed by the gravity of a universe that doesn't tolerate impactful mystics for too long and demands everything from its wizards or prophets.

Elvis's power came from performing, from shaman ritual magic, by which he could fully unleash his totems and sorcery into the world, assuring his tribe that the witch doctor was in control of their destiny in the jungles of a dangerous world of communism, nuclear bombs, corrupt governments, and blossoming cults. As Bob Dylan said, "Hearing Elvis for the first time was like busting out of jail." Elvis was a headliner in the collective expansion of the American psyche that included race inclusivity, female empowerment, high technology adoption, and exploration of alternative spirituality. He became the center, the Anima Mundi and Axis Mundi of a new world order.

Yet it is still impossible to comprehend or describe his impact and magnetism. One might as easily put down on paper the beauty of Aphrodite or the melodies of Orpheus. Elvis's aura and charisma were so intoxicating that he could wriggle "his little finger lasciviously in a move that sent his audience into paroxysms of ecstasy."[1]

Taking the view of Elvis as both a historical and mythical shaman performing necessary tasks for the greater good, we can understand him better.

As mentioned in chapter 2, the shaman is his people's magic user, a role that involves healing, wisdom, and protection from spiritual wickedness in high places. Like the Trickster, the shaman is a psychopomp—the being who walks between all worlds and crosses the boundaries between the living and the dead, often in the service of accompanying souls to their next life. Music and high drama are part of the shaman's toolkit, not to mention endless toying with mind-altering substances. As also discussed, shamanism influenced the Greco-Egyptian and Greco-Roman worlds through mystery religions and Gnosticism, which employed elaborate theatrics and music in their rhapsodic sacraments.

As detailed in chapter 5, Elvis falls under the "wounded healer" category that appears worldwide, throughout history. History fits this shamanistic credential like a wizard's glove, beginning with the primal trauma of his twin's death, his subsequent lethal enmeshment that was part of a severely dysfunctional family system, his Pentecostal exposure to glossolalia and healing by "laying on of the hands," and his sudden, mystical experience in the Arizona desert."[2]

Paul Levy explains more about the wounded healer in *Undreaming Wetiko*, stressing that *only* the wounded healer can heal. In the myth of the wounded healer found in various lores, this sensitive and vulnerable individual is easily damaged but gifted enough to bring to consciousness their wounds that, in effect, bestows them with the priestly power to heal, physically or psychically. The wounded healer "must suffer through the sickness in order to be able to cure it." Only those who truly suffer can alleviate the suffering of others. These healers "have healing abilities not in spite of their wounds, but because of them."[3]

Summarizing this, we can quote Rachel Naomi Remen: "A shaman is someone who has a wound that will not heal. He sits by the side of the road with his open wound exposed."

Elvis was built to be the nation's shaman. Elvis was the personification of a charged magical life, and like any able shaman, always had one foot in the land of the dead. *Shamanism, An Encyclopedia of World Beliefs, Practices, and Culture* states that many "shamanic initiations mimic the dying experience."[4]

With Elvis, the magic of the devilish blues and the devastating and premature passing of Jesse and Gladys tethered part of him to the domain of Hades. Red West claimed that Elvis's fascination with human corpses was terrifying. Elvis once stood calmly while a mortician embalmed the body of a recently deceased friend. He knew by heart the embalming process better than most doctors, which is creepy to modern sensibilities but merely another sepulchral shamanistic duty in many traditions, which involve funerary rights, autopsies, and the state of the dead's soul. After watching a horror movie, *Diabolique*, Elvis took Priscilla to the Memphis morgue to inspect bodies. Priscilla was both horrified and thrilled at the experience until she noticed the corpse of a baby no more than three months old. She began crying and questioning life, and Elvis answered, "Sometimes God works in strange ways. I guess it was just meant for the little fellow to be with Him." Both held the dead child's hand and prayed for its soul.[5]

Elvis was also the kind of person who laughed or cracked jokes at funerals and enjoyed walking for hours at night through cemeteries. According to journalist and author Tom O'Neill, Elvis visited the Tate-Polanski residence on Cielo Drive shortly after the Manson murders, the location being at the time the "morbid mecca for Hollywood's elite."[6] Once, he broke into a funeral home with Linda Thompson and some members of the Memphis Mafia to examine corpses, acting cooly like a tenured professor in an anatomy class.[7] Recall the story of Elvis inviting himself to a hospital and pushing to be present for the birth of a baby—this was one instance of Elvis's opposite fascination with the miracle of birth.

In some cultures, shamans serve as substitutes for the dead to speak to their families.[8] Elvis took on the persona of his dead twin. Beyond hearing voices (Jesse's) and naturally going into trances (at the Assembly of God Church and concerts), it is also not uncommon for a shaman to gain his abilities at a young age due to a close brush with death.[9] Elvis's birth was difficult, and hunger was part of his growing life. As an infant, a historic tornado in 1936 leveled much of Tupelo and killed 236 people. It was a collective traumatic event for the town. The tornado struck on a Sunday when much of the population was in the various churches, and the Assembly of God Church saw it as a sign of the apocalypse.[10]

Early trauma and trauma-inducing rituals are part of the shaman's initiation and acquisition of powers that include the knowledge to heal others and serve as the therapist/soul mender of the tribe. As music writer Dave Marsh said, "Elvis Presley was more than anything a spiritual leader of our generation."[11]

Across many cultures, a shaman must die and be born again in some intense ritual. Some ceremonies have the initiate travel to the underworld, to ultimately be torn apart by spirits and then find a way to rebuild himself, echoing the myth of Osiris.[12] Elvis's standing between two worlds, being the Lord of the Crossroads, can further be stressed by the lonely ritual he practiced later in his life where he "would light candles, sit on the floor of his hotel room or his bedroom at Graceland, and meditate himself back into that world of the child, and beyond, to the womb, that safe haven where once upon a time so very long ago all had been so right."[13]

Indeed, Elvis's attraction to the shamanistic Pentecostal rites and his reinventions were part of his witch doctor role. It's already been established that, as a teen, his hairstyle mimicked that of Captain Marvel Jr., the great symbol of a human undergoing a magical transformative rite. It parallels the shaman after they return from the dead in a new body. No recorded explanation is given why, during that time, Elvis began to wear pink and black, regardless of the continued mocking, fruit thrown at him, and even being called a "nigger lover."[14] He continued wearing those colors after becoming a star and utilized those colors in decorations such as cars. Whitmer deduces that the baby color, pink, and the death color, black, symbolize Elvis carrying Jesse as his daemon. From a shamanistic lens, it means that Elvis was forever between the states of birth and death.[15]

Beyond extravagant costumes, some shamans, such as certain Siberian sects, are known to be gender fluid, to cross-dress, and even to act as the opposite sex. Ambiguity and wholeness are keys to navigating the spirit world and relating to all members of the tribe. Some stories claim that male shamans can give birth, and Inuit male and female shamans undergo a mock-birthing ritual. Shamans are sexual and responsible for mediating between couples, often considered a "third gender" by the tribe.[16]

Before we turn to the spicy topic of Elvis's sexuality and its shamanistic (and esoteric) aspects, it should be noted that even Elvis's devolved ending perfectly matches the shamanic prototype, specifically circumpolar shamans. These healers begin to lose their mystical powers at the same time as their physical bodies deteriorate, and they must resort to heavy drug use to keep serving their people.[17]

It's never a good ending for these shamans, and neither was it for Fat Elvis, but how could it be? The demand of the gods, the weight of the spirit world, and the village's dependency take a horrible toll on the body. Even more, the seeker cannot stop seeking regardless of the price. As Gordon White writes:

> Properly used, magic will destroy your life. This is a feature, not a bug. Ever since modern humans first emerged into full consciousness those who worked with spirit, be they shamans or witches or magicians, moved into their tribal function only after some kind of Otherworld trauma experience. Some event has to occur that provides the magician with a lasting, visceral, unshakable *knowing* that the universe extends beyond what can be physically observed.[18]

We have yet another possible reason for Elvis's demise. The great sacrifice of the shaman has to happen, as it has from ancient times to Jesus to America's Magician. Goes with the job.

SEXUALITY, KUNDALINI, AND ANDROGYNY

Understanding Elvis's sexuality may seem akin to mopping the ocean floor. Within the context of magic, however, some mysteries make more sense.

We can start with Vernon. He claimed that precisely nine months before Elvis and Jesse's birth, he blacked out after orgasm.[19] Had Vernon been possessed by some alien force? Was he a proxy shaman? In some Amazonian traditions, the initiation ceremony centers on the penetration of the cosmic uterus that ends in orgasm.[20] Was this some call to an old soul, as certain Buddhist traditions contend a spirit is drawn to reincarnate by seeing the conjugal act of its parents-to-be?[21]

Passing out after an orgasm does happen, typically caused by stress, hyperventilation, heart issues, or sexually induced syncope (when a person's blood pressure suddenly drops, temporarily depriving the brain of oxygen, resulting in unconsciousness). We are talking about Elvis here, though. Magical sex is common in esoteric circles, from ancient Egyptians to some classical Gnostic sects to shamanistic groups to practitioners of modern traditions like Thelema—although blacking out during sexual climax is rare.

An orgasm is a form of ecstasy, that *petite mort* or "little death" of the French when the ego momentarily melts into the ocean of being. It's impossible to separate Elvis's anxiety, magic, and sexuality. The King's libido erupted from a young age. Billy Smith, a cousin, related a story about Elvis looking at women dancing when he was four or five. When he caught a glimpse under their skirts, he would yell, "Oh, my peter!"[22]

Keep in mind the women were in the act of dancing, which Elvis associated with the Divine.

Elvis's *Comeback Special* is arguably one of the highlights of his career, doubling as the magic ceremony that transformed Movie Star Elvis into Vegas Elvis. From its inception, he saw it, after a long dry spell of performing live, as his opportunity to do what he did best: connect directly with people. He rehearsed endlessly and gave it everything he had, as they say. It paid off. A massive 42 percent of television sets were tuned in, making it the highest-rated holiday show and NBC's biggest hit of 1968. Critics and tens of millions of fans knew that Elvis's magic was still potent.[23]

What barely anyone knew was that Elvis's libido was just as potent: he orgasmed while performing live.

After the first session, Elvis went backstage and quickly shed his now-legendary black leather jumpsuit. He called over his costume designer Bill Belew, who had personally tailored his outfit. "We've got a problem," Elvis told him. "It's all wet inside." He wasn't talking about perspiration. Belew took the suit without a word and worked it with a few paper towels and a hair dryer. Elvis went out again without a word for the second act.[24]

Elvis's tantric currents must have been in overdrive that night as he shapeshifted again.

Fig. 9.1. Still from *Girls! Girls! Girls!*,
Paramount Pictures (1962).

It wasn't the first time something like this happened, though, and we can wager there were other times never recorded. It is known that during the 1962 filming of his fourth movie, *Girls! Girls! Girls!*, Elvis sported an erection during a tango dance scene with costar Laurel Goodwin. "Damn pants were rubbing me the wrong way and I couldn't stop the feeling," Elvis confessed to Joe Esposito, adding that "Little Elvis" was out of control.[25]

The scene was never edited because the director thought a reshoot would affect the budget. So even today, anyone can view "Little Elvis" online.

Beyond his psychological hangups discussed already (having sex with women who had conceived, projecting Gladys onto other women, having issues with commitment), Elvis lived a typical rock star whirlwind life when it came to women, though he tended to make long-lasting female friends and relished women intellectually. Beyond Deborah Walley, Daya Mata, and others mentioned, he interacted spiritually and philosophically with his *Frankie and Johnny*

(1966) costar, Donna Douglas, best known as Elly May Clampett in *The Beverly Hillbillies*.

During and after his split with Priscilla in the early 1970s, his relationships focused less on sex and more on companionship and spiritual discussion. Singer Kathy Westmoreland and Elvis spent weeks-worth of nights together as friends before they had sex (she was a virgin at the time). His chief interest was reciting poetry to her and reading aloud books on spirituality. Joyce Bova, a House Armed Services Committee staff member, also claimed that Elvis often chose to talk metaphysics and read *The Impersonal Life* instead of having a romantic evening. Predictably, there were fights with girlfriends, centered on Elvis's anxiety-ridden creepiness and bad jokes, taxing work schedule, and commitment expectations, but nothing too out of the norm as far as couples dating (considering he was married during some dating sessions, and was peaking as Vegas Elvis during this period).[26]

George Klein writes that during one of his dating sprees in the mid-1970s, Elvis, at night, "just wanted to sit on his bed and talk with his date" and was not "interested in any encounters that were strictly sexual." One Playboy model who spent the night with Elvis said they only "talked and joked around." Elvis had to counter this story in a typical macho way, saying they talked and joked so much they "broke the damn bed."[27] Elvis was always intent on connecting on different levels with women.

Elvis's sexuality was intense, sporadic, and unpredictable. From the previous chapter, one might agree with David Schoen that Elvis represented Adonis or some other loverboy god more than any Trickster god. Yet once again, Elvis is closer to Hermes. Primal and roguish sexual powers are attributed to Mercury, more akin to that of an underdeveloped teen (Jung's *Puer Aeternus*), whose true orgasm stems from getting an adolescent reaction or stealing something unique and timeless from his partner. It's the child Elvis who gets excited about peeking under a girl's skirt because it is a shameless, dangerous action more than anything. In the old myths, Hermes is represented as a chthonic phallus, meaning his sexual power deals with that perilous but exciting journey between the spiritual and material realms. In his singing and playing, Hermes always honors the divine feminine (including the mother), even if he can never reach her inner sanctums because of being at the Crossroads. He also honors "the servants of his mother and becomes the god of servants because he serves the gods."[28]

To understand Elvis's Hermes love act, we may consider another partner, actress actress Peggy Lipton, who openly shared stories of her three-weekend tryst with Elvis. Lipton had a friend who had dated the King, and despite his "fragile, outsized, damaged ego" and "problems and weirdness," it was impossible not to fall in love with him. So, she gave it a chance and met the "supposedly sexiest, most sensual celebrity of [her] time."[29]

Lipton met Elvis in Tahoe and Las Vegas in 1971, but her nervousness quickly changed to perplexity. Despite the flashiness and always-present retinue, Elvis was the perfect gentleman, witty and charming. And he was trapped, isolated in his vast kingdom. Elvis was an incredible kisser in their private moments, but "he just wasn't up to sex," as Lipton put it. She assumed it was the drugs. At one point, after some failed attempts, Elvis left embarrassed to go to the bathroom for a long spell (which typically meant he needed to read or meditate). While waiting, she remembered a piece of cardboard on which he had scribbled a poem for her, a traditional Irish blessing:

> *May the road rise to meet you*
> *May the wind be always at your back*
> *The sun shine warm upon your face*

When he exited the bathroom, Elvis was outfitted for the night show in "full ceremonial dress." Lipton felt he was a different being and was amazed that later, when she watched him sing, he exuded that sexual dynamism lacking in their bed. Women went wild, and the energy of the concert was tangible. Elvis was focused and professional yet knew when to play around with his audience. With this show and others she witnessed, it would take him hours to shift from Vegas Elvis to mortal Elvis Presley, who enjoyed hearty meals, socializing, and playing pranks on the Memphis Mafia. Ultimately, Lipton ended the relationship because she was scared. The final straw was one night when Elvis began to gag and choke in his sleep because of the usual galaxy of pharmaceuticals in his system. Lipton pulled Elvis up and punched him in the back until he heaved into a breathing condition (and vomited all over his silk pajamas). He wasn't fully conscious, though; white as a ghost, he kept calling out for his mother. Lipton cleaned and held the weeping man until the sun came up.

He was still unmatched as a shaman—Hermes at his zenith with music, tricks, and saving souls—but it was apparent that his mortal self was showing cracks like those of the circumpolar shamans. Lipton felt he was beyond saving.[30]

What truly defines Hermes's sexuality is his androgyne quality. The same went for Elvis, beyond the typical shamanic gender-bending.

Like many early rockers, Elvis was called a "safe-sex" hero. High on a stage or behind a television screen, women worshipped a godlike Elvis, who allowed them to bring out their desires, and even their Shadows. He understood them and taught them to become sovereign over their bodies. Females could scream, cry, and shake their hips cathartically. Elvis himself denied he shook his hips as any mating call or was ever lewd, but "Elvis the Pelvis" and his shamanistic aura were enough to initiate women. This dynamic resulted in women feeling both liberated and equal, or as a music culture writer said: "When females shook and sobbed at the seductive spectacles onstage, they in a sense endorsed the sexual status quo, reassuring their dates they wanted only those things boys already assumed they wanted."[31]

Elvis was sexy, deep, and talented, but he was also approachable to women because of his soft features ("female eyes or lips," stylish hair, serpentine moves, and pink colors). Two of his heroes, James Dean and Rudolph Valentino, were different than, let's say, Cary Grant, for they didn't exude that assertive male aura but allowed themselves to be the passive object of the female gaze (and sometimes of the male gaze too). They provided receptive auras instead of penetrative ambiances. The great Trickster thief Elvis took that quality from the two movie stars. However, Elvis never acted in any way feminine, even if he could be "active and passive, an object of adoration and at the same time someone engaged in demanding physical work." More than Dean or Valentino, Elvis, throughout his career, allowed himself to be vulnerable to his audience (and *vulnerable* comes from the Latin "to wound," as in the wounded healer).[32] For a woman, Elvis was the type of partner that you could love as a man and be a mother to at the same time (which is probably what he wanted in his lethal enmeshment state of proxy spouse and frozen child).

This shift in sexuality was a hard pill to swallow as America shifted to its postwar identity. Still, it allowed the macho, cold, and distant John Wayne type to give way to a generation of men, rocks stars or not, who could bond deeply with the opposite sex. Without Elvis, many androgynous giants of pop might not have succeeded or hit their full potential—stars like David Bowie, the Beatles, Mick Jagger, Iggy Pop, Grace Jones, Freddy Mercury, Annie Lennox, Michael Jackson, Marilyn Manson, or Prince, to name a few. Singer K. D. Lang had no problem appropriating Elvis's looks, costumes, and sounds a few times, as he was her idol and she called him a "total androgynous beauty."[33]

Elvis might have done a great deed for culture if viewed in the context of the Jungian ideas of Animus/Anima. For Jung, the Animus (male) and the Anima (female) were two archetypes essential for the process of individuation (his term for wholeness or self-actualization). In every person, solar and lunar forces exist dynamically, and it is imperative for a person to balance them and seek them for different personas. For example, a female figure might appear in the dream of a male during a depression, and thus he must access a more feminine approach to heal, or perhaps look deeper into a feminine archetype like that of the Mother.

Sometimes, seeking out synchronicities or figures in real life is a portent, as happened to Jungian analyst James Hollis. He told about undergoing a great depression and crisis in his early days, while studying to become an analyst in Zurich, Switzerland. His dreams spoke of an angry witch who needed to be faced. His therapist told him he needed to confront this Anima force inside and outside.

Hollis's reconciliation dream to access his Anima actually had to do with Elvis. In this dream, he met a goddess-like woman standing under an arch at the entrance of Graceland. Later, his analyst told him he had done his inner work, and the woman would come to him in the outer world. Hollis encountered the woman a few days later; she had been working in the Bibliothek of the Jung Institute all along. They eventually get married. He later reflected on how difficult journeys can lead to happy outcomes and mentioned that a trip to Hades was worth it."[34]

Hollis' Anima was urging him, sometimes painfully, to face the real-world manifestation of her to heal and set him on the next stage of his life.

Every individual must find how much Animus or Anima permeates their psyche beyond integrating the two archetypes for individuation. Times and roles change across history, but these two forces extend back into ancient mythology and are as present as the sun and the moon.[35]

Still, the question of the exact difference between male and female psychic forces might linger for many. Ultimately, these forces exist on a spectrum; to understand them is to understand our everpresent psychological dualities and their attempt to unify in a sacred marriage. This said, Jung was black and white in his definition, if slightly politically incorrect:

If I were to attempt to put in a nutshell the difference between man and woman in this respect, i.e., what it is that characterized the animus as opposed to the anima, I could only say this: as the anima produces moods, so the animus produces opinions.[36]

In Gnosticism, the Animus manifests as the Logos/Divine Reason (Jesus), while the Anima is Wisdom/Divine Understanding (Sophia). Both entities encompass all sexualities and genders, but their playing off each other as distinct polarities remains an important map or grand drama to soul liberation.

Elvis ignited a grander courtship between the Animus and Anima in the American psyche. The question is not whether this was for better or worse, but that it was essential for self-knowledge, collective and personal, and part of a necessary evolution that would keep up with technology and emerging spiritualities.

Perhaps America's growing power allowed the Animus and Anima to rise, especially in their conjoined aspect of the androgyne, manifested in the flesh with Elvis.

It is written that Hermes and Aphrodite conceived a son, Hermaphroditus, whose body merged with that of a water nymph

Fig. 9.2. The god Hermaphroditus.

and became both male and female.[37] In Plato's *Symposium*, we find the famous myth of the Hermaphrodite, the original male-female form of humans. According to the myth, humans were extremely powerful but also extremely arrogant. These four-legged, four-armed beings were split by Zeus (some say out of fear) into male and female. Thus, all men and women seek to join completely with their missing half to reach an original state of wholeness. This androgyne being appeared many times in ancient myths, from the Adam Kadmon of the Kabbalah to the Purusha of the Hindus. The book of Genesis seems to have two creation stories, and in the first one, God creates man and woman simultaneously, meaning the original Adam and Eve might have been none other than Hermaphroditus.

In Gnosticism, the ultimate consciousness is depicted as a complete unity of male and female, often with both genitalia (this also goes with its cosmic antagonists, the archons). The Living Jesus is no exception. In the Secret Book of John, an ancient Gnostic text, Jesus appears to the apostle John, saying that part of his essence is "The Mother."

When reading the Gospel of Thomas, Elvis surely read saying 22, where the apostles ask how they can enter the Kingdom. Jesus answers (note my italics):

> When you make the two into one, and when you make the inner like the outer and the outer like the inner, and the upper like the lower, and when you make male and female into a single one, so that *the male will not be male nor the female be female*, when you make eyes in place of an eye, a hand in place of a hand, a foot in place of a foot, an image in place of an image, then you will enter the kingdom.[38]

This is not some outward process—although it can be expressed as a persona—but the ancient motif of the Animus and Animus: transcendence is attained by becoming unified by becoming a total human, with all psychic and sexual energies in harmony. Then anything is possible;

even the gods will fear to tread where humans shake their hips.

Did Elvis take his Anima even further in the material domain? Linda Thompson said, "He had a very open attitude about homosexuality. I never heard him say anything denigrating about gays. I don't think there was any possibility that he could have been bisexual."[39] Other accounts detail how Elvis interacted normally with gay people. On the occasions a gay man made sexual advances toward him, he would laugh and firmly say, "Hey, that just ain't my style."[40]

There are salacious rumors about a close friendship with actor Nick Adams, who himself was a friend of bisexual James Dean. June Juanico complained of Elvis's obsession with Adams, and Elvis loved to party with him and Dennis Hopper when in Hollywood.[41] During the mourning period after Gladys's passing, Adams was the one person who was alone with Elvis in his bedroom.[42]

There is also the incident with Laurenz Landau, the man who provided Elvis with aromatherapy treatments in his first few months serving in Germany. Elvis had flown Landau from Johannesburg, South Africa, and gave him room and board, seeking some spark for his being after the recent death of Gladys, just as he'd found reading *The Prophet*. However, during one of the treatments—which involved Elvis shirtless and lying on a table in a dark room—Landau moved his hand from his client's chest and down his pants to grab "Little Elvis." Elvis blew a fuse and threw him out. Landau later attempted to blackmail Elvis in two ways: through secret pictures and recordings. This evidence threatened to publicly compromise Elvis's sexuality, getting him into hot water with the army and exposing to the world that he was dating a young teenage girl (Priscilla). After some hush money exchanged in a ham-fisted way by Elvis and Vernon, the situation ended with the FBI getting involved and Landau being kicked out of Germany. After an investigation, the army concluded that Elvis had been the victim in the affair and was a stand-up officer.[43]

There's not much else, and it doesn't matter.

What matters is that Elvis exuded his Anima effectively, and within, his Anima and Animus were in balance. He was Hermes and the cross-dressing shaman, but he was also Hermaphroditus, who had a beautiful sexuality, rather than a rugged one. Phyllis Diller, who knew Elvis as an adult, once said, "If his twin had lived, I am sure that Elvis's twin would have been gay."[44] She understood the androgynous forces within Elvis and the polarity of his daemon.

If anything, Elvis's balanced Anima and Animus made him an embodiment of the outdated term *metrosexual*: a fashion-conscious male who interested in grooming, fashion, and personal care, often knowledgeable about beauty products, clothing trends, and styling—of both sexes. Beyond his obsession with his looks and style, Elvis was "nothing less than a master at knowing what the feminine mind wanted" and was so embedded in Priscilla's fashion choices that she became a sort of Pygmalion figure.[45]

In Luhrmann's film *Elvis* we find a suitable example of Elvis's tantric shamanism. It occurs in the *Louisiana Hayride* scene. Historically, it happened on October 1954, and Colonel Parker wasn't present. Elvis had long adopted his "Elvis the Pelvis" moves. Luhrmann presents the scene as Elvis's induction into the live music industry (we could call it a mystery religion initiation). The scene shows Elvis in his pink-and-black (life-and-death) costume (historically accurate), nervous before an indifferent crowd. As Elvis starts to sing "Baby, Let's Play House," he finds those channels to Heaven and Hell, instantly blossoming into a rock star, electrified with his gyrating legs and electrifying the crowd. Parker walks in and sees a magician a million times more powerful than he could ever be—the greatest show on Earth.

The scene perfectly summarizes the power and intent of Elvis as a shaman, the androgynous Hermes. As Parker (Tom Hanks) narrates, "He became a superhero" (*Captain Marvel Jr., of course*). One by one, women in the audience rise to their feet and become hysterical. This spectacle is a mass sexual awakening that suggests the Mysteries of Dionysus, with the female attendees turning into the dangerous maenads of ancient times who would tear living things limb by limb and even devour them. In that scene, Gladys is convinced that the young women present are in a psychotic frenzy and want to kill her son. Elvis and the women were being commenced into higher mysteries, as in many shamanic rituals.

As the fictional narrative continues, Parker becomes more fascinated by the reaction of Elvis's female audience than by the singer himself. He focuses on one young lady who is still sitting down, but her face is on the verge of ecstasy. Parker gives this internal monologue: "Now, I don't know nothing about music, but I could see in that girl's eyes she was having feelings she wasn't sure she should enjoy. Yes. It was a taste of the forbidden fruit. She could have eaten him alive."

The girl gives in and becomes a maenad of Dionysus, not eating Elvis but screaming and reaching out for their new androgynous demigod. The forbidden fruit reference is perfect, as in many Gnostic texts, the serpent is the bringer of wisdom; his convincing Adam and Eve to eat the fruit from the Tree of the Knowledge of Good and Evil is what wakes them up to their true destiny. They don't realize their nakedness but understand that they are trapped in a fool's paradise of Jehovah/Saturn/Ahriman, and by leaving, they can become whole once again. They can return to being the Hermaphrodite that Zeus was so worried about.

This scene also reflects an Eastern idea of divine awakening in certain tantric traditions. As Joanna Kujawa explains in *The Other Goddess*: "In esoteric Hinduism, this energy is called *Kundalini*. . . . Kundalini energy is described as a coiled serpent which, upon spiritual awakening, moves upward." By upward, she means from the lower spine and up through the chakras.

Kujawa goes on to share her experience during a tantric ceremony:

An inner gate flung open within me and I began feeling the upward movement of energy along my spine. An invisible wave crawled upward in a slow but persistent motion. It kept moving until it reached my heart and exploded there. The initial feeling of pleasure and lust disappeared. Briefly, we became bound together in a strange state of bliss, expanded beyond pleasure and lust, beyond woman and man. A great space had opened up in front of us, magnificently impersonal yet tender.[46]

A similar experience likely happened to women during Elvis performances. In short, this notion of stimulating the kundalini serpent (the Gnostic snake of the Garden?) or Shakti energy (cosmic creativity) is what Elvis was gifted with and destined to do with his female audience, like any good Hindu esoteric shaman.

The results of kundalini awakening are bliss and cosmic liberation. To have this experience, one needs to "engage with the feminine energy," as Shakti is seen as a goddess and an aspect of the Anima archetype. Women needed Elvis to get Shakti, and Elvis needed their energy/presence to have the rising of the Kundalini and pass it back to them.[47]

Was Elvis aware of Kundalini energy? He was indeed aware of its serpentine gifts of bliss and cosmic liberation, practicing with Ginger's spine to release its charged energy, but without the success of Kujawa or other yogis. Elvis also sought sex magic from Betty Bethards's *Sex and Psychic Energy.*[48]

We can add sex magic to the occult repertoire of America's Magician. In addition, we can mention an inner revelation he had with respect to his issues with women, which became clear toward the end of his life. During a conversation with Charlie Hodges about his troubles with Ginger, Elvis admitted that he sought to fill a void with all the women he romantically encountered. "It's my fault," Elvis said, "I needed to love somebody so desperately that I read something into it that wasn't there."

His Gnosis also came from the old spiritual standby, *The Prophet*, and one passage that he read out loud: "For even as love crowns you so shall he crucify you."[49]

CEREMONIAL CLOTHING

It has been established how Captain Marvel Jr. influenced Elvis's early hairstyle and later Vegas persona, how Jesse and the life/death shaman

Fig. 9.3. Elvis and Liberace, 1956.
Photo by Associated Press.

motif informed his pink-and-black taste, and how natural introversion
and fantasy worlds determined his idiosyncratic clothing style. His old
mentor and friend (and twinless survivor), Liberace, may have influenced his Vegas Elvis style, starting in 1956 when Liberace pushed him
to wear flamboyant jumpsuits.[50]

In his early days, whether he was attired as a hillbilly or rockabilly
star, Elvis leaned towards rhythm and blues styles, especially what was
on sale at Black-centric Beale Street in Memphis. Elvis favored pleated
pants with wide legs that vibrated when he bounced on the balls of his
feet while performing. He liked trousers with stripes down the sides—
with oversized baggy suit coats in white or black draped around his thin
body, finished with brightly colored ties in gaudy patterns. At times,
he might prefer tight, high-collared shirts in intense colors with sleeves
rolled up. When not mimicking African American singers, Elvis could
appear as a traditional country-western musician.[51]

Bill Belew, the costume designer with the dubious honor of cleaning Elvis's pants during the *Comeback Special*, was largely responsible for his Vegas Elvis style. Beyond the Liberace and Captain Marvel Jr. influence, a karate belt and Napoleonic-collar vibe also informed the outfits. As the year passed and the shows grew in scope, the costumes became more baroque. They were more varied in colors, including silk capes that sometimes reached the floor (although they were retired because of too many incidents in which maenad fans attempted to grab them and pull Elvis into the crowd). Gems, gold chains, and rivets could add as many as thirty pounds to the outfit (which later shortened his live acts as his health deteriorated). It was common for Elvis to throw items or his clothing or even his capes to adoring fans, the mark of Dionysus or Jesus sharing his flesh with devotees.[52]

According to Larry Geller, Elvis's habit of wearing high-collared shirts came from one of his favorite books, *Through the Eyes of the Masters* by David Anrias, which showcased illustrations of various spiritual masters wearing high collars.[53]

Motifs/iconography for his Vegas Elvis garb included eagles, karate, tigers (based on his karate name), and sundials. Fans began to name his costumes: the Mexican Sundial, the King of Spades, the Rainbow Swirl, the American Eagle, the Red Flower, the Gypsy, and the Dragon. Some of his costumes earned their names because of a specific event, like the Burning Love, a bright red costume worn during the fall of 1972 when Elvis incorporated "Burning Love" in shows—or the Aloha Eagle, a white jumpsuit with an American eagle patterned in red, gold, and blue gems, worn during his *Aloha from Hawaii* landmark television special, telecast live to millions across several countries via satellite in January of 1973.[54] Of course, the lord of Memphis, that land of Crossroads, the new Thoth-Hermes who was a patron of Egyptian magic, had to have a "Pharaoh," "Egyptian," and "Egyptian Bird" suit.[55]

One of his favorite costumes during a 1974 tour was the Peacock: a white jumpsuit with a V-neck and high collar, accentuated with stylized features of a blue and gold bird on the front and back. The birds

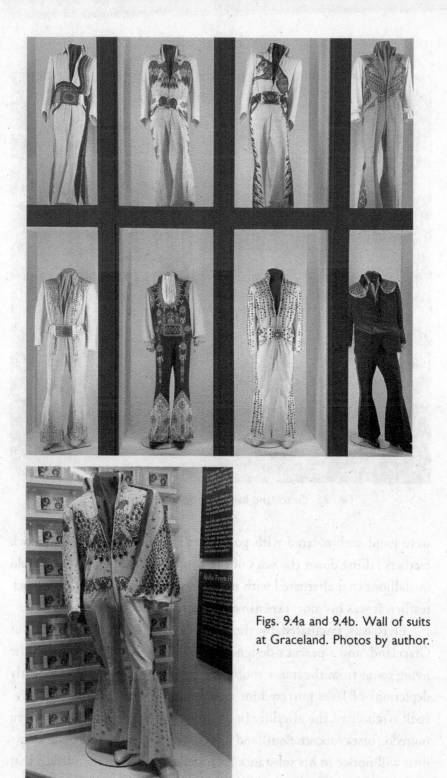

Figs. 9.4a and 9.4b. Wall of suits at Graceland. Photos by author.

Fig. 9.5. Graceland living room. Photo by author.

were hand embroidered with gold thread, showing outlined peacock feathers falling down the sides of the pant legs. The belt included gold medallions that alternated with motifs resembling the eye of a peacock feather. It was his most expensive suit, costing $10,000.

Elvis was fascinated by the peacock. He kept live peacocks at Graceland, and a peacock-designed stained-glass window separated the living room from the music room.[56] From a Christian standpoint, early depictions of Jesus portray him as a peacock.[57] Elvis believed the peacock symbolized the afterlife. In alchemy, in the pivotal stage between nigredo (black/unconscious) and albedo (white, awakening), the alchemist will notice in his substance an iridescent glow on the surface that is often called a "peacock's tail."[58]

The peacock is a potent mystical symbol in many cultures across the world. Still, as the Trickster at the Crossroads, it makes sense that Elvis would be unconsciously attracted to an occult symbol of being in a liminal, border place (that "peacock tail" in between states). From an even more arcane point of view, we can tap into the ideas of the Yezidi, an ancient Middle Eastern people, still surviving today, who worship a being called Malek Taus or the Peacock Angel. This entity was originally part of an angelic assembly, who fell from grace and into chaos. He fashioned the material world and will be redeemed along with all living beings at the end of time.[59]

Belew revealed that shortly before Elvis died, the two were innovating the show suits to include emitting lasers. That pivot was inevitable: Elvis was constantly pushing to find ways to connect with the tribe. More than entertainment, the shows were a series of "rituals and ceremonies" where Elvis engaged in "dramatic actions and gestures" during the performance, all to give rise to collective emotion in the "illusion of intimacy." In an Elvis show, only you (the devotee) and him (the shaman) were there.[60]

Fig. 9.6. Elvis's Peacock suit at Graceland. Photo by author.

Many believe Elvis's costumes and behavior signified his patriotism. That's not altogether accurate. Elvis *embodied* America, and America flowed through him. He was here, like Captain Marvel, to save the souls of the country—like Nietzsche's Super-man or *Übermensch*. In time Elvis's shows started with Richard Strauss's "Also sprach Zarathustra," with him propelled into the stage by a seemingly supernatural force, his first song being "See See Rider."[61]

The shaman is always dressed and prepared for magic and mystery. When it was time for Elvis to travel to the underworld, he was ready. On August 16, 1977, after communing with clouds before his racquet-ball game and summoning the alien blue light by playing "Blue Eyes Crying in the Rain," the King was on his symbolic throne. He read about the face of Jesus, a preparation for the daemon he would meet face to face soon, along with Jesse, wearing exactly what he needed for the journey: electric-blue silk pajamas, and around his neck, the protective wards of an ankh, a Star of David, and a crucifix.[62] The afterlife journey had to happen in Memphis, "Ankh-Tawy" or "Life of the Two Lands," which always symbolized Elvis's reality as a shaman and magician. This event was no sudden tragedy but a funerary rite orchestrated by an aging shaman.

Elvis knew, for he always had one eye on the underworld and on what fate had in store for him.

AN AMERICAN EGREGORE IN MEMPHIS

Elvis once said: "A live concert to me is exciting because of all the electricity that is generated in the crowd and onstage. It's my favorite part of the business—live concerts."[63]

Elvis was onto something arcane about the electricity shared during his performances. Energy was indeed transferred; it goes beyond mere metaphors. This energy created something alive, independent, and sentient starting when Elvis first came on the scene as America's Magician and the shaman of our age.

Chris Knowles writes that Elvis has "come to embody an archetype all his own, one that is instantly recognized by people all around the world."[64] In the previous chapter, I argued that Elvis being the American Dream archetype was wrong. Elvis is recognized as a demigod worldwide and indeed represents the American Dream. But the American Dream is not an archetype; it is an *egregore*.

The concept of the egregore is among the most occult topics in occultism. It's that obscure. In my view, the reason is probably in the egregore itself, which by nature is a secret invisible force that is often only understood by the leader, or the more knowledgeable, of an organization. To show the egregore behind the curtain, Mark Stavish clarifies and summarizes this notion in his book, *Egregores*. The word *egregore* comes from the ancient Greek *égrégoros*, meaning "wakeful" or "watcher." The term is found in the Book of Enoch, referring to the Watchers or those fallen angelic beings influencing humanity.[65] The Watchers promote technology, female empowerment with cosmetics, and forbidden magic, so it wouldn't be surprising if they appeared with Captain Marvel Jr.–style hairstyles and jumpsuits.

Stavish quotes Wiktionary for the standard definition of egregore as "an autonomous psychic entity that is composed of, and influences, the thoughts of a group of people." He then adds a second definition that is more startling, writing that an egregore is also the "home or conduit for a specific psychic intelligence of a nonhuman nature connecting the invisible dimensions with the material world in which we live."[66]

An egregore, in short, is a collective thoughtform fueled by the emotional will, spiritual aura, and psychic energy (electricity) of a unified group or population. In Tibetan Buddhism, one might think of a *tulpa*, an independent thoughtform or ghostly mind secretion that rises from our cognition, often with its own agenda. An egregore is a tulpa for the masses. Like a tulpa or an archetype, it possesses a certain amount of agency that can move beyond a group's physical boundaries or structure.

Stavish describes how an egregore can be manifested intentionally or unintentionally and can be found in diverse contexts like in religious traditions, political movements, and even in corporate culture. Ritual, sacrifices, and beliefs feed this entity, while symbols and logos establish its force. Its power can cross material, mental, and spiritual domains. All gods and daemons might be egregores, a concept echoed in Neil Gaiman's *American Gods,* where all deities are simply projections of our brain electricity that creates independent beings that feed off human adulation and sacrifice. As Elvis said: "My moment of glory is being on that stage and singing and feeling all the love the audience sends to me. It's a completed circle of love we send each other. It's beyond any mortal high. . . . It's like a surge of electricity going through you. It's almost like making love, but it's even stronger than that. . . . Sometimes I think my heart is going to explode."[67]

Here is a quick summary of an egregore:

- Its name means that it is a "watcher" and "watches" or "presides" over some earthly business or collectivity.
- Belief and ritual supplement its presence, but sacrifice might be its best fuel.
- With enough nourishment, it can take on a life of its own and appear independent with limited power on behalf of its devotees, who believe it to be a divine being.
- It has an unlimited appetite for devotion.[68]

How an egregore acts depends (at least at first) on the mutual desires of a group. In Alcoholics Anonymous, for example, an alcoholic might feel safe from the call of the Devil archetype (for example, being in a meeting provides comfort and relief from addiction while simultaneously fueling one's capacity not to relapse afterward). In a Pentecostal church, the egregore might focus on healing through the hands of a pastor. In magician or cult circles, a group might send an egregore to punish a politician or church leader threatening their existence. On a corporate level, as Stavish writes, the egregore ensures the company thrives at any cost, as with Coca-Cola, where "you can rot your teeth and expand your belly with the illusion of sophistication and refreshment as you invoke the epidemic of diabetes—this, in virtually any country in the world!"[69] Think of the example of a company with its enchanting logos and fake promises, embedded like a parasite on the public consciousness. With its mystical culture and cultic employees, Apple, for example, seems to have a magical quality as it continues to grow and grow in people's hearts. The company's founder, Steve Jobs, was akin to Elvis in that he was sometimes more of a shaman than a businessman (and was personally influenced by mystic thought).

Jobs indeed manifested an egregore from his wizard mind, and sometimes, an egregore will use an individual as a vessel for its "prime directive," if you will. To understand the darkest side of an egregore, we can return to National Socialism. The movement was as occult as it was political or social. It drained, controlled, and nurtured the minds of its followers with propaganda, symbols, and neopagan rituals. There was something almost supernatural about Nazism's growth and success, not wholly unlike that of Apple or McDonald's. The Nazi egregore was seemingly autonomous in how it rapidly enveloped the German population and granted Hitler break after break in his rapidly expanding empire. The vessel of a genuinely global or continental egregore, whether it's Jobs or Hitler or Lenin, can be gradually crushed physically or eroded mentally with a shift in public consciousness.

And it can get worse. As Stavish writes, "Egregores that have existed for a period of time will become independent and no longer obey their earthly masters. An egregore may easily turn into 'a fierce tyrant' and cause its associated organization or movement to deviate from its original purpose."[70]

An apt example is the French Revolution, in which the collective passion for freedom turned into a violent thirst for authoritarianism. Nobody was safe when this egregore began sending people to the guillotine.

An argument could be made that an egregore is an outward Jungian complex, a semi-sentient constellation cloud of brain electromagnetic force that overtakes every individual ego that bows to its power. It is a "honeycomb with its numerous cell divisions. While a number of cell divisions can occur or even change, as long as they maintain the core principles then the same egregore is simply being tweaked."[71]

Leaving an egregore is very difficult, whether it's a cult or kicking a Diet Coke habit. Individuals can feel drained and manipulated, perhaps never truly safe, as the egregore always seeks that person's life.

In the context of an egregore, let us return to early postwar America. The country's collective psyche had been under siege for decades by the Great Depression and World War II. Suddenly, the ostensible desert ended, and the Promised Land appeared on the other side of two atomic bombs. The collective psyche of Americans shifted and yielded all its energy to the bounty and comfort that was for the taking. A different egregore rose, and we may call it the American Dream. The force needed a vessel to create magical sigils (symbols and logos) to harness psychic currents and steer the population forward, not back into the desert. The chosen vessel needed to be open to the higher worlds, a gifted individual full of witch power, who would represent the rag-to-riches core of the egregore. The vessel would represent the WASP ethos of work-as-salvation and syncretic innovation regardless of race or religion. Again, sometimes those broken vessels are the best conduits for eldritch energies, the will of the gods we perhaps create.

Ladies and gentlemen, allow me to introduce you to Elvis Presley. As Thomas Moore wrote in the foreword of *The Tao of Elvis*:

> Many said that Elvis was the mirror image of America, meaning that when Americans gazed at Elvis we were seeing ourselves and maybe a caricature of ourselves. America itself is an eternal adolescent, playing at love and full of virtuous ideals while hiding a menacing, ferocious capacity for aggression and self-destruction. This is not yin and yang. This is a split personality.[72]

Fig. 9.7. Elvis's private jet, the Lisa Marie, at Graceland.
Photo by author.

Elvis pied piped the egregore effectively, leveraging stage, television, jukebox, and the movie screen to siphon human essence into the American Dream egregore, and siphoning back the coding to continue growing the nation into unparallel prosperity. Elvis represented "both the best and worst of the American dream" and "American and world myth gone amuck."[73] Challenges and interruptions loomed at every corner, but the American Dream egregore never lost its post as the protector of its people.

As music critic Bill Holdship said: "Elvis is loved, and he is hated. He was a genius, a fraud. A saint, the devil. The king, the clown. Even more than when he was alive, Elvis has come to symbolize everything great and everything hideous about America."[74]

Elvis was right about electricity, and you can almost hear fate laughing when learning that he had been studying to be an electrician before Sun Records allowed him to be an egregore electrician. He was right about adopting the motto "TCB" or "Taking Care of Business" with the lightning logo. The wizard turned Billy Batson into Captain Marvel with a magic lightning bolt, and the American Dream egregore turned Elvis into its superhero to care for the people.

But what happened when the American Dream's vessel finally shattered for good? Did it have enough energy, or did it utilize other receptacles like Ronald Reagan or Bruce Springsteen? Were the continued explosion of mass media and the gradual adoption of the internet enough for the egregore to move through its vast, fleshy organism? Perhaps with the fall of the other mighty egregore, communism, globalization caused the entity to extend beyond the borders and tap more power from places like China or India. What happened? As Elvis himself said, "Once I go, the world is going to really start changing. That's when it will all start."[75]

Esoteric speculation is fascinating, but as always, we shouldn't make the mistake of falling under the material reductionistic rubric. What happened when Elvis died is the wrong line of thinking. You can't kill an idea; a god just won't stay down as long as humans worship him.

After his passing, Elvis was more alive, present, and divine than ever.

10
FUNERAL FOR A FRIEND AND RETURN OF THE KING

I Am with You Always

There is the word icon, and I don't think anybody has topped that. . . . not one single person has ever topped Elvis.

DAVID LYNCH, FILM DIRECTOR

I'll tell the world, Elvis was the greatest of all time.

MUHAMMAD ALI

Saw the ghost of Elvis
On Union Avenue
Followed him up to the gates of Graceland
Then I watched him walk right through

"WALKING IN MEMPHIS"
MARC COHN, SINGER-SONGWRITER

LONG BEFORE QANON predicted that John F. Kennedy Jr. would rise from the dead, long before Alex Jones, long before fringe ideas became as ubiquitous as they now are, Elvis Presley was a cottage industry of legends, fables, and constant tabloid sensationalism. His death was a collective shock for the country, and his fame in many ways only increased afterward. He remained a global conspiracy theory factory. It reminds me of that infamous quote that circulated after Elvis died: "Good career move."

With Elvis, everything was so damn magical. Even his age at death, forty-two, has esoteric meaning. Beyond "forty-two" being the answer to the universe, according to Douglas Adams's *The Hitchhiker's Guide to the Galaxy*, 42 was an important number in ancient Egypt. When the soul left the body, it eventually stood before the judging deity Maat or Osiris. One of these gods would weigh the individual's heart on a scale against a feather while they orated forty-two "negative confessions" (sins they had not committed). The heart would be lighter or heavier than a feather on the scale. Weighing lighter meant a joyous afterlife, and heavier meant being devoured into extinction by the fierce god Ammit. In other occult traditions, 42 is the number gleaned from the vesica piscis, considered a symbol of divine feminine energy, birth, and creation, while in other systems, specifically numerology, 42 is associated with the balancing of the spiritual and material planes (we're back at the Crossroads, yet again, although you and I have never really left).

On the material plane, his death was genuinely seen as the fall of a King. An astonishing crowd of 50,000 congregated outside Graceland the day after Elvis passed away. Thousands of people were eventually granted access to see his body. Souls traveling the Crossroads continued even with the physical form of the shaman not present: one man had a fatal heart attack, a woman went into labor and had to be rushed to the hospital, and two women were killed when a teenager lost control of their car and plowed into a crowd. Many others required medical treatment under the oppressive Memphis afternoon heat. All the florists in Memphis sold out of flowers while offerings of condolence were amassed around the King's palace.[1]

The emotion and sentiment that spread throughout the world was something never witnessed before, a collective psychic tsunami of "hysteria, voyeurism, and nostalgia."[2] Massive congregations around the globe were formed to honor the fallen liege, especially in Europe. President Jimmy Carter delivered a sorrowful address, followed by hundreds of other influential people. Elvis's funeral on August 18 was befitting of nobility and well attended by celebrities and politicians alike. His initial resting place was Forest Hill Cemetery in Memphis. However, due to an attempted body-snatching two weeks after the burial, Vernon relocated his son's body to the grounds of Graceland.

Then came the blame game and the fight over finances. After the passing of Vernon and his grandmother Minnie Mae, after Colonel Parker had finally been exorcised legally and financially, the estate went to Lisa Marie. Elvis Presley became a company, a trademark, a business empire with a logo—an egregore that made many people rich and powerful. Beyond clubs, merchandise, and events, Graceland is one of the most visited homes in the country, second only to the White House. Thousands of people visit Graceland daily, and a traditional vigil and all-night candlelit procession around the grounds attracts more than 70,000 fans annually.[3] No other deceased pop star receives this sort of religious adulation or financial success. None ever will (sorry, not sorry, Swifties).

ELVIS REDIVIVUS

The apparitions (or Elvis sightings) began right after his death.

On that fateful night, the entire Graceland community gathered to watch the ten o'clock news and learn how the day's events would be reported. Oddly, the television suddenly lost sound, adding to the thick unease and tension in the air. The following day, as Elvis was being carried to his hearse by pallbearers, a limb from an oak tree broke off and landed on Ginger Alden's car, a grim reminder of the tragic day. George Klein attempted to lift his spirits by playing a cassette of Elvis's greatest hits, but the tape broke right after the rendition of "Can't Help Falling in Love," the song that Elvis used to close his shows. Meanwhile, another Elvis friend and bodyguard, Alan Fortas, experienced frustration when the tape he was playing in his car, featuring "Blue Hawaii," jammed. In Los Angeles, Linda Thompson received the tragic news and immediately lost power in her apartment.[4] The American Dream egregore and his electricity were everywhere.

Elvis's disrupting electrical powers and aura went beyond his loved ones and friends. (Bear in mind that in the following examples the names of witnesses have been altered by the researcher, who will be mentioned, to protect their privacy.)

In the afternoon of the day Elvis died, Tennessee farmer "Claude Buchanon" was tending to an injured cow on a slope behind his house. Claude and Elvis had previously crossed paths. The King had helped Claude purchase a pickup truck when he couldn't afford it. As Claude worked on the slope, he suddenly spotted Elvis walking up the far slope toward him, surrounded by a blue mist (no surprise on the color by now). It struck Claude as odd that he hadn't noticed him earlier. The King came within ten feet of Claude, who said, "Elvis, what are you doing here, boy?"

Elvis smiled. "I've come to say goodbye for a while, Claude."

As he finished speaking, Claude's wife called out from behind, frantically yelling that Elvis had passed away, and it was all on the radio. When he turned back to look, Elvis had vanished into thin air.[5]

At 5:30 p.m. on the day of Elvis's death, his devoted fans "Arthur" and "Marian" returned home to a bizarre scene. They found all the windows in their house shut tight. The front door was locked with a deadbolt. As they stepped inside, the pair noticed a statue of Elvis sitting at the center of their coffee table was now toppled. Two pictures of the King, one of which had been autographed, had been knocked off the wall, their glass frames shattered. No other objects in the room were disturbed. The couple had no children or pets who could have caused the mess. Miriam wanted to call the police, but Arthur said, "Call the police and tell them a shelf fell?" (Instead of the poltergeist shenanigans of an elf on a shelf, such a disturbance might have been, as Chris Knowles calls the King, "elfish," but what else do you expect from the Trickster?).

After surveying the damage, the couple turned on the television to catch the news, and their hearts shattered to learn of Elvis's death.[6]

Meanwhile, another Elvis fan, "Ruth Ann Bennett," and her friend decided to spend the evening mourning Elvis by listening to his records together. When Ruth went to pick out some of her favorite albums, she found that almost half of them were warped and unplayable. Strangely, the records were still warm to the touch. The odd occurrence only added to the eerie feeling that befell many Elvis fans after his untimely death.[7]

"Hilda Weaver" had met Elvis when she was a child. She didn't exactly meet him, but the King had walked by her one day and, with a wave, said, "Hi, honey." She was thrilled then, but with more time, she lost interest in Elvis or anything magical, growing up to be a serious and secular clinical psychologist. One night, Hilda was working on an article for a professional journal. It was November 17, 1977. She looked up at one point, and Elvis sat across the desk. He looked concerned but overall appeared to be very happy. Of course, he was wearing a blue suit. Hilda was urged to do what she did with all patients and ask him how she could help, but instead blurted out, "What can you help me with?"

He smiled, immediately grasping her good humor in the situation, and said, "Are you satisfied with your life, Missy?" He used a name only her family called her when she was younger.

"You're a better psychologist than I am," she responded, "and you've never been to school."

His smile grew. "I've been to the best school."

It hit her then that Elvis had died, *really died*, some months ago. How was this happening?

Not understanding why, she said, "Am I satisfied with my life? Oh, me! You know something about me that I don't know, that I'm not facing, don't you?"

Elvis didn't answer, looking into her eyes kindly. Hilda began to cry, and Elvis said, "Hilda, you must open up your perspective on what you are doing with your life."

They chatted very personally for a while, Hilda understanding that she had sold her soul for a career, money, and safety—but that she was not truly living. She was not a full human being as Elvis had been when in the flesh, warts and all.

At one point, Hilda explained that she had been disturbed by the incident of the two young women at Graceland being killed when struck by a car the day after Elvis had passed. Hilda expressed her confusion about life and its injustices and random tragedies.

"I was deeply concerned about them, too," Elvis admitted seriously. "I was there to greet them and to be with them when they passed over into heaven."

Hilda immediately felt peace, bowing her head and holding her hands in prayer, knowing that the Lord of the Crossroads doesn't take days off, that Hermes and the shaman never truly leave their people. When she looked up, he was gone. Her life was changed forever.

How did she know it was November 17? She immediately wrote on her calendar in green ink for that day: "EP dropped by."[8]

On December 20, 1980, long-haul trucker "Jack Matthews" had stopped to fuel and relax at a station in Arkansas. He was about one hundred miles from his destination in Memphis. He noticed a glowing light and cloud suddenly coming from the woods across the highway. A man appeared out of the light and walked down the highway, wearing an overcoat and carrying a bundle under his arm. For some reason, Jack went to him and asked where he was headed. "Memphis," the man answered with a Tennessee accent. Jack couldn't see his face because of a hood over his head and face.

"Going to Memphis for the holidays?" Jack asked.

"Yeah, I'm going home to see my momma and daddy."

Jack eventually offered him a ride since he was heading in that direction. During the hundred-mile journey, they engaged in friendly conversation. He still couldn't see the hitchhiker's face. Nevertheless, he was struck by the man's impeccable manners, always addressing him with "Yes, sir" and "No, sir." As they chatted, he knew his passenger was close to his mother. The man admitted he was once a trucker like him, although Jack didn't buy his story of owning several Cadillacs. At one point, Jack admitted to struggling with alcohol issues, and the hitchhiker confessed to abusing pills. As they approached Graceland, for some reason, Jack finally introduced himself. The man looked directly into his eyes for the first time and said, "I'm Elvis Presley, sir."

Jack had no doubt it was Elvis. In a state of pure shock and drenched in cold sweat, he somehow drove another mile to where Elvis wanted to be dropped off. Elvis got out, leaving the trucker paralyzed and with a pounding heart. Jack had been enjoying a period of sobriety at that time.[9]

Another eerie incident occurred with a woman named "Janice," who had met Elvis several times. He had even given her one of his jackets one time when she was cold and not dressed for the weather (giving was something he did automatically, Janice admitted). She found it amusing that Elvis stored a penny in the right pocket because why would a multimillionaire care about such a coin? (Perhaps the Archon of Poverty makes one never forget.) Right after his death, she noticed it repeatedly falling off the hangar and onto the closet floor. One day, while watching the jacket hanging in broad daylight, it fell again without apparent reason. Another time, Janice woke up in the middle of the night to find the right sleeve of the jacket moving up and down on its own, sending shivers down her spine. Fearing for her safety, she rented a room to another woman named "Mary," who owned a miniature collie. The dog would often bark at the closet where the jacket hung and avoided going near it, further adding to the creepy atmosphere in the house.

Janice was not listening, so Elvis had to come in person, more or less. Shortly later, she dreamt she and Elvis were walking through picturesque country woods, surrounded by green mountains and topped by a beautiful blue sky. They held hands, and Elvis led her to a calm brook on a stone bridge. He hugged her tenderly but then let her have it, "Janice, you are kinda slow, aren't you? Don't you remember how we used to talk about death? We wanted to know whether we lived after we die. I've been trying to get through to you through the jacket, honey, but you keep getting scared. It didn't work. I want to let you know that we do live after we die. So go on and live."

He held her again and said goodbye.[10] A penny for your Gnosis, Janice.

One of the most extraordinary occurrences involving Elvis fans happened to a Georgia police officer and his estranged son. On February 11, 1982, the son, "Tony," left for Los Angeles after arguing with his parents about his reckless behavior. He had two thousand dollars in savings, and his father, "Harold," was concerned that he would soon become involved with drugs. After more than two weeks with no word from Tony, Harold and his other son decided to fly to Los Angeles to search for him. Before they could leave, Harold dreamed of Elvis coming to his office. In the dream, Elvis wore a police jacket and showed Harold a badge (some complexes die hard, even in death). He said that he was worried about Tony and wanted to guide Harold to him. Elvis pointed to a Los Angeles map, but Harold had difficulty focusing on the street names. Elvis led him to a corner drugstore with a small hamburger stand across the street. He directed Harold to a rooming house on the block and urged him to look at the front door. When Harold struggled to focus, Elvis grabbed him by the arm and shook him, saying, "Look, man, you gotta look at this. This is important, man. Your son is on drugs." Harold remembered the front of the building and thanked Elvis. He woke up with a headache and ringing in his ears.

Harold and his other son flew to Los Angeles on March 3 after seeking advice from local police about the neighborhoods to search. They rented a car and began looking for Tony. On March 9, at two o'clock in the afternoon, Harold saw the corner drugstore from his dream. Directly across the street was the hamburger stand. After finding three similar-looking rooming houses midway down the block, Harold identified the one Elvis had shown him. When he knocked on the door, an older woman answered. Harold asked her, "Ma'am, do you have a Tony Welch living here?" She replied, "Well, yes, I do." He introduced himself as Tony's father, and she directed him to the boy's room upstairs.

Harold knocked on the door, and Tony told him to come in. He was lying on his bed reading a magazine. He went pale at the sight of his father in the doorway. After a moment of mutual emotion, Tony confessed that he was ready to come home. As Elvis had warned Harold in the dream, Tony was using drugs and was on dangerous ground. Finding him helped turn his life around.

At the time, Harold was too embarrassed to tell either son about his dream. But that evening, while they talked in a hotel, Tony revealed, "Dad, it's the funniest thing. Two times since I've been out here I've had dreams about Elvis Presley. In both dreams, he told me you would be coming to get me. He said he was worried about me. He said he would work it out."

These occurrences merely scratch the surface, with Elvis taking so many roles at the Crossroads. For a woman named "Bess," single and pregnant and cast out from her conservative Christian family, Elvis appeared in the delivery room. He smiled and winked at her behind a wall of nurses and doctors. "Relax, Bess, it's OK. I'll be here with you." When the child came out, Elvis boomed, "It's a boy!" The child arrived safely and healthy, and Elvis vanished, finally seeing a human birth.

Elvis was there for "Jennifer," a girl born with Down syndrome and several health issues, including a weak heart. Jennifer's greatest joy was listening to Elvis, and all in all, she lived a happy life. She even saw Elvis live in Las Vegas and never understood when the King had passed. Years later, in 1980, when she was only ten, her health finally failed. Dying in her hospital bed with her parents, she spread her arms and screamed joyously, "Here comes Elvis. Here comes Elvis." She passed away with a big smile on her face.

And Elvis was there for "Beverly Wilkins," who clinically died during surgery. In a typical near-death-experience walkabout, she floated out of her body, away from the physicians trying to resuscitate her, and up beyond the material world. She arrived at a beautiful meadow landscape, meeting several of her deceased family members. The energy was holy and peaceful, so Beverly was somewhat disappointed when she learned that she would have to return to Earth. She was glad she would see her husband and children again, though. As she was about to leave, she was startled to see Elvis approaching her. "Hi, Beverly, remember me?" he asked.

She did remember meeting him years ago during a concert. They chatted for a while, and Elvis thanked her for treating him like an average person and not a celebrity. That treatment was something he had always craved since becoming famous.

"Yes, Elvis, I do remember you, of course," Beverly said. "And many people all over our world still remember and love you, too."

In the middle of Paradise, they enjoyed more casual conversation until it was her time to return to Earth. Elvis was absorbed into a bright light, and Beverly was sent back to samsara.

These and more examples are found in *Elvis After Life*, by Raymond A. Moody, Jr. Moody contends that after Elvis's death, hundreds of such psychical experiences transpired. He remains agnostic and open about supernatural implications.[11]

Of the many Elvis visitations, the most famous might have happened in 1988 when multiple sightings of Elvis were reported in Kalamazoo, Michigan. This paranormal event captured national attention. One of the sightings occurred at a Burger King in the town, where Elvis was reportedly seen eating. Another happened at the local Columbia Hotel that Elvis had patronized. The sightings were witnessed by several people, including a woman named Louise Welling. She claimed to have seen Elvis at a supermarket in Vicksburg, Michigan, wearing a white jumpsuit and paying for an electrical fuse (gotta keep feeding that egregore, electrician).

Why Kalamazoo? Beyond enjoying a burger like any loyal American and visiting his old office downtown, Elvis enjoyed the Gibson guitar factory while alive. He also performed several times at the Wings Stadium.[12] But your ghost guess is as good as mine.

Not all notable Elvis apparitions are old news, as they say. When Billy Stanley, another Elvis stepbrother, suffered a heart attack, stroke, and seizure at once at his house in 2018, he legally died for approximately fourteen minutes. He survived and recovered but experienced a near-death experience where, like Beverly Watkins, he took a short tour of Heaven. Stanley stood above clouds, dressed in white and surrounded by bright light. He beheld a city in the distance tinged with a golden glow and topped by steeples. A voice urged him to go to the city. He obeyed, filled with love and glad the clouds took on his weight. He came up on none other than his stepbrother.

"Billy." Elvis smiled and looked directly at him.

"Elvis," Stanley said nervously.

Elvis hugged him and said, "It's good to see you." A darkness crossed Elvis's form, but he kept talking, "Tell all of my family, friends, and fans I love them. And I'll see them when they get here. I love you, Billy."

"I love you too," Stanley said, wishing he had told him this decades earlier when they had their last conversations.

Then he heard God's voice informing him that Heaven was real, fear was unnecessary, and he would return if he believed in Jesus. The darkness swallowed Elvis, and Stanley returned to samsara, led to his body by the desperate screams of his wife as he lay on the floor in his house, the paramedics rushing to save his life.[13]

Sightings are still common enough today that the Graceland website houses a page to record anyone encountering the risen king—like Cleopas meeting Jesus on the road to Emmaus.[14] Along with Bigfoot, the Virgin Mary, and UFOs, Elvis has been very photogenic for decades. He may not appear on toast like Jesus, but his image once suddenly appeared on a pantry door in front of a family (and Moody himself visited the "holy site" and verified it was Elvis's face eerily imprinted on the wood).[15]

INFOWARS ELVIS

The more "tabloid" or "conspiratorial" variations of Elvis sightings are also extraordinary—from appearing in an airport line in the film *Home Alone* to allegedly being the groundskeeper of Graceland the

Fig. 10.1. Still from *Home Alone*,
with Elvis supposedly in the background.
20th Century Studios (1990).

entire time. Entire books and documentaries solely focus on Elvis as a ghost or person who staged his death for different reasons. A 2002 poll implied that seven percent of Americans believed Elvis was still alive.[16]

The sudden death of a famous person and ensuing maelstrom never help bring closure. As with anything concerning Elvis, it was larger than life. Even his cause of death was questionable. After Elvis's passing, his family requested a private autopsy to establish the cause of death. Tennessee's Chief Medical Examiner, Jerry Francisco, released Elvis Presley's official death certificate a few days later. The document stated that the cause of death was a coronary issue unrelated to drugs. He informed *American Medical News* that even if the drugs were not present, Elvis would still have died from heart disease. However, several pathologists involved in the autopsy later criticized Francisco's methods. They claimed he favored the family's privacy with his swift announcement and conclusion. Multiple doctors contended that the musician's cause of death should have been attributed to a toxic combination of pharmaceuticals. Remember that Elvis's game of Russian roulette with drugs was mainly hidden from the public, and his doctor,

George Nichopoulos, gave him what he wanted because if he did not, the King would always find another physician or buy from the streets.[17]

Furthermore, a spokesman from Baptist Memorial Hospital made a statement that they never agreed with the conclusion of natural causes. No gross evidence of a heart attack was apparent. What's more, autopsy officials declared that, in their view, Elvis was still years away from serious heart disease.[18]

Perhaps one of the strangest anomalies around Elvis's death is the medical examiner's report, which Elvis apparently signed—the handwriting is blatantly like his. Throughout the years, handwriting experts have stated that only Elvis could have signed it, basing this claim on other materials that feature his original writing. Just as peculiarly, the body in the casket, according to photos and witnesses, appears like a young Rockabilly Elvis, with a pug nose—when Elvis's nose was straight. Sweat was seen coming down the face of Elvis's corpse, and the fact that ten male pallbearers struggled with the coffin led many to believe that what was being carried was a wax figure with an elaborate and heavy cooling system.[19]

Stories abound about a black helicopter picking someone up the day of Elvis's death, taking him to an airport where he bought a ticket to Buenos Aires, Argentina. The name on the ticket was Jon Burrows, the name Elvis gave when checking in at hotels incognito.[20] Did Elvis get to live his dream of meditating forever and away from the demands of stardom?

Another account involves a sample from Elvis's biopsy in 1975 to check for hepatitis. That sample allegedly does not match the DNA obtained from Elvis's 1977 autopsy.[21] And the investigations go on and on, from why Elvis was playing racquetball the day he died (and manipulating the weather)—not something one does on the threshold of death—to why Vernon never went to the hospital with his son's body. Combing through every detail of Elvis's death is something only matched in intensity by the ends of John F. Kennedy, Princess Diana, and Jeffrey Epstein.

Like many great singers with roots in Las Vegas, Elvis rubbed shoulders with the mob and other underground elements. Unlike any other pop star, Elvis was a former US Army soldier obsessed with being a law enforcement agent, even undercover. This running in both crime and law circles is yet another duality of the Lord of the Crossroads that provided more fodder for fringe aficionados—especially when considering the many threats and extortion attempts, along with Elvis's penchant for fighting or brandishing his weapons on people (or vehicles, as with Linda Thompson). The idea of an assassination or a quick Witness Protection migration was always in the air for those who couldn't believe their demigod was felled by mere drugs or a lackluster heart.

Rumors abound that Elvis received more than an honorary badge after meeting Nixon. Some claim he was appointed as a secret DEA agent. Elvis then served as an undercover agent to gather intel which led to his direct involvement with the FBI. He provided high-level information on the illegal trafficking of drugs, which began his involvement as a federal informant.

On a more plausible level, Elvis was allegedly engaged in Operation Fountain Pen, an investigation targeting Frederick Peter Pro for various scandals, including defrauding Vernon out of over one million dollars in 1976 in a scheme to sell and refurbish one of Elvis's Lockheed Jetstar airplanes. The Jetstar was bleeding money from Elvis and wasn't airworthy. Vernon, always the poor businessman, was introduced to Pro in May 1976. Pro encouraged Vernon to get involved with a complex leasing agreement with his company. Pro explained he would facilitate the repairs needed, sell the plane on Elvis's behalf , and then lease it back to him. Yet Pro was a conman and a member of a criminal group called the Fraternity.

Elvis's case was the catalyst that enabled the FBI to temporarily stop the illegal activity of at least two of the group's members. On July 26, 1977, the FBI stated that they possessed enough evidence to prosecute Frederick Peter Pro and his group. In early August of 1977, Elvis allegedly tried to reach President Carter. On August 15 the US Attorney advised that the FBI was ready to go to the Grand Jury. On August 16, Elvis was found dead—the same day four Fraternity members were arrested. Coincidence? By this account, placing Elvis into a witness security program for his safety would have made sense.[22] The FBI *was* investigating Pro and his organization, but Elvis and his family were out of the loop, victims more than anything.

Not surprisingly, in this Game of Thrones conjecture, Colonel Parker is also a suspect in many of these stories—though why kill the person who was still a massive money machine for him? Maybe, instead, mobsters got Elvis—like they eventually got Tony Soprano at the end of the fabled HBO television series.[23]

When did the Elvis conspiracies take flight in the public imagination? With Mercury's winged feet, they gained traction as soon as 1978 when the world was introduced to the release of *Orion*, written by Gail Brewer-Giorgio. The protagonist of this "novel" is a famous Southern singer, bearing striking similarities to Elvis, who ultimately fakes his death to escape the rigors of fame. This fiction-becoming-fact theory gained even more traction when singer Jimmy Ellis donned a mask and adopted the stage name Orion. His first album, "Reborn," featured an Elvis-esque figure in a coffin on the cover. Additionally, his uncanny vocal resemblance to Elvis convinced many listeners he was the King himself. His record label did nothing to quell the rumors, viewing the stunt as a profitable opportunity.

Orion eventually established himself as a successful artist, but he sparked an Elvis impersonation phenomenon that continues today. One of the most notorious imitations occurred in 1981, with the emergence of a singer calling himself Sivle Nora (Aron Elvis spelled backward). He released a book, album, and even a video purportedly proving that Elvis was still alive and right before the world's eyes. However, it was revealed that Sivle was nothing more than a talented Elvis impersonator named David Darlock.

In 1988, Brewer-Giorgio released the nonfiction version of *Is Elvis Alive?*. The book was bundled with a cassette tape featuring

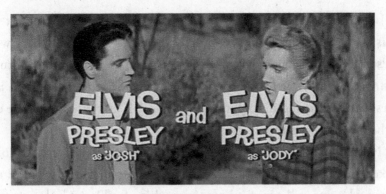

Fig. 10.2. Still from *Kissin' Cousins*,
Metro-Goldwyn-Mayer (1964).

an exclusive interview with none other than Elvis himself. Yet it was once again revealed that the voice on the tape belonged to David Darlock. Nevertheless, the book was a commercial success, leading Brewer-Giorgio to appear on television shows like *Geraldo* and *Larry King Live*.[24]

Along with Elvis impersonators, the persistent belief that Elvis faked his death continues to this day, with countless sightings and supposed evidence cropping up over the years. The King may be gone, but his legend lives on, and the conspiracy theories surrounding his supposed demise only add to his enduring legacy.

Even Jesse makes it into some conspiracy theories. Perhaps he lived, and Vernon and Gladys gave him up for adoption as they could not care for two children. A third child was born that night of the blue light, named Clayton, or the Presleys conceived a third surviving child later named Franklin. If Jesse lived, he acted as Elvis's body double on certain occasions, even if his eyes were brown instead of blue (and somehow colored contact lenses existed then instead of being invented in the 1980s, but whatever). Could the heavy casket at Elvis's funeral contain either Franklin, Jesse, or Clayton? Inquiring conspiracists want to know! It would explain why showing three verions of Elvis in advertisements was a staple of the King's promotions.[25] Perhaps Elvis's film *Kissin' Cousins* didn't show split screens in which Elvis played two identical people, but it was really Jesse helping his bro out!

I am reminded of the 1992 film *Death Becomes Her*, with Bruce Willis, Meryl Streep, and Goldie Hawn. The plot centers on a magical elixir that grants immortality and an elite society that benefits from this alchemy. At a gathering of this group, a leader warns that some members who staged their deaths should be more careful while they enjoy their eternal life. The camera pans to a parting crowd to reveal Elvis with two girls at each side. "Just trying to have fun," Elvis mumbles. Later, we also run into Jim Morrison by a pool.

Sorry, Jim, but Elvis is still the brightest star in a constellation of figures society cannot accept as physically absent. This list also includes James Dean, Kurt Cobain, Paul Walker, Princess Diana, Tupac Shakur, Michael Jackson, Bruce Lee, Andy Kaufman, and Steve Jobs. Even if you put them all together in terms of continued interest, from books to television shows to sightings, they still wouldn't reach the level of attention Elvis has received.

Elvis is probably amused, regardless of what state he currently finds himself in. Like Philip K. Dick, paranoia was often his coping skill, and he did enjoy an occasional snifter of conspiracy theory. During the 1960s, in an interview, going against the grain of public opinion, he asserted there were possible links between the assassinations of John Kennedy and Robert Kennedy. He was convinced that the government was withholding evidence proving Lee Harvey Oswald did not act alone. It became one of his many obsessions, which included speculating that foul play was involved in the death of Bruce Lee.[26]

Beyond *2001: A Space Odyssey*, Elvis was fascinated with another of Stanley Kubrick's films. One of his habits as Movie Star Elvis was renting an entire movie theater after hours, paying the staff to work extra. He would sit in the center row with Joe Esposito and Priscilla on each side of him, with the rest of his entourage behind. Sometimes, he might invite the crowd of fans outside to join in the back as long as they kept quiet. His favorite film of that time was *Dr. Strangelove*, which he watched three times in a row, then requested for the last reel to be screened six more times (his favorite line of the film was, "Gentlemen, you can't fight in here! This is the War Room.").[27] For good measure, he was also an avid *Star Trek* fan and even named one of his horses "Star Trek."[28]

I AM WITH YOU ALWAYS

Could Elvis have survived? Is any of the evidence above valid? Does it matter? Hermes is the god of both the mind and tricks, so the mind will see what it wants, individually and collectively. An egregore can turn a fallen people into a murderous regime that almost consumes Europe or make a population eat poisonous food under a golden and red sigil. Magic is the altering of consciousness in accordance with will. We believe what we want to believe, regardless of whether it's Alex Jones or the US military telling us UFOs are now real.

Shock is one reason people cannot accept the passing of a great figure. Heroes are larger than life, and their sudden vanishing sends Hermes to convince us that death was avoided or that a resurrection is possible. Additionally, acclaimed figures can rise into mythic stature, often symbolizing a more idyllic time. King Arthur represents an era of order and peace for all, and despite his sins and ultimate failure, his return could herald a return to more fair times. Jesus briefly walked the Earth, his presence providing a safe space of wisdom, wholeness, and eternal life for anyone who kept him company. His return means a new age where the meek and poor finally get a break.

Elvis ushered in a safe and prosperous era, and he symbolizes the American condition. As long as he might be alive, the collective dream of a nation remains possible. Arthur is England's savior, Jesus is the world's savior, but Elvis will always be America's savior.

Elvis has attained a divine stature, expressed today by a robust industry of Elvis impersonators, clergy, conferences, Graceland tourism, and content creation. A 2017 poll stated that 47% of Americans see themselves as Elvis fans.[29] Mother Dolores Hart, Elvis's costar in 1957's *Loving You* who later became a Catholic Benedictine nun, said that she would listen to Elvis singing on the film set and "couldn't believe the charisma. This man is going to live forever, that voice is not just for us, that voice is for the people of God."[30] Cinda Godfrey's *The Elvis–Jesus Mystery* claims that Adam, Jesus, and Elvis are all the same soul. As a matter of fact, Elvis is the Messiah to return, even predicted by famous prophets Nostradamus and Edgar Cayce. Like Jesus, he not only showed the way to heaven but carried the sins of a country by taking on addiction, gun violence, rank materialism, and a legion of mental disorders. During a standup performance, comedian Bill Burr stated that Elvis was meant to break virgin ground and make those mistakes so other musicians and celebrities would learn. "This man kicked open all of those fucking doors for the rest of us," he said.

For a darker interpretation, I am reminded of Phil's high school classmate, Ursula LeGuin, and her short story, "The Ones Who Walk Away from Omelas." In the story, the utopian city of Omelas depends for its happiness and peace on the suffering of a single, abused child locked in a basement. Some citizens stay because it's a fair bargain, while others leave because it's too much for one child to be sacrificed for the collective. What would you choose? Would you be okay with the Archon of Poverty eternally tormenting a child in Tupelo, or would you help him find his marble under the house and escape?

Elvis is America's "Hero with a Thousand Faces" who is expected to return home. As Ernest Becker wrote in his Pulitzer Prize-winning *The Denial of Death*: "The hero was the man who could go into the spirit world, the world of the dead, and return alive."[31] A hero is a shaman and teaches that life is not life because it is lived but because it is experienced at its fullest, warts and all.

As Marilyn Monroe became the mythological embodiment of the Anima archetype, Elvis became the mythical embodiment of the

Animus Archetype. Both figures are living myths, and this does not mean as characters in a fable or story, as Joseph Campbell explained:

> Mythology is not a lie, mythology is poetry, it is metaphorical. It has been well said that mythology is the penultimate truth—penultimate because the ultimate cannot be put into words. It is beyond words. Beyond images, beyond that bounding rim of the Buddhist Wheel of Becoming. Mythology pitches the mind beyond that rim, to what can be known but not told.[32]

Like archetypes and egregores, myths are as close as we can get to that place of pure experience, the numinous or sublime, what some have called God. In that thin membrane that separates the known from the unknown, in that liminal place or Crossroads stands the magician always there to show us the way. This is where the real magic happens, and the Trickster holds court. At the beginning of this love letter I am writing for Elvis, I detail various forms of interpreting magic. But the best definition might come from Gordon White:

> Magic is the felt sense that our role in the cosmos is co-creative.[33]

I don't have to explain how Elvis embodies this definition, whether as a musician or an eternal seeker. He was a magician, the greatest, and he helped co-create the reality we all live in now. His magical system is far greater than Aleister Crowley's Thelema or John Dee's Enochian magic. You know it as rock 'n' roll. His ceremonial temple remains the greatest mystical wonder of the West since the Hagia Sophia, the very capital of American culture and where Heaven and Hell will never stop meeting, and it is named Las Vegas.

You may call Elvis a messiah as well. David, Israel's first messiah, was a rags-to-riches fellow who mesmerized crowds with his music and danced naked in a transgressive way as the Spirit of God entered him. His relationships were disastrous, and his family was broken by his ego,

Fig. 10.3. Author posing for photo at
Elvis Presley's grave, Graceland.

but he played a tune that a nation followed into a new era. You may also refer to Elvis as the Trickster, the Changer, Lord of the Crossroads, a shaman, or whatever, but it doesn't matter as his role encompasses and transcends all labels and eventually just means, if you grasp his sorcery, that your soul is ready to go on an adventure through the spheres of imagination and co-creation.

He had a name, though. His name was Elvis Presley.

11

GNOTHI SEAUTON

~~~~~~~~~~~

Know Thyself, Honey

"WHO ARE YOU? Who are you, man?"

That's what Elvis asked Larry Geller that fateful day they met. The question would send Elvis on a spiritual quest culminating with two intense mystical events (and a lot of high weirdness spread throughout for good measure).

"Who am I?"

That's what Elvis asked his stepbrother David Stanley shortly before his death, knowing his earthly mission was coming to an end. Time had run out. The question was a bookmark to his chat with Larry.

Who are you?

Who am I?

These questions might be the greatest lessons of America's Magician. The forces on Earth, the forces from above—the magic, the money, the myth, the rise and fall of a King who now sleeps under a hill—it all pales in comparison to the big questions, and Elvis knew this. He never stopped asking these questions. As an illustration, we can see his annotation on yet another book he treasured, *Living the Infinite Way* by Joel S. Goldsmith.

"Look into your inner self to find the truth."

In the Greek town of Delphi, located on the flank of Mount Parnassus and underneath its craggy peaks in an olive-lined valley, the great and the small in a bygone era sought the wisdom of the oracle in

COD IS   51

according to the appearance, but judge righteous judgment."

We have been seeing with our eyes and hearing with
our ears, when we should have been seeing with our inner eyes, hearing with our inner ears, with that spiritual
awareness that judges not by appearances, but judges
spiritual judgment. Then we will know that all of the
sin, disease, death, lack, limitation, and chaos in the
world today come for only one reason, and that they
come only to those who are living through material sense;
to those still desiring and wanting to get, to acquire, and
to achieve; to those who, as yet, do not know the infinite
nature of their own being and the fact that, because of
this infinite nature, they must let it pour out *from them*
instead of trying to make it add more to them.

The commonly accepted prayer, both orthodox and
metaphysical, must fail, because it is an attempt, in most
cases, to add something, achieve something, accomplish
something, or receive something; whereas the infinite nature of your own being as one with God means that your
"vessel" is already full. All that the Father has is already
yours. Can more be added? The great poet, Browning,
gave us a beautiful secret when he wrote, "Truth is
within ourselves . . . and to know . . . consists in
opening out a way whence the imprisoned splendor may
escape. . . ."

In judging by appearances, we come upon a phase of
belief which causes the entire trouble and inharmony of
human existence: the judgment of good and evil. This,
we say, is good and this is evil. Of course, the very thing

LOOK INTO YOUR INNER SELF TO FIND THE TRUTH

Fig. 11.1. An annotated page of Elvis's copy of *Living the Infinite Way* by Joel S. Goldsmith, as seen in *Leaves of Elvis' Garden* by Larry Geller.

the Temple of Apollo. For the ancient Greeks, this was the center of the world, a place where Zeus once released two eagles from the two ends of the Earth to mark the place as the omphalos, or "navel of the world." No one knows how Apollo came to consecrate this magical place, but some say he arrived personally as a dolphin while leading Delos or Hyperborean shamans here.

Within his temple are several important inscriptions like "Nothing in Excess." Yet Apollo's most important command was:

"Know Thyself."

Such knowledge is not an ego inventory, nor is it the sort of surface-level introspection found in an astrology app or endless tweaking of your internet bio. It's far deeper. Recall the quote from Elaine Pagels in chapter 3:

"Yet to know oneself, at the deepest level is to know God; this is the secret of Gnosis."

That's what Elvis wanted more than anything, as Gnosis is ultimately an experience with the transcendental, the integration of all complexes and daemons, an ecstatic, untethered union with undivided divinity. Gnosis is the ultimate achievement for any human and the ultimate way to find the means to live a noble purpose on Earth and help others find their way to their celestial origins.

The road to Gnosis is more like a labyrinth teaming with Colonel Parker minotaurs, and there are no guarantees of lasting rhapsody, even for the most experienced adepts. Aleister Crowley died a heroin addict and penniless. Alan Watts ended his days in physical pain and suffering from alcoholism. John Dee finished his own days poor and forgotten by the world. This universe wouldn't suffer bright, kind lights like Jesus of Nazareth, Joan of Arc, Hypatia of Alexandria, or Al-Hallaj. Sometimes, the world corrupts the mystic's teachings or hides them until it can no longer.

The perilous journey of Gnosis is worth it for those who won't accept that humanity is an accident. It was worth it for Elvis to find the "Christ in you, the hope of glory," as Paul wrote in Colossians.

"Know thyself" was also a warning by Elvis, who clothed himself in the two-edged sword or Shadow of the American Dream egregore: materialism, consumerism, violence, insanity, and addiction.

Did this country listen? It couldn't have totally, of course, as this is the first time this message from Elvis has been made public to any full degree. Indeed, his magic helped a nation to cope and even thrive during the changing of an era; simultaneously, countless individuals found healing, liberation, and destiny because they followed the Lord of the Crossroads. Now, perhaps, it's time to go even deeper into the ethos of the King.

On a personal level, I don't know if it was channeled or some daemon came over me. It's just something I needed to do for a new friend, someone I never knew until recently. I was honored and humbled to take on this task and, gratefully, I've learned so much about my own life, the many roads I took that led me to meet the Changer at the latest stage of my journey in this wonderful illusion. If I'm delusional, at least I know the tale of Elvis, Jesse, Parker, and Vernon has helped me understand my own father, whom I didn't know well while he was alive. And my brother, who, like Elvis, was forty-two years old when he died. And, Gladys, who did her best and loved as she should have. . . .

"Know thyself."

This country didn't listen totally and perhaps missed an opportunity when it rose from the brutal bloodshed and atomic ashes of World War II. The USA could have led the world by fully embracing its nature of dynamic innovation, enlightenment-era benevolence, and the experiential quest for the divine. Instead, like Elvis and many of us, it refused to look inward and ignored its Shadow. Poverty, war, and disease could have been but temporal stumbling blocks instead of continual global issues.

The toll has been gradual but heavy on the economy, the environment, and the collective psychic health of the population. In the twenty-first century, the USA has been in decline, senile in creativity and less unified with each passing election season, only able to instigate war and bleed the working classes a bit more. Technology and mass media exist in it now as a River Lethe, a river of forgetfulness, a dark enchantment hiding the last remnants of the American Dream egregore. The blue mothership or comet isn't dropping any more saving technology.

Yet the Trickster archetype is more active than ever, for his alchemical laboratory thrives most in those times of great transition, in which the USA and other Western nations now find themselves. Dennis Merritt said this was the "Age of Hermes," and he is right.[1] The Trickster has manifested recently as a reality television host, as a pandemic that perplexed the best and the brightest, in quicksilver cryptocurrency and artificial intelligence, and as a mercury-fluid understanding of identity and gender. No mortal can take the Trickster force on his shoulders and show the population that the perils are always opportunities for transmuting lead to gold. No one can tap into the ancient primordial shamanic witchcraft, can live at the Crossroads between death and life, or or can wrestle all extremes to ensure the nightmares of Philip K. Dick don't come true (although they already have, some might argue). There are no salvific magicians anymore, and both Elvis and Merlin are frozen in the crystal cave of some YouTube algorithm. Other androgynous Changers like David Bowie, Michael Jackson, and Prince have left the building (and the last two in similar ways to Elvis).

Without being able to harness the Trickster archetype, with the death of the American Dream egregore, the best we can do is move beyond the Crossroads and reach the Temple of Apollo to realize that essential maxim that removes all traps.

"Know thyself."

Who are you?

Perhaps Elvis, Jesse, and Jesus will greet us at the entrance, along with Apollo. A blue light will shine, and we'll all look at clouds and their faces from the ghetto.

I pray so because we need Elvis more than ever. The West is crumbling. A few years before he died, Elvis spoke of a terrible dream. In it he and Lisa Marie are somewhere in the Holy Land. They travel in a large, armored vehicle, a tank perhaps, with destruction and Mad Max–looking scenery everywhere as the world has just come out of Armageddon. Lisa begins crying. Elvis looks at her and says, "Don't worry, honey. Don't worry, honey. Nothing's going to happen to your daddy. There's always going to be an Elvis."[2]

I hope so, even as Lisa Marie also left the building in 2023. There must be an Elvis. Is there another means of collective individuation and unity?

As you finally leave the Crossroads, know the definitive answer: no.

"Know thyself."

At the beginning of the book, I quoted *Pulp Fiction*'s Mia Wallace and her declaration that there are only Elvis or Beatles people in the world. "Somewhere you have to make a choice," she said. "And that choice tells you who you are."

More than ever, I know who I am.

I am an Elvis person. I am a magician.

And so are you. If you will only *know thyself, honey*. It might be our only chance.

IF I COULD DREAM
HOW IT ENDS

SOMETIME IN THE SPRING OF 1975, Elvis was in the hospital. Linda Thompson had found him struggling to breathe at home. The reason was his guts, punished by laxatives and other drugs. He had been getting better, but Vernon soon joined him. It was Vernon's first heart attack and first time in a hospital as a patient. Elvis had Vernon stay in the same wing once he was out of intensive care. They bonded while recuperating, reminiscing about more innocent times. Such journeys always run into ghosts, complexes, traumas, and the Shadow. During one tense discussion, Vernon decided to stab his son through the heart with a psychic dagger. "I can thank you for this," Vernon said, referring to his heart attack. "You worried your mama right to the grave."[1]

Elvis broke down crying, feeling like he wasn't alive anymore. He cried and cried, and suddenly . . .

Elvis was so excited. He was thirteen and going to see his first movie, *Abbott and Costello Meet Frankenstein*. He stood in the ticket line with his dad on a hot July day. He couldn't wait to go inside.

"Remember," Vernon said, putting his arm around his son's shoulder. "Don't tell nobody about this. You know how mama and the church feel about them pictures. And I am deacon at Assembly of God, Elvis."

"Why, Daddy?" Elvis asked. "Movies ain't real. Aren't they just make-believe?"

"It's all make-believe, son," his father responded, briefly remember-ing a blue light that brought his children to Earth. "All of it. God's dream. Religions, governments, the land . . . this film we're seeing . . . Frankenstein . . . in the story he ain't no monster. He's like Prometheus, a Trickster. Brings fire to keep us warm on January winter nights."

Elvis was glancing at the movie poster. They were so close to the counter. "I don't understand, Daddy."

Vernon blinked. "I don't either."

"I hear this movie will later inspire Tarantino to create *Pulp Fiction*," Elvis said, not knowing why either. "And then we pick me or some bug band with bad teeth. Ah, Daddy. I was going to get *Star Wars* for Lisa Marie the day before practicing my ritual to see Jesus face to face."

"Last movie you saw was *The Spy Who Loved Me*," Vernon said, narrowing his eyes.

Elvis was looking up at his father. "You knew all about this trick called life. You always smile with your eyes, Daddy. You knew. This whole book. It's just my long love letter to you. That don't make no sense."

"Love letters rarely do, son," Vernon said. "But the lovin' sure is fun."

Elvis squeezed his father's hand. "You did your best."

Vernon looked down at his precious child. "So did you. And you're just gettin' started, Elvis. Books don't ever end. Linear time don't make no sense either."

"We're there!" Elvis exclaimed as they got to the ticket counter.

"Two," Vernon told the young lady in the booth.

They paid and went inside the theater.

THE KING'S NATAL CHART

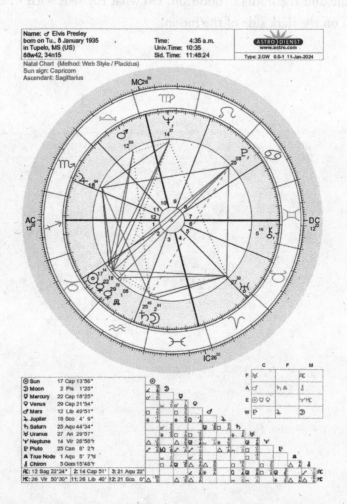

Fig. 12.0. Elvis's natal chart: Capricorn sun, Pisces moon, Sagittarius ascendant. Chart generated by Astro.com.

I HAVE NOWHERE NEAR THE SKILL of the King when it comes to mining the zodiac. So I thank the stars (and my bad puns) that two brilliant astrologers and daemon-hunters came together for Elvis's natal chart: Cat Rose Neligan and Maja D'Aoust. Thank you, thank you very much, ladies.

I felt this esoteric information is necessary for the book, as astrology remains even more popular and relevant today than in the 1960s, when Elvis and Larry Geller were consulting charts to understand the mysteries of life and the human condition. Do what thy wilt with it, and I'll see you on the dark side of the moon.

NOTES

INTRODUCTION

1. Guralnick, *Careless Love*, xi.
2. Greer, *The King in Orange*, 4.
3. Webb, *How to Become A Modern Magus*, 6.
4. Webb, *How to Become A Modern Magus*, 6.
5. Conner, *Magic in Christianity*, 5.
6. Pinch, *Magic In Ancient Egypt*, 16.

CHAPTER 2. THE APOCALYPTICAL WORLD THAT CREATED ELVIS

1. Guralnick, *Last Train to Memphis*, 13; Nash, *Baby, Let's Play House*, 12.
2. Tillery, *The Seeker King*, 7–8.
3. Tillery, *The Seeker King*, 18; Guralnick, *Last Train to Memphis*, 13; Whitmer, *The Inner Elvis*, 108, 114, 148.
4. Whitmer, *The Inner Elvis*, 13, 108.
5. Peake, *The Daemon*, 198–202.
6. Yeats, "The Words upon the Window-Pane, a Commentary."
7. Neligan, *Discovering Your Personal Daimon*, 13.
8. Peake, *The Daemon*, 111, 170.
9. Neligan, *Discovering Your Personal Daimon*, 44–45.
10. Hollis, *Prisms*, 70.
11. Stearn, *Elvis' Search for God*, 12.
12. Whitmer, *The Inner Elvis*, 34–35.
13. Whitmer, *The Inner Elvis*, 148.

245

14. Whitmer, *The Inner Elvis*, 91.

15. Whitmer, "Leading to the 'Elvis Story.'"

16. Nash, *Baby, Let's Play House*, 1.

17. Whitmer, *The Inner Elvis*, 47, 54.

18. Nash, *Baby Let's Play House*, 5; Seay and Neely, *Stairway to Heaven*, 47.

19. Whitmer, *The Inner Elvis*, 50.

20. Nash, *Baby, Let's Play House*, 6–7; Tillery, *The Seeker King*, 17.

21. Whitmer, *The Inner Elvis*, 32, 48.

22. Whitmer, *The Inner Elvis*, 82.

23. Whitmer, *The Inner Elvis*, 35, 94.

24. Nash, *Baby, Let's Play House*, 17.

25. Nash, *Baby, Let's Play House*, 14–15.

26. Guralnick, *Last Train to Memphis*, 20–21; Nash, *Baby, Let's Play House*, 22–23.

27. Rosen, *The Tao of Elvis*, 19.

28. Guralnick, *Last Train to Memphis*, 13.

29. Whitmer, *The Inner Elvis*, 104.

30. Whitmer, *The Inner Elvis*, 164.

31. Whitmer, *The Inner Elvis*, 165.

32. Rosen, *The Tao of Elvis*, 143.

33. Whitmer, *The Inner Elvis*, 29.

34. Maté, *The Myth of Normal*, 59–60, 64–65, 66–67.

35. Tillery, *The Seeker King*, 8–9; Guralnick, *Last Train to Memphis*, 12–15.

36. Guralnick, *Last Train to Memphis*, 28.

37. Tillery, *The Seeker King*, 17.

38. Whitmer, *The Inner Elvis*, 28–29.

39. Tillery, *The Seeker King*, 22; Guralnick, *Last Train to Memphis*, 44–46, 50.

40. Guralnick, *Last Train to Memphis*, 19.

41. Guralnick, *Last Train to Memphis*, 29.

42. Tillery, *The Seeker King*, 10; Whitmer, *The Inner Elvis*, 126.

43. Dunleavy, *Elvis: What Happened?*, 94.

44. Moscheo, *The Gospel Side of Elvis*, 90.

45. Klein, *Elvis: My Best Man*, 182.

46. Kripal, *Mutants and Mystics*, 45.

47. Jeansonne, Luhrssen, Sokolovic, *Elvis Presley, Reluctant Rebel*, 56.

48. Knowles, *Our Heroes Wear Spandex*, 11.

49. Kripal, *Mutants and Mystics*, 220–24.

50. Kripal, *Mutants and Mystics*, 230.

51. Tillery, *The Seeker King*, 135; Sonny West, *Still Taking Care*, 248; Nash, *Baby, Let's Play House*, 500.

52. Geller, *Leaves of Elvis' Garden*, 57.

53. Jeansonne, Luhrssen, Sokolovic, *Elvis Presley, Reluctant Rebel*, 57.

54. Knowles, *Our Gods Wear Spandex*, 111.

55. Knowles, *Our Gods Wear Spandex*, 18.

56. Guralnick, *Careless Love*, 484.

57. Shirey, "Elvis' Captain Marvel Jr. Connection & Inspiration Explained."

58. Guralnick, *Careless Love*, 429.

59. Stephens, *The Devil's Music*, 88.

60. Stephens, *The Devil's Music*, 88.

61. Altschuler, *All Shook Up*, 100.

62. Altschuler, *All Shook Up*, 103.

63. Tillery, *The Seeker King*, 51.

64. Scaruffi, *A History of Rock Music, 1951-2000*, 11.

65. Scaruffi, *A History of Rock Music, 1951-2000*, 12.

66. Altschuler, *All Shook Up*, 14–15.

67. Shumway, *Rock Star*, 24.

68. Shumway, *Rock Star*, 25.

69. Guralnick, *Last Train to Memphis*, 266–67.

70. Altschuler, *All Shook Up*, 45.

71. Altschuler, *All Shook Up*, 24.

72. Doll, *Elvis for Dummies*, 84.

73. Knowles, "Lucifer's Technologies: Fallen from the Sky."

74. Corso, *The Day After Roswell*, 85.

75. Corso, *The Day After Roswell*, 59.

76. Knowles, "Lucifer's Technologies: Fallen from the Sky."

77. Guralnick, *Last Train to Memphis*, 52.

78. Frederick, *A Meeting at The Crossroads*, 13.

79. Frederick, *A Meeting at The Crossroads*, 14.

80. Frederick, *A Meeting at The Crossroads*, 10–11.

81. Frederick, *A Meeting at The Crossroads*, 10.

82. Geller, *Leaves of Elvis' Garden*, 62.

83. Frederick, *A Meeting at The Crossroads*, 75.

84. Frederick, *A Meeting at The Crossroads*, 28–29.

85. Milward, *Crossroads*, xv.

86. Frederick, *A Meeting at The Crossroads*, 58–59.

87. Milward, *Crossroads*, 15.

88. Frederick, *A Meeting at The Crossroads*, 128–29.

89. Geller, *Leaves of Elvis' Garden*, 62.

90. Marshall, "Elvis Presley."

91. Frederick, *A Meeting at The Crossroads*, 94–95.

92. Geller, *If I Can Dream*, 81.

93. Frederick, *A Meeting at The Crossroads*, 92.

94. Frederick, *A Meeting at The Crossroads*, 67.

95. Klein, *My Best Man*, 20–22; Stephens, *The Devil's Music*, 41.

96. Stearn, *The Truth about Elvis*, 65.

97. Tillery, *The Seeker King*, 22.

98. Guralnick, *Last Train to Memphis*, 430.

99. McIntosh, *Occult Russia*, 123.

100. McIntosh, *Occult Russia*, 123–24.

101. DeConick, *The Gnostic New Age*, 63–64.

102. McIntosh, *Occult Russia*, 123.

103. Horwatt, *The Shamanistic Complex*, 128, 131–33.

104. Stephens, *The Devil's Music*, 42.

105. "African American Gospel."

106. Stephens, "God Gave Rock and Roll to You."

107. Tillery, *The Seeker King*, 25.

108. Knowles, *The Secret History of Rock 'n' Roll*, 81.

109. Knowles, *The Secret History of Rock 'n' Roll*, 83.

110. Stephens, *The Devil's Music*, 63.

111. Stephens, *The Devil's Music*, 46.

112. Stephens, *The Devil's Music*, 43–44, 47.

113. Stephens, *The Devil's Music*, 45, 53, 62; Dunleavy, *Elvis: What Happened?*, 131–32.

114. Knowles, *The Secret History of Rock 'n' Roll*, 96.

115. Tillery, *The Seeker King*, 40.

116. Tillery, *The Seeker King*, 51.

117. Knowles, "Something Happened on the Day He Died."

118. White, *The Chaos Protocols*, 59.

119. Kusiaks, "Were Elvis & B.B. King Really Friends?"

120. Harrison, *Death and Resurrection of Elvis Presley*, 31–32.

121. Milward, *Crossroads*, 18.

122. Harrison, *Death and Resurrection of Elvis Presley*, 33.

123. Whitmer. *The Inner Elvis*, 140–43.
124. Knowles, *The Secret History of Rock 'n' Roll*, 152.
125. Shumway, *Rock Star*, 25.
126. Jeansonne, Luhrssen, Sokolovic, *Elvis Presley, Reluctant Rebel*, 18.
127. Doll, *Elvis for Dummies*, 39.

CHAPTER 3. THE KING'S ESOTERIC STUDIES AND OCCULT INFLUENCES

1. Geller, *If I Can Dream*, 42.
2. Geller, *If I Can Dream*, 25.
3. Tillery, *The Seeker King*, 81.
4. Dunleavy, *Elvis: What Happened?*, 107.
5. Tillery, *The Seeker King*, 58.
6. Geller, *Leaves of Elvis' Garden*, 106.
7. Geller, *If I Can Dream*, 42–43.
8. Geller, *If I Can Dream*, 131, 191.
9. West, *Still Taking Care*, 339.
10. Priscilla, *Elvis and Me*, 204.
11. Tillery, *The Seeker King*, 78.
12. Rosen, *The Tao of Elvis*, 135.
13. Guralnick, *Careless Love*, 646–47.
14. Tillery, *The Seeker King*, 176; Brinn, "Elvis fans all shook up for Holy Land theme tour."
15. Guralnick, *Last Train to Memphis*, 474.
16. Geller, *If I Can Dream*, 38.
17. Tillery, *The Seeker King*, 56–57; Geller, *If I Can Dream*, 38.
18. Guralnick, *Last Train to Memphis*, 313.
19. Stearn, *The Truth About Elvis*, 248.
20. Gibran, *The Prophet*, 22.
21. Gibran, *The Prophet*, 7.
22. Gibran, *The Prophet*, 60–61.
23. Geller, *Leaves of Elvis' Garden*, 8.
24. Stearn, *The Truth about Elvis*, 242.
25. Guralnick, *Careless Love*, 178.
26. Geller, *If I Can Dream*, 42.
27. Tillery, *The Seeker King*, 77.

28. Sonny West, *Still Taking Care*, 163.

29. Ostjysk TV, "A Talk About Elvis."

30. Guralnick, *Careless Love*, 173–74.

31. Geller, *Leaves of Elvis' Garden*, 35.

32. Geller, *If I Can Dream*, 157.

33. Sonny West, *Still Taking Care*, 88, 214.

34. Guralnick, *Careless Love*, 176–77.

35. Sonny West, *Still Taking Care*, 164; Whitmer, *The Inner Elvis*, 718.

36. Tillery, *The Seeker King*, 77.

37. Tillery, *The Seeker King*, 77; Geller, *If I Can Dream*, 9–12, 14–16, 18; Geller, *Leaves of Elvis' Garden*, 39.

38. Geller, *If I Can Dream*, 104–5.

39. Tillery, *The Seeker King*, 112–13.

40. Tillery, *The Seeker King*, 109.

41. Stearn, *Truth about Elvis*, 175; Geller, *If I Can Dream*, 17.

42. Geller, *If I Can Dream*, 161.

43. Geller, *If I Can Dream*, 59; Schilling, *Me and a Guy Named Elvis*, 299–300.

44. Tillery, *The Seeker King*, 113–14; Guralnick, *Careless Love*, 266.

45. Geller, *If I Can Dream*, 180–83, 415; Rosen, *The Tao of Elvis*, 166.

46. Geller, *If I Can Dream*, 334.

47. Geller, *If I Can Dream*, 43.

48. Geller, *If I Can Dream*, 43–45.

49. Tillery, *The Seeker King*, 80.

50. Geller, *If I Can Dream*, 180.

51. Vonnegut, "The Mysterious Madame Blavatsky."

52. Greer, *Ceremony of the Grail*, 164.

53. Goldman, *Elvis*, 436.

54. Lachman, *Madame Blavatsky*, 8–10.

55. Tillery, *The Seeker King*, 102; Harrison, *Death and Resurrection of Elvis Presley*, 236.

56. Geller, *If I Can Dream*, 136.

57. Selvidge, *For the Love of Elvis*, 42; Stearn, *The Truth About Elvis*, 252.

58. Selvidge, "Elvis Presley Studied Alice Bailey to Find Health."

59. Stearn, *The Truth About Elvis*, 157.

60. Martin, *The Gnostics*, 82.

61. The Gnostic Society Library, "The Gospel of Thomas."

62. Hoeller, *Gnosticism*, 238.

63. Pagels, *The Gnostic Gospels*, xix.

64. The Gnostic Society Library, "The Gospel of Thomas."

65. Martin, *The Gnostics*, 81.

66. Geller, *If I Can Dream*, 138.

67. Smith, *A Dictionary of Gnosticism*, 105.

68. Davies, *The Gospel of Thomas and Christian Wisdom*, 18–19.

69. Stearn, *The Truth About Elvis*, 242.

70. Geller, *Leaves of Elvis' Garden*, 49–50.

71. Alden, *Elvis and Ginger*, 77, 335.

72. Bloom, *The American Religion*, 22.

73. Tillery, *The Seeker King*, 161.

74. Geller, *Leaves of Elvis' Garden*, 125.

75. Geller, *Leaves of Elvis' Garden*, 118.

76. Tillery, *The Seeker King*, 84.

77. Geller, *Leaves of Elvis' Garden*, 118–19.

78. Geller, *Leaves of Elvis' Garden* 119–20.

79. Geller, *Leaves of Elvis' Garden*, 101.

80. Geller, *Leaves of Elvis' Garden*, 103.

81. Geller, *If I Can Dream*, 61.

82. Geller, *If I Can Dream*, 62–65.

83. Priscilla, *Elvis and Me*, 205.

84. Sahagun, *Master of the Mysteries*, 227.

85. Nash, *Baby, Let's Play House*, 513.

86. Geller, *If I Can Dream*, 134–35.

CHAPTER 4. EASTERN INFLUENCES

1. Rosen, *The Tao of Elvis*, 139.

2. Stearn, *The Truth About Elvis*, 173.

3. Geller, *Leaves of Elvis' Garden*, 87, 90, 93–94, 96–98, 100, 120; Guralnick, *Careless Love*, 197–200, 513; Presley, *Elvis and Me*, 210; Tillery, *The Seeker King*, 94–95; Rosen, *The Tao Elvis*, 3.

4. Geller, *Leaves of Elvis' Garden*, 92.

5. Rosen, *The Tao of Elvis*, 75.

6. Harrison, *The Death and Resurrection of Elvis Presley*, 165–66.

7. Dunleavy, *Elvis: What Happened?*, 65.

8. Tillery, *The Seeker King*, 94–95.

9. Alden, *Elvis and Ginger*, 176.

10. Rosen, *The Tao of Elvis*, 1.

11. Stearn, *The Truth About Elvis*, 83.

12. Nash, *Baby, Let's Play House*, 482–83; Tillery, *The Seeker King*, 103.

13. Nash, *Baby, Let's Play House*, 472.

14. Geller, *If I Can Dream*, 119–22; Tillery, *The Seeker King*, 100.

15. "The Untold Truth of Elvis Presley," 12:24.

16. Tillery, *The Seeker King*, 60; Guralnick, *Careless Love*; Presley, *Elvis and Me*, 45.

17. "The Untold Truth of Elvis Presley," 12:24.

18. Tillery, *The Seeker King*, 157.

19. Whitmer, *The Inner Elvis*, 333.

20. Priscilla, *Elvis and Me*, 210.

21. Klein, *Elvis: My Best Man*, 132; Presley, *Elvis and Me*, 210–11.

22. Guralnick, *Careless Love*, 639.

23. Irwin, "When Alice Cooper Pointed a Loaded Gun"; "Alice Cooper on Meeting Elvis."

24. Guralnick, *Careless Love*, 504.

25. Guralnick, *Careless Love*, 448–49; Tillery, *The Seeker King*, 140.

26. Tillery, *The Seeker King*, 157–58.

27. Presley, *Elvis and Me*, 296.

CHAPTER 5. A NATURAL HEALER AND SORCERER

1. Whitmer, *The Inner Elvis*, 186–87.

2. Geller, *Leaves of Elvis' Garden*, 126–27.

3. Alden, *Elvis and Ginger*, 69–70.

4. Alden, *Elvis and Ginger*, 55.

5. Geller, *Leaves of Elvis' Garden*, 127–128.

6. Geller, *If I Can Dream*, 136; Tillery, *The Seeker King*, 96; Geller, *Leaves of Elvis' Garden*, 131.

7. Presley, *Elvis and Me*, 197.

8. Alden, *Elvis and Ginger*, 110.

9. Stearn, The Truth About Elvis, 259–60.

10. Geller, *Leaves of Elvis' Garden*, 130; Schilling, *Me and a Guy Named Elvis*, 123–24.

11. Stearn, *Truth about Elvis*, 255–56.

12. Geller, *If I Can Dream*, 137; West, *Still Taking Care*, 164, 295.

13. Dunleavy, *Elvis: What Happened?*, 161–62.

14. Simpson, "Elvis Presley MIRACLE?"

15. Stanley, *My Brother Elvis*, 207–9.

16. Dunleavy, *Elvis: What Happened?*, 129–130.

17. Whitmer, *The Inner Elvis*, 377.

18. Whitmer, *The Inner Elvis*, 803.

19. Tillery, *The Seeker King*, 104–5; Stearn, *Elvis' Search for God*, 116–18.

20. Whitmer, *The Inner Elvis*, 235–36; Tillery, *The Seeker King*, 12.

21. Peake, *The Daemon*, 35–36.

22. Dunleavy, *Elvis: What Happened?*, 171–72.

23. Whitmer, *The Inner Elvis*, 101.

24. Whitmer, *The Inner Elvis*, 289.

25. Whitmer, *The Inner Elvis*, 290.

26. Whitmer, *The Inner Elvis*, 477.

27. Nash, *Baby, Let's Play House*, 575–76.

28. Whitmer, *The Inner Elvis*, 854.

29. Rosen, *The Tao of Elvis*, 165.

30. Whitmer, *The Inner Elvis*, 855.

31. Rosen, *The Tao of Elvis*, 165.

32. Stanley, *My Brother Elvis*, 298–99.

33. Guralnick, *Last Train to Memphis*, 313.

34. Presley, *Elvis and Me*, 215.

35. Presley, *Elvis and Me*, 115–16.

36. Tillery, *The Seeker King*, 149–151.

37. Klein, *My Best Man*, 163; Tillery, *The Seeker King*, 96.

38. Tillery, *The Seeker King*, 175.

39. Stearn, *The Truth About Elvis*, 246.

40. Alden, *Elvis and Ginger*, 177–78.

41. Alden, *Elvis and Ginger*, 153–54.

42. Whitmer, *The Inner Elvis*, 834.

43. Presley, *Elvis and Me*, 213–14; Dunleavy, *Elvis: What Happened?*, 228; Geller, *If I Can Dream*, 149–50.

44. *Elvis and Me*, 213; Guralnick, *Careless Love*, 217–18.

45. Guralnick, *Careless Love*, 231.

46. Geller, *Leaves of Elvis' Garden*, 64.

47. Geller, *Leaves of Elvis' Garden*, 70.

48. Geller, *I Can Dream*, 104.

49. Geller, *Leaves of Elvis' Garden*, 11–16; Geller, *If I Can Dream*, 104, 190–192; Whitmer, *The Inner Elvis*, 722; Stearn, *The Truth About Elvis*, 52–54.
50. Tillery, *The Seeker King*, 158-59, 182; Stearn, *The Truth About Elvis*, 83, 101–2.

CHAPTER 6. CLOSE ENCOUNTERS AND THE ALIEN BLUE LIGHT

1. Pasulka, *American Cosmic*, 12.
2. Strieber and Kripal, *The Super Natural*, 3.
3. Geller, *If I Can Dream*, 60.
4. Geller, *If I Can Dream*, 98.
5. Smith, *A Dictionary of Gnosticism*, 102.
6. Strieber, *Communion*, xv–xvi.
7. Jorjani, *Closer Encounters*, 13–14, 66–67, 67–76, 134, 159, 337, 398.
8. Luckman, *Alien Rock*, 5; Harrison, *Death and Resurrection of Elvis Presley*, 168.
9. Hill, "Elvis Face to Face."
10. Luckman, *Alien Rock*, 16.
11. Luckman, *Alien Rock*, 17.
12. Luckman, *Alien Rock*, 11.
13. Dunleavy, *Elvis: What Happened?*, 136.
14. Tillery, *The Seeker King*, 97–98.
15. Luckman, *Alien Rock*, 5, 31–32.
16. Tillery, *The Seeker King*, 98.
17. Strieber and Kripal, *The Super Natural*, 257–58.
18. Geller, *Leaves of Elvis' Garden*, 146–148.
19. Stanley, *Elvis, My Brother*, 209–10.

CHAPTER 7. ELVIS AND PHILIP K. DICK

1. Gopnik, "Blows Against the Empire."
2. Verk, *The Simulation Hypothesis*, 241.
3. Davis, *High Weirdness*, 267.
4. Peake, *A Life of Philip K. Dick*, 12–14.
5. Gopnik, "Blows Against the Empire."
6. Peake, *A Life of Philip K. Dick*, 15.
7. Sutin, *Divine Invasions*, 12, 16.

8. Peake, *A Life of Philip K. Dick*, 17, 46; Sutin, *Divine Invasions*, 16–17.

9. Sutin, *Divine Invasions*, 50, 99.

10. Sutin, *Divine Invasions*, 19.

11. Peake, *A Life of Philip K. Dick*, 46.

12. Davis, *High Weirdness*, 275–77.

13. Suton, *Divine Invasions*, 110.

14. Peake, *A Life of Philip K. Dick*, 135.

15. Tillery, The Seeker King, 127–32.

16. Whitmer, *The Inner Elvis*, 787; Tillery, *The Seeker King*, 132–33.

17. Hanson, "Ricky Stanley Recalls Life with Elvis Presley," Elvis History Blog.

18. Dunleavy, *Elvis: What Happened?*, 241.

19. Tillery, *The Seeker King*, 134–35.

20. Dunleavy, *Elvis: What Happened?*, 241.

21. Presley, *Elvis and Me*, 287.

22. Whitmer, *The Inner Elvis*, 132.

23. Whitmer, *The Inner Elvis*, 764.

24. Suton, *Divine Invasions*, 204.

25. Tillery, *The Seeker King*, 99.

26. Presley, *Elvis and Me*, 29, 151–52; West, *Still Taking Care*, 134; Geller, *If I Can Dream*, 101.

27. Tillery, *The Seeker King*, 166–67.

28. Davis *High Weirdness*, 272.

29. Tillery, *The Seeker King*, 158.

30. Davis, *High Weirdness*, 284–85.

31. Peake, *A Life of Philip K. Dick*, 8.

32. Davis, *High Weirdness*, 274.

33. Farrell, "Philip K. Dick and the Face Humans."

34. Yogananda, "The Dream Nature of the World."

35. Dick, Lethem and Jackson, *The Exegesis of Philip K. Dick*, 276.

36. Douglas, *Apocalypse of the Reluctant Gnostics*, 51.

37. Dick, *VALIS*, 84.

38. Peake, *A Life of Philip K. Dick*, 95–96

39. Suton, *Divine Invasions*, 288–289.

40. Peake, *A Life of Philip K. Dick*, 76–77.

41. Erik Davis, *High Weirdness*, 272.

42. Lachman, *The Quest for Hermes Trismegistus*, 215.

43. Davis, *High Weirdness*, 333.

CHAPTER 8. WHY ELVIS FELL

1. Robertson, *Inner Voices*, 60–61.

2. Robertson, *Inner Voices*, 6–7.

3. Kastrup, *Decoding Jung's Metaphysics*, 33–34.

4. Robertson, *Inner Voices*, 60–61.

5. Robertson, *Beginner's Guide to Jungian Psychology*, 38–39.

6. *Aeon Byte*, "Jungian Complexes," 41:00; Hollis, The Broken Mirror, 37–38.

7. Priscilla, *Elvis and Me*, 193–95.

8. Whitmer, *The Inner Elvis*, 774.

9. Whitmer, *The Inner Elvis*, 637.

10. Whitmer, *The Inner Elvis*, 772.

11. Priscilla, *Elvis and Me*, 176–77.

12. Hollis, *Under Saturn's Shadow*, 60.

13. Robertson, *Inner Voices*, 108–9.

14. Hollis, *The Broken Mirror*, 40; and Robertson, *Inner Voices*, 2.

15. *Speaking of Jung*, "Episode 51: Ann Casement"; London, "The Shadow."

16. Whitmer, *The Inner Elvis*, 290.

17. Jung, *Aion*, 70–71.

18. Schoen, *The War Of The Gods In Addiction*, 16.

19. Schoen, *The War Of The Gods In Addiction*, 30; "The Bill W.–Carl Jung Letters."

20. Wilson, *Alcoholics Anonymous*, 59.

21. Schoen, *The War Of The Gods In Addiction*, 43.

22. Schoen, *The War Of The Gods In Addiction*, 43, 47.

23. Schoen, *The War Of The Gods In Addiction*, 21.

24. Schoen, *The War Of The Gods In Addiction*, 50.

25. Schoen, *The War Of The Gods In Addiction*, 54, 62.

26. Schoen, *The War Of The Gods In Addiction*, 62.

27. Rosen, *The Tao of Elvis*, 123.

28. Rosen, *The Tao of Elvis*, 144.

29. *Good Morning Britain*, "Priscilla Presley Admits Elvis Could Never Have Beaten His Demons."

30. Rosen, *The Tao of Elvis*, 145.

31. Schoen, *The War of The Gods In Addiction*, 68.

32. Jung, "The Shadow," 32

33. Kastrup, *Decoding Jung's Metaphysics*, 34.

34. Jung, *Archetypes of the Collective Unconscious*, 40.

35. Schoen, *The War Of The Gods In Addiction*, 124.

36. Schoen, *The War Of The Gods In Addiction*, 126.

37. Schoen, *The War Of The Gods In Addiction*, 126–27.

38. Greer, *The King in Orange*, 133.

39. *Speaking of Jung*, "Episode 59: Jungian Analyst Dennis Merritt."

40. Hynes and Doty, *Mythical Trickster Figures*, 34.

41. Lang, *The Trickster Gods*, 77.

42. Harrison, *The Death and Resurrection of Elvis Presley*, 30–31.

43. Sharp, *Jung Lexicon*, 27, 109–10.

44. Harrison, *The Death and Resurrection of Elvis Presley*, 48.

45. Tillery, *The Seeker King*, 86.

46. Guralnick, *Careless Love*, 448–49.

47. Whitmer. *The Inner Elvis*, 601.

48. Geller, *If I Can Dream*, 98.

49. Sonny West, *Still Taking Care*, 60.

50. Geller, *If I Can Dream*, 81.

51. Gary Lachman, *Rudolf Steiner*, 132–33, 146–47.

52. Tillery, *The Seeker King*, 86.

53. Gary Lachman, *Rudolf Steiner*, 186–87.

54. Twyman, *Money Grows on the Tree of Knowledge*, 36.

55. Meisfjord, "The Untold Truth of Elvis' Last Show."

56. Jung, *Mysterium Coniunctionis*, 474.

CHAPTER 9. THE LIVE SHAMAN

1. Guralnick, *Last Train to Memphis*, 322.

2. Whitmer, *The Inner Elvis*, 803.

3. Levy, *Undreaming Wetiko*, 83.

4. Namba and Fridman, *Shamanism*, 217.

5. Presley, *Elvis and Me*, 195–96.

6. O'Neill, *Chaos*, 86.

7. Dunleavy, *Elvis: What Happened?*, 158–59.

8. Namba, Fridman, *Shamanism*, 377.

9. Namba, Fridman, *Shamanism*, 217.

10. Whitmer, *The Inner Elvis*, 102.

11. Rosen, *The Tao of Elvis*, xviii.

12. Namba, Fridman, *Shamanism*, 64.

13. Whitmer, *The Inner Elvis*, 302.

14. Whitmer, *The Inner Elvis*, 256.

15. Whitmer, *The Inner Elvis*, 258, 302.

16. Namba, Fridman, *Shamanism*, 133.

17. Whitmer, *The Inner Elvis*, 815.

18. White, *The Chaos Protocols*, 59.

19. Stearn, *The Truth About Elvis*, 239.

20. Namba, Fridman, *Shamanism*, 133.

21. Merritt, *Hermes, Ecopsychology, And Complexity Theory*, 11.

22. Selvidge, *For the Love of Elvis*, 100.

23. Guralnick, *Careless Love*, 324–25.

24. Whitmer, *The Inner Elvis*, 753.

25. Whitmer, *The Inner Elvis*, 689.

26. Guralnick, *Careless Love*, 408, 434–35.

27. Klein, *Elvis: My Best Man*, 269–70.

28. Merrit, *Hermes, Ecopsychology, and Complexity Theory*, 11–12.

29. Lipton, *Breathing Out*, 154.

30. Lipton, 157–62; Nash, *Baby, Let's Play House*, 514.

31. Altschuler, *All Shook Up*, 87.

32. Shumway, *Rock Star*, 32–33.

33. "KD Covers Elvis," *ElvisNews.com* website, June 18, 2006.

34. Hollis, *The Broken Mirror*, 79.

35. Robertson, *Jungian Archetypes*, 187–190.

36. Jung, *Collected Works, Vol. 7*, 331.

37. Twyman, *Money Grows on the Tree of Knowledge*, 21–22.

38. The Gnostic Society Library, "The Gospel of Thomas."

39. Whitmer, *The Inner Elvis*, 177.

40. Whitmer, *The Inner Elvis*, 395.

41. *Guralnick, Last Train to Memphis*, 347–48.

42. Dunleavy, *Elvis: What Happened?*, 117.

43. Whitmer, *The Inner Elvis*, 622–25.

44. Whitmer, *The Inner Elvis*, 175.

45. Whitmer, *The Inner Elvis*, 395, 695.

46. Kujawa, *The Other Goddess*, 51, 86, 283.

47. Kujawa, *The Other Goddess*, 60.

48. Alden, *Elvis and Ginger*, 176–77, 339.

49. Stearn, *The Truth About Elvis*, 130–31.

50. Whitmer, *The Inner Elvis*, 780.

51. Doll, *Elvis for Dummies*, 52.

52. Doll, *Elvis for Dummies*, 130, 211.

53. Geller, *If I Can Dream*, 118.

54. Doll, *Elvis for Dummies*, 211–12.

55. Rosen, *The Tao of Elvis*, 130.

56. Doll, *Elvis for Dummies*, 212.

57. White, *Star.Ships*, 155.

58. Bartlett, *Real Alchemy*, 117.

59. Smith, *Secret History of the Gnostics*, 184; Smith, *John the Baptist and the Last Gnostics*, 15.

60. Doll, *Elvis for Dummies*, 213–14.

61. Doll, *Elvis for Dummies*, 214.

62. Whitmer, *The Inner Elvis*, 855.

63. Doll, *Elvis for Dummies*, 215.

64. Knowles, *The Secret History of Rock 'n' Roll*, 96.

65. Stavish, *Egregores*, 2.

66. Stavish, *Egregores*, 3.

67. Rosen, *The Tao of Elvis*, 32.

68. Stavish, *Egregores*, 5.

69. Stavish, *Egregores*, X.

70. Stavish, *Egregores*, 53.

71. Stavish, *Egregores*, 52.

72. Rosen, *The Tao of Elvis*, x.

73. Rosen, *The Tao of* Elvis, xx.

74. Rosen, *The Tao of Elvis*, xix–xx.

75. Rosen, *The Tao of Elvis* 171.

CHAPTER 10. FUNERAL FOR A FRIEND AND RETURN OF THE KING

1. Jeansonne, Luhrssen, Sokolovic, *Elvis Presley, Reluctant Rebel*, 201.

2. Jeansonne, Luhrssen, Sokolovic, *Elvis Presley, Reluctant Rebel*, 201.

3. Harrison, *The Death and Resurrection of Elvis Presley*, 90.

4. Klein, *My Best Man*, 286–87.

5. Moody, *Elvis After Life*, 25–26.

6. Moody, *Elvis After Life*, 68–72.

7. Moody, *Elvis After Life*, 63–66.

8. Moody, *Elvis After Life*, 16–21.

9. Moody, *Elvis After Life*, 34–39.

10. Moody, *Elvis After Life*, 74–80.

11. Moody, *Elvis After Life*, 45–46, 52–55, 57–61.

12. Gonzales, "Happy Birthday Elvis Presley."

13. Stanley and Sanders, *The Faith of Elvis*, 204–5.

14. Graceland, "Elvis Sightings."

15. Moody, *Elvis After Life*, 96–99.

16. Jeansonne, Luhrssen, Sokolovic, *Elvis Presley, Reluctant Rebel*, 203.

17. Hubbard, "Inside the Enduring Mysteries of Elvis Presley's Death."

18. Beckett, *I Just Can't Help Believin'*, 44.

19. Beckett, *I Just Can't Help Believin'*, 38.

20. Beckett, *I Just Can't Help Believin'*, 49.

21. Beckett, *I Just Can't Help Believin'*, 48.

22. Beckett, *I Just Can't Help Believin'*, 66–7.

23. Indigo, *Suspicious Minds*, 22.

24. Vinyl Rewind, "Did Elvis Presley Fake His Death?," 12:51.

25. Beckett, *I Just Can't Help Believin'*, 69–70.

26. Whitmer, *The Inner Elvis*, 739–40; Alden, *Elvis and Ginger*, 153.

27. Stearn, *Truth about Elvis*, 36–37; Schilling, *Me and a Guy Named Elvis*, 220.

28. Encyclopedia Britannica, "Elvis Presley was Such a Star Trek Fan."

29. Bat, "Americans Still Love Elvis 40 Years After His Death."

30. Harrison, *The Death and Resurrection of Elvis Presley*, 166–68.

31. Becker, *The Denial of Death*, 12.

32. Campbell and Moyers, *The Power of Myth*, 163.

33. White, "Towards a Definition of Magic."

CHAPTER II. *GNOTHI SEAUTON*

1. *Speaking of Jung*, "Episode 59: Jungian analyst Dennis Merritt," 31:00.

2. Rosen, *The Tao of Elvis*, 52.

EPILOGUE

1. Guralnick, *Careless Love*, 558.

BIBLIOGRAPHY

Aeon Byte Gnostic Radio (podcast). "Jungian Complexes." October 20, 2020.

Alden, Ginger. *Elvis and Ginger: Elvis Presley's Fiancée and Last Love*. New York: Berkley Books, 2014.

Altschuler, Glenn C. *All Shook Up: How Rock 'n' Roll Changed America*. Oxford: Oxford University Press, 2003.

Bat, John. "Americans Still Love Elvis 40 Years After His Death." CBS News, August 16, 2022.

Bartlett, Robert Allen. *Real Alchemy: A Primer of Practical Alchemy*. Lake Worth, FL: Ibis Press, 2009.

Becker, Ernest. *The Denial of Death*. New York: Simon and Schuster, 2007.

Beckett, Lee. *I Just Can't Help Believin' . . . : Conspiracy Theory Book One—Elvis Presley*. N.p.: Self-published, 2020. Kindle edition.

Bloom, Harold. *The American Religion: The Emergence of the Post-Christian Nation*. New York: Simon & Schuster, 1992.

Brinn, David. "Elvis fans all shook up for Holy Land theme tour." *The Jerusalem Post*, March 29, 2012.

Campbell, Joseph, and Bill Moyers. *The Power of Myth*. New York: Doubleday, 1988.

Conner, Robert. *Magic in Christianity: From Jesus to the Gnostics*. Oxford: Mandrake of Oxford, 2014.

Corso, Philip J., and William J. Birnes. *The Day After Roswell*. New York: Pocket Books, 1998.

Davies, Stevan L. *The Gospel of Thomas and Christian Wisdom*. New York: Seabury Press, 1983.

Davis, Erik. *High Weirdness: Drugs, Esoterica, and Visionary Experience in the Seventies*. Cambridge, MA: MIT Press, 2019.

DeConick, April D. *The Gnostic New Age: How a Countercultural Spirituality*

Revolutionized Religion from Antiquity to Today. New York: Columbia University Press, 2016.

Dick, Philip K. *The Exegesis of Philip K. Dick*. Edited by Pamela Jackson and Jonathan Lethem. Boston: Houghton Mifflin Harcourt, 2011.

Dick, Philip K. *VALIS*. New York: Bantam Books, 1981.

Doll, Susan. *Elvis for Dummies*. Hoboken, NJ: Wiley Publishing, 2009.

Douglas, Stuart. *The Apocalypse of the Reluctant Gnostics: Carl G. Jung and Philip K. Dick*. London: Routledge, Taylor & Francis Group, 2018.

Dunleavy, Steve, Red West, Sonny West, and Dave Hebler. *Elvis: What Happened?* New York: Ballantine Books, 1977.

"Elvis Presley was Such a Star Trek Fan, He Named One of His Horses Star Trek." Encyclopedia Britannica, accessed February 27, 2023.

Eternalised. "The Shadow—Carl Jung's Warning to The World." Youtube. Last updated October 1, 2021.

Farrell, Henry. "Philip K. Dick and the Face Humans." *Boston Review*, January 16, 2018.

Frederick, Matt. *A Meeting at The Crossroads: Robert Johnson and The Devil*. N.p.: Chicken Feet Press, 2022. Kindle Edition.

Geller, Larry. *If I Can Dream: Elvis' Own Story*. New York: Simon & Schuster, 1989.

Geller, Larry. *Leaves of Elvis' Garden: The Song of His Soul*. Beverly Hills, CA: Bell Rock Publishing, 2007. Kindle Edition.

Gibran, Kahlil. *The Prophet*. New York: Alfred A. Knopf, 1923.

Goldman, Albert. *Elvis*. New York: McGraw-Hill Book Company, 1981.

Gonzalez, John. "Happy Birthday Elvis Presley, thanks for the Kalamazoo memories." *Michigan Live*, last updated January 8, 2019.

Good Morning Britain. "Priscilla Presley Admits Elvis Could Never Have Beaten His Demons." August 16, 2017.

Gopnik, Adam. "Blows Against the Empire." *The New Yorker*, August 13. 2007.

Graceland website. "Elvis Sightings."

Greer, John Michael. *The Ceremony of the Grail: Ancient Mysteries, Gnostic Heresies, and the Lost Rituals of Freemasonry*. Woodbury, MN: Llewellyn Publications, 2022.

———. *The King in Orange: The Magical and Occult Roots of Political Power*. Rochester, VT: Inner Traditions, 2020.

Grunge. "The Untold Truth of Elvis' Last Show." YouTube. June 24, 2022.

Guralnick, Peter. *Last Train to Memphis: The Rise of Elvis Presley*. Boston: Little, Brown and Company, 1994.

———. *Careless Love: The Unmaking of Elvis Presley*. Boston: Little, Brown and Company, 1999.

Hanson, Alan. "To Step-brother Rick Stanley . . . Life with Elvis Was Truly Sex, Drugs, and Rock 'n' Roll." Elvis History Blog, November 2014.

Harrison, Ted. *The Death and Resurrection of Elvis Presley*. London: Reaktion Books, 2016.

Hill, Wanda June. "Elvis Face to Face." PDF available online.

Hoeller, Stephan A. *Gnosticism: New Light on the Ancient Tradition of Inner Knowing*. Wheaton, IL: Quest Books, 2002.

Hollis, James. *Prisms: Reflections on This Journey We Call Life*. Asheville, NC: Chiron Publications, 2021.

———. *The Broken Mirror: Refracted Visions of Ourselves*. Asheville, NC: Chiron Publications, 2022.

———. *Under Saturn's Shadow*. Toronto: Inner City Books, 1994.

Horwatt, Karin. "The Shamanic Complex in the Pentecostal Church." *Ethos: Journal of the Society for Psychological Anthropology* 16, no. 2 (1988): 128–45.

Hubbard, Lauren. "Inside the Enduring Mysteries of Elvis Presley's Death." *Town & Country*, August 8, 2022. Available online.

Hynes, William J., and William G. Doty. *Mythical Trickster Figures: Contours, Contexts, and Criticisms*. Tuscaloosa, AL: University of Alabama Press, 1993.

Indigo, Aiden. *Suspicious Minds: The Sinister Side of Elvis Presley*. N.p.: Self-published, 2023. Kindle Edition.

Irwin, Corey. "When Alice Cooper Pointed a Loaded Gun at Elvis Presley." *VCR: Classic Rock and Culture* website, last updated April 19, 2021.

Jeansonne, Glen, David Luhrssen, and Dan Sokolovic. *Elvis Presley, Reluctant Rebel: His Life and Our Times*. Santa Barbara, CA: Praeger, 2011.

Jorjani, Jason Reza. *Closer Encounters*. Budapest, Hungary: Arktos, 2021.

Jung, C. G. "Archetypes of the Collective Unconscious," in *The Collected Works of C. G. Jung*, edited by Sir Herbert Read, Michael Fordham, and Gerhard Adler, vol. 9, part 1, 3–41. Princeton, NJ: Princeton University Press, 1968.

———. *Mysterium Coniunctionis: An Inquiry Into the Separation and Synthesis of Psychic Opposites in Alchemy*. London: Routledge, 2014.

———. "The Shadow," in *The Collected Works of C. G. Jung*, edited by Sir Herbert Read, Michael Fordham, and Gerhard Adler, vol. 9, part 2, 1–41. Princeton, NJ: Princeton University Press, 1963.

———. "Two Essays on Analytical Psychology," in *The Collected Works of*

C. G. Jung, translated by Gerhard Adler and R. F. C. Hull, vol. 7. Princeton, NJ: Princeton University Press, 1966.

———. *Aion: Researches Into the Phenomenology of the Self*. London: Routledge, 1959.

Kastrup, Bernardo. *Decoding Jung's Metaphysics: The Archetypal Semantics of an Experiential Universe*. Winchester, England: Iff Books, 2021.

"KD Covers Elvis." *ElvisNews.com* (blog). Last updated June 18, 2006.

Klein, George, and Chuck Crisafulli. *Elvis: My Best Man*. New York: Three Rivers Press, 2010.

Knowles, Christoper. "Lucifer's Technologies: Fallen from the Sky." The Secret Sun Blog, April 27, 2016.

———. *Our Gods Wear Spandex: The Secret History of Comic Book Heroes*. San Francisco: Weiser Books, 2007.

———. "Something Happened on the Day He Died." The Secret Sun Blog, January 10, 2022.

———. *The Secret History of Rock 'n' Roll*. Jersey City, NJ: Cleis Press, 2010.

Kripal, Jeffrey J. *Mutants and Mystics: Science Fiction, Superhero Comics, and the Paranormal*. Chicago: University of Chicago Press, 2011.

Kujawa, Joanna. *The Other Goddess: Mary Magdalene and the Goddesses of Eros and Secret Knowledge*. Fort Lauderdale, FL: Haniel Press, 2022.

Kusiaks, Lindsay. "Were Elvis & B. B. King Really Friends? The True Story Is Complicated." Screenrant website, March 6, 2023.

Lachman, Gary. *Madame Blavatsky: The Mother of Modern Spirituality*. New York: Penguin Random House, 2012.

———. *Rudolf Steiner: An Introduction to His Life and Work*. New York: TarcherPerigee, 2007.

———. *The Quest for Hermes Trismegistus: From Ancient Egypt to the Modern World*. Edinburgh, UK: Floris Books, 2018.

Lang, Jeffrey David. *The Trickster Gods and Their Influence on the Development of Human Culture*. Asheville, NC: Chiron Publications, 2018.

Levy, Paul. *Undreaming Wetiko: Breaking the Spell of the Nightmare Mind-Virus*. Rochester, VT: Inner Traditions, 2023.

Library of Congress. "African American Gospel." *Library of Congress Magazine*, vol. 6, no. 3, June 2017, 22–23.

Lipton, Peggy, David Dalton, and Coco Dalton. *Breathing Out*. New York: St. Martin's Press, 2005.

Luckman, Michael C. *Alien Rock: The Rock 'n' Roll Extraterrestrial Connection*. New York: Pocket Books, 2005.

Marshall, Matt. "Elvis Presley—A Man That Simply Wanted to Play The Blues." American Blues Scene, August 2011.

Martin, Sean. *The Gnostics*. Harpenden, England: Pocket Essentials, 2012.

Maté, Gabor, and Daniel Maté. *The Myth of Normal: Trauma, Illness, and Healing in a Toxic Culture*. New York: Penguin Random House, 2021.

McIntosh, Christopher. *Occult Russia: Pagan, Esoteric, and Mystical Traditions*. Rochester, VT: Inner Traditions, 2022.

Merritt, D. L. *Hermes, Ecopsychology, and Complexity Theory*. Carmel, CA: Fisher King Press, 2012.

Milward, John. *Crossroads: How the Blues Shaped Rock 'n' Roll (and Rock Saved the Blues)*. Boston: Northeastern University Press, 2013.

Moody, R. A. *Elvis After Life: Unusual Psychic Experiences Surrounding the Death of a Superstar*. Atlanta: Peachtree Publishers, 1987.

Moscheo, Joe. *The Gospel Side of Elvis*. New York: Center Street, 2014.

Nash, Alanna. *Baby, Let's Play House: Elvis Presley and the Women Who Loved Him*. New York: HarperCollins Publishers, 2009.

Neligan, Cat Rose. *Discovering Your Personal Daimon: An Accessible Astrological Guide to Fate and Destiny*. N.p.: Self-published, 2021.

Never Mind the Buzzcocks. "Alice Cooper on Meeting Elvis." YouTube. October 22, 2016.

O'Neill, Tom, and Dan Piepenbring. *Chaos: Charles Manson, the CIA, and the Secret History of the Sixties*. New York: Little, Brown and Company, 2019.

Ostjysk TV. "A Talk About Elvis. Larry Geller—A Look at Elvis's Spiritual Journey" November 5, 2021. 18:00.

Pagels, Elaine. *The Gnostic Gospels*. New York: Vintage Books, 1989.

Pasulka, Diana Walsh. *American Cosmic: UFOs, Religion, Technology*. Oxford, UK: Oxford University Press, 2019.

Peake, Anthony. *The Daemon: A Guide to Your Extraordinary Secret Self*. London: Arcturus Publishing, 2008.

———. *A Life of Philip K. Dick: The Man Who Remembered the Future*. London: Arcturus Publishing, 2013.

Pinch, Geraldine. *Magic in Ancient Egypt*. Austin: University of Texas Press, 1994.

Presley, Priscilla Beaulieu, and Sandra Harmon. *Elvis and Me*. New York: Berkley Books, 1985

Robertson, Robin. *Beginner's Guide to Jungian Psychology*. Toronto: Inner City Books, 1992.

———. *Inner Voices: and Other Essays on Jungian Psychology*. Cheshire, MA: Manyhats Press, 2017.

———. *Jungian Archetypes: Jung, Gödel, and the History of Archetypes*. Nicolas-Hays, 1995.

Rosen, David H. *The Tao of Elvis*. San Diego, CA: Harcourt, 2002.

Sahagun, Louis. *Master of the Mysteries: New Revelations on the Life of Manly P. Hall*. Port Townsend, WA: Process Media, 2016.

Scaruffi, Piero. *A History of Rock Music, 1951-2000*. Bloomington, IN: iUniverse, 2003

Schilling, Jerry, and Chuck Crisafulli. *Me and a Guy Named Elvis*. New York: Penguin Publishing Group, 2006. Kindle Edition.

Schoen, David E. *The War of the Gods of Addiction*. 2nd edition. Asheville, NC: Chiron Publications, 2009. Kindle Edition.

Seay, Davin, and Mary Neely. *Stairway to Heaven: The Spiritual Roots of Rock 'n' Roll*. New York: Ballantine Books, 1986.

Selvidge, Marla J. "Elvis Presley Studied Alice Bailey to Find Health." *For the Love of Elvis*, March 17, 2007.

———. *For the Love of Elvis*. N.p.: Roseville Publications, 2014. Kindle edition.

Sharp, Daryl. *Jung Lexicon: A Primer of Terms and Concepts*. Toronto: Inner City Books, 1991.

Shirey, Paul. "Elvis' Captain Marvel Jr. Connection & Inspiration Explained." Screenrant website, June 27, 2022.

Shumway, David R. *Rock Star: The Making of Musical Icons from Elvis to Springsteen*. Baltimore, MD: Johns Hopkins University Press, 2014.

Simpson, George. "Elvis Presley MIRACLE? His Las Vegas backing singer makes INCREDIBLE claim of The King." *Express*, February 12, 2020.

Smith, Andrew Phillip. *A Dictionary of Gnosticism*. Wheaton, IL: Quest Books, 2009.

———. *John The Baptist: The Secret History of the Mandeans*. London: Watkins Publishing, 2016.

Smith, Andrew Phillip. *The Secret History of the Gnostics: Their Scriptures, Beliefs and Traditions*. London: Watkins Publishing, 2015.

Speaking of Jung (podcast). "Episode 51: Ann Casement." December 4, 2019.

———. "Episode 59: Jungian analyst Dennis Merritt, Ph.D. on COVID-19." April 2020.

———. The Bill W.–Carl Jung Letters." Last updated November 14, 2015.

Stanley, Billy, and Kent Sanders. *The Faith of Elvis*. Nashville, TN: Thomas Nelson, 2022. Kindle Edition.

Stanley, David E. *My Brother Elvis: The Final Years*. Scotts Valley, CA: CreateSpace Independent Publishing Platform, 2016. Kindle Edition.

Stavish, Mark. *Egregores: The Occult Entities That Watch Over Human Destiny*. Rochester, VT: Inner Traditions, 2018.

Stearn, Jess, and Larry Geller. *Elvis' Search for God*. Murfreesboro, TN: Greenleaf Publications, 1998.

———. *The Truth About Elvis*. New York: Jove/HBJ, 1980.

Stephens, Randall J. *The Devil's Music: How Christians Inspired, Condemned, and Embraced Rock 'n' Roll*. Cambridge, MA: Harvard University Press, 2018.

Strieber, Whitley, and Jeffrey J. Kripal. *The Super Natural: A New Vision of the Unexplained*. New York: TarcherPerigee, 2017.

Strieber, Whitley. *Communion: A True Story*. New York: Avon Books, 1987.

Sutin, Lawrence. *Divine Invasions: A Life of Philip K. Dick*. Cambridge, MA: Da Capo Press, 2005.

The Gnostic Society. "The Gospel of Thomas." Gnosis.org.

Tillery, Gary. *The Seeker King: A Spiritual Biography of Elvis Presley*. Wheaton, IL: Quest Books, 2013.

Twyman, Tracy R. *Money Grows on the Tree of Knowledge*. Scotts Valley, CA: CreateSpace Independent Publishing Platform, 2010.

Vinyl Rewind. "Did Elvis Presley Fake His Death? The Elvis Is Alive Theory Explained." Youtube. January 12, 2022.

Virk, Rizwan. *The Simulation Hypothesis*. Mountain View, CA: Bayview Books, 2019.

Vonnegut, Kurt. "The Mysterious Madame Blavatsky." *McCall's*, March 1970.

Walter, Mariko Namba, and Eva Jane Neumann Fridman (Editors). *Shamanism: An Encyclopedia of World Beliefs, Practices, and Culture*. Santa Barbara, CA: ABC-CLIO, 2004.

Webb, Don. *How to Become a Modern Magus: A Manual for Magicians of All Schools*. Rochester, VT: Inner Traditions, 2023.

West, Sonny, and Marshall Terrill. *Elvis: Still Taking Care of Business: Memories and Insights About Elvis Presley from His Friend and Bodyguard*. Chicago: Triumph Books, 2007.

White, Gordon. *The Chaos Protocols: Magical Techniques for Navigating the New Economic Reality*. Woodbury, MN: Llewellyn Publications, 2016.

———. *Star.Ships: A Prehistory of the Spirits*. London: Scarlet Imprint, 2016.

———. "Towards a Definition of Magic." *Runesoup*, March 14, 2022.

Whitmer, Peter O. *The Inner Elvis: A Psychological Biography of Elvis Aaron Presley.* New York: Hyperion, 1996. Kindle Edition.

———. "Leading to the "'Elvis Story.'" Twinlesstwins.org, February 2020.

Wilson, Bill. *Alcoholics Anonymous: The Story of How Many Thousands of Men and Women Have Recovered from Alcoholism.* 4th ed. New York: Alcoholics Anonymous World Services, 2001.

Yeats, William Butler. "The Words upon the Window-Pane, a Commentary," in *Explorations*, edited by Mrs. W. B. Yeats, 251–84. New York: Macmillan & Co., 1962.

Yogananda, Paramahansas, "The Dream Nature of the World." N.p.: n.p, n.d.

INDEX

Page numbers in *italics* refer to illustrations.